SADIE'

A NOVEL

To Caitlyn,
May Sadie speak
to you from her
silence and inspire
you as her daughter
has! Aunt Libby
Love
Libby Layne

BY

LIBBY LAYNE

First Printing

Author - Libby Layne

Publisher
Wayne Dementi
Dementi Milestone Publishing, Inc.
Manakin-Sabot, VA 23103
www.dementimilestonepublishing.com

Cataloging-in-publication data for this book is available from The Library of Congress.

ISBN: 978-1-7350611-1-5

Cover design: Jayne Hushen

Graphic design by Dianne Dementi

Printed in U.S.A.

Sadie's Silence is a work of fiction. References to real people, events, establishments, organizations or locales are intended only to provide a sense of authenticity, and are used fictitiously. All other characters, incidents and dialogue are drawn from the author's imagination and are not to be construed as real.

Sadie's Silence

DEDICATION

Sadie's Silence is dedicated to all "Pilgrim" women whose journeys were interrupted by the times in which they lived, the duties to which they were called, and most of all the circumstance of their gender.

"I fancy I can hear you say…'You know I never did the things you made me do in your story.'"

"Well, to tell the truth, I don't care so very much what people think if only they will love you…"

"You must remember, too, that you will have been gone almost 100 years, and it is therefore quite time that someone put you in a book."

The Re-Creation of Brian Kent

Harold Bell Wright

1919

From lonely silence,
From rich quiet,
Words rise from our hearts to be shared.
Unspoken and spoken, the words tell our stories.
They free and bind us. Describe and define us.
We search for the right ones,
The ones that will tell the truth.
Words of both law and poetry are truthful,
But when we put our lives into words,
Facts are the mere skeleton that supports the living
story.
Music may express the truth of our lives far better
than logic.
A tear may reveal more of our reality than economical
prose.
Words can sing, dance, weep, laugh if we let them -
if we go beyond what we are afraid of saying.
To do that we must stop covering our silence with
words.
We must let silence have its home in us.
Beyond our fear
is a quiet depth, a stillness of the soul
where words give birth to the language of our
true stories.

Sadie (Maybe)

Prologue

AUGUST 7, 1921

A woman's true story is not always written with words in the pages of a book, but is woven into the fabric of the family she leaves behind and the generations that follow.

I sit in the lonely silence of my bedroom pondering the life that I have lived these forty years and what manner of tapestry I have fashioned on my own loom. Like the clothing, carpets and blankets we wove on the looms upstairs in the old smokehouse in Broadway, Virginia, there are many colors and textures that make up the finished product. Some individual pieces are beautiful in and of themselves, while other scraps only become beautiful when woven into the whole.

Some facts of my life, including my obsession with learning and my stubborn drive for independence, are the scraps that become lovely only in the context of my faith which has colored every choice, or lack of choice I have made through the years. And there is the secret that I keep. Certainly, since it is a lie, this secret would be considered a tattered scrap, perhaps not even to be included, but this lie is beautiful and adds necessary texture to the tapestry.

I sense a certain fear in these moments of silence, wondering whether the choices I made were worth the sacrifices. Sacrifice is a tricky word. It can mean giving up something cherished or hoped for or it can mean, as it does in scripture, killing something to appease or as atonement to some Deity. It seems to me that the only thing that gives any sacrifice meaning is love. Love alone makes the sacrifice sacred. So was love always my motivation?

And what of the loves of my life: the love of family, love of my husband and children, love of friends, and the love that defied category and can't be described easily? Did I love well or did I cheat myself or anyone else?

I am aware that I have used the word "fear" in my musings, a word I rarely, if ever, use, but I am indeed afraid of the changes that are manifesting in my body. I have told no one, not Charles, not his sister, Pearl, and certainly not the children. Yet another secret that I keep.

I wonder if I return to that farm in Broadway, Virginia, and begin gathering up the earliest scraps of my life's tapestry, would they perhaps hold some answers and provide me some idea of whether I indeed found my purpose in life and followed it? Might some reflection give me insight and a sense of peace about where I am on this day, facing an uncertain future?

PART ONE
BROADWAY, VIRGINIA

"It is the combination of land and family that makes me declare the Zigler homestead a sacred and holy place."

M. R. Zigler

LIBBY LAYNE

CHAPTER ONE
1887

T he sprawling brick house and what transpired there shaped who I became every bit as much as the family into which I was born.

The house itself, as most Brethren homes of the period, was fairly plain. Sturdily built of red clay brick, it had been added to several times by previous owners. There were small porches on two sides of the house. On one two–story addition, there was a double deck porch with wooden lattice–work, a decorative feature that varied from other more traditional Brethren homes.

"Sarah," said Papa one evening as we sat in the combination living room/dining room that had been worship space for the early Brethren Church, "Can you tell me who first built this house?" By the age of five, I was expected to know the rich history of our home. Periodically, I was quizzed by my father on the details.

"Yes, Papa," I answered, sitting on the bottom step of the staircase that led to the second floor. I looked up to the ceiling where there were large wooden panels on hinges that were designed to be lowered for service here. "Brother Benjamin Yount and his wife Barbara," I said trying to imagine someone else living in our house. I glanced right above me where a photograph of my family hung.

In it, I stand on the top of the gatepost in a white dress, supported by my sister Lizzie. I was about two years old. My curly mop of hair sits on the crown of my head like a halo and the smile on my face is that of a child who is confident at this time in her life, that she is the center of the universe. That would, of course, soon change. I am not positive whether I recall this particular event or just remember always seeing it as I climbed the stairs each day, but whichever it was, the memory is visceral – this is my family – this is who I am.

In the photo Lizzie is fourteen, twelve years older than I was then, and the only other girl in the family. She is rather short and a bit plump – she wears a bright plaid dress with ruffles, a stark contrast to all of the older women in the picture. Her dark hair is parted down the middle and pulled back in a bun on her neck. Her expression tells the story as she looks at me adoringly, perched like her dolly on the gatepost, "This one is MINE!"

Outside the white picket fence is Edgar, who is twelve. He stands behind my baby carriage in a suit and vest that strains over his ample body.

Dressed in full Brethren garb are my grandparents. Grandfather Zigler sits in a rocking chair in the middle of the sidewalk. His long, full, greying beard covers the high collar of his plain, dark coat. There are no buttons on his jacket, but hooks and eyes instead. The Brethren Church felt that buttons were too worldly. The style of the jacket is clerical and all men in the church wore them – this was to convey the belief at the time that every man who was a member of the Christian church was a minister—the Bible adage, "the priesthood of all believers" was taken literally. Beside him stands my Grandmother Mary who wears the required long, homespun plain dress, topped off with the prayer veil and bonnet on her head.

Behind Grandfather and Grandmother Zigler are my parents, both young in this picture, sitting on the steps of the porch. My Papa, Michael, has dark hair and his beard is short and trimmed with no moustache, the style expected of a young family man. To have a moustache was considered by the church as being associated with the military and as a Peace Church, this was frowned upon. Mama is wearing, like my grandmother, a plain dull–colored handmade dress, but in this photo wears no prayer veil.

The farm hands are also in the picture and, standing away from the rest of the family is Alice Madden, who helps us in the house and out in the garden. She is the wife of Ned Madden, among several other Negroes hired on our farm. Their tradition is always to maintain their distance, even though, as Brethren, our family believes them to be equals.

In the photograph I take note that the door and almost all of the windows stand wide open, which pretty much describes what has transpired here all my life. Our door was always open, as it had been constantly since 1800 when other Brethren families had lived here. It had been built not only for the comfort of its owners, but for the weary sojourner, the traveling preacher, the religiously persecuted, the freed slave and the hobo or tramp. All were welcome in this home on Linville Creek where they were fed and housed by their hosts.

"Very good," said Papa after waiting patiently for me to cease my musings over the family picture. This too was part of our history sessions and he seemed to read my thoughts as I stared at the photograph before he asked the next question. "And in what year did the Yount's build this house?"

"I forget," I said nervously twirling a strand of my curly hair that had escaped from the long pigtail hanging down my back. I was always very proud of myself when I knew the answers to these questions and embarrassed when I didn't. Papa never seemed to mind.

"In 1800," he reminded me, raising his eyebrows and scratching his beard, which he had just trimmed that morning. "And what did they build it for?"

"To live in," I said with just a touch of five–year–old sass.

"And what else?" Papa said, ignoring my attempt at cheekiness.

I thought for a minute, beginning to get restless with the never–ending questions. "Oh, yes, I remember, to be a meeting house for the church people." For many years there were no church structures available for services – several homes in the area were designated for this purpose. Ours had always been one of these.

"And who was the first Zigler live in this house?" Papa frowned as he saw me starting to slide off the step getting ready to stand up. I quickly sat back down, knowing he was not yet finished with me.

The history of the Ziglers here in Broadway had begun four generations back in 1746 when my great–great grandfather, Philip Ziegler, came to Lancaster County, Pennsylvania from Bern, Switzerland. The Zieglers were then and have been to this day, members of the Church of the Brethren which traces its roots to the Anabaptist/Pietist Movement in Germany in the early 1700's. These early Brethren believed that both the Lutheran and Reformed churches were taking liberties with New Testament theology and what it meant to be Christian. They rejected especially the sacrament of infant baptism—this stance had been at the center of the formation of our church and its move to America. In the state churches of Europe, such as Catholic and Lutheran, the threat to parents of their babies going to hell if they were not baptized and charging them a fee to perform the rite was abhorrent to the newly reformed churches such as Brethren and Mennonite. Since there was no separation of church and state, the government used the registration of baptisms as a means of tracking the population, whom they would then tax.

By the time Phillip Ziegler arrived in Pennsylvania at twelve years of age, the Brethren Church in Germantown was well established. They, like the Mennonites and Quakers, were a Peace Church who believed in plain living and dress and an outrageous hospitality. When Grandfather Zigler and his wife, Mary bought this farm, the house already had a rich heritage handed down with each new owner, every one of whom had been Brethren. The spelling of the Ziegler name, according to Papa, had changed when Grandfather Zigler was trying to label a feed bag he had just filled. When the original spelling of the name didn't fit on the sack, he had dropped the "e." Papa always told this tale with a smile and a wink.

"Grandfather John Zigler and Grandmother Mary Miller Zigler purchased the farm in about 1850." I stated confidently as I stood up, knowing we were getting to the most sacred question of all that went to the heart of the legacy of this home.

"One more thing," said Papa, as always, controlling the situation, "Why is it important that we remember what has happened here through the years?"

I stood straight and tall and recited the mantra, "We must always remember what good folks did back then in this house so we don't forget to keep on doing God's work of taking care of the people who stop by here and need food and shelter."

"Sadie," I heard Lizzie yell from the dining room, "I need you to help me set the table for supper."

I looked at Papa who smiled proudly and nodded my dismissal.

"I'm coming, Lizzie," I replied, grinning with pleasure as Papa patted me on the back indicating I had done well once again.

As Lizzie handed me a stack of dishes, she said, "We've got someone real special coming for supper tonight." And for some reason I did not understand, she turned beet red.

CHAPTER TWO

April 1887

"Good evening, John," said Papa, opening the door to a man I had never seen before. "Haven't seen you around for a while, yet."

Even at my age, I could see this was no ordinary young man. John Samuel Flory was tall and slender. His dark hair was parted on the side, not down the middle like most Brethren men and he was beardless. His hair clearly had not been cut by a pair of shears at home in the kitchen as the men in our family, but by a real barber. His eyes were kind and twinkling as if he held a big secret. He was not at all like the Brethren men I was used to seeing at Church and around the farm in dress or in demeanor.

"Well, Mr. Zigler, I've been busy with my college work, you know. Takes about all the time I have these days," he said, his eyes darting around the room. His gaze rested on Lizzie for a moment then he looked at Mama. "Good evening Mrs. Zigler, Lizzie – and who is this bright-eyed young lady?" he said, looking over at me as I got up from the chair by the wood stove and walked over to him to get a closer look.

"My name is Sarah Edna Rebecca Zigler and I am five years old—Mama and Papa call me Sarah, but Lizzie and my brothers call me Sadie. You may call me Sadie, if you wish."

"Well, Miss Sadie," he said in a quiet but strong voice that was refined and elegant. "It is a pleasure to make your acquaintance, and you may call me John." He reached out his hand to shake mine—a very unusual gesture for a young man towards a five–year–old girl. He was definitely not a farmer and I was smitten.

As this was going on, Lizzie stood across the room with the strangest look on her face. She finally said, "Hello John, it's nice to see you again after so long," and once again she turned that shade of red from earlier in the day. I knew about her having a few dates with a boy named John in high school and their breakup over something she kept to herself. This must be the same John.

"Lizzie, Sarah, I need you two, please," called Mama, waving a dish towel like a flag from the kitchen where she was preparing the meal.

As always, when we had people for meals, there was a mountain of food we had been cooking all day. Tonight we were having fried pork tenderloin in gravy, mashed potatoes, green beans cooked in smoked pork side–meat, applesauce we had made from the apples in the orchard, sliced ham, baking powder biscuits with butter we had churned and strawberry preserves we had put up last year. For dessert there were two mince meat pies. Most of the time we had this big meal in the middle of the day for everybody who worked on the farm and we called it "dinner." When we had company we waited until in the evening to have "supper."

"Edgar, Ben, John, come on in and wash up for supper," Papa yelled from the porch. My brothers came bounding in from the barn where they were finishing up their chores. They all wore denim bibbed overalls and were dirty with farm dust. The contrast between them and our guest was stark and I took note of it. "Go wash up, boys, we have company and a feast tonight."

We carried in the dishes of steaming hot food and placed them on the table at the end of the large room that served as living room and dining room. Dividing the two areas was a black iron stove standing on a large wooden block. The long rectangular table was set with our best china and I had picked some early spring flowers from the garden and placed them in the center.

We gathered around the table and with a nod from Papa, all sat down.

"Father in Heaven," Papa began his traditional grace, "We thank Thee for this food and for the hands that have prepared it. We are grateful for Thy bounty and ask that you bless this family and our guest who has joined us this evening."

He then stole a quick gaze at John as he said, "We ask that you guide the conversation, that it may be your best will for us as faithful Brethren. In Jesus name we pray, Amen."

John smiled and nodded as we began passing the food around. He spooned something from every single dish until there was not one bit of room on his plate. The conversation was mostly about the weather, the crops, and praise for the country cooking that John had missed while he was away at school.

The women cleared the table before serving the warmed minced meat pie with vanilla ice cream dribbling down into the plates—John practically groaned with delight. Usually we washed the dishes immediately, but when we had a special guest, we rinsed and stacked them to do later in the evening.

The adults moved to the other end of the room for fellowship. A sofa and several comfortable chairs were strategically placed around the brick fireplace to accommodate the tradition of stimulating conversation that had always transpired there and would continue tonight. Too young yet to be invited to these sessions, I took my customary place on the bottom step of the staircase where I wouldn't miss a word.

"Education, that's the ticket," said John, his dark eyes lighting up with excitement, "the most valuable thing we can do for ourselves and the world we must build for those who come after us. And I'm not just talking about high school, I believe..."

"I agree with you to a point," said Papa, sitting up very straight in his chair facing John. "But a college education is not meant for everyone. It's important to learn to read and

not only with Lizzie but with Papa. I had an ally in my plans for the future.

Lizzie got up from the sofa and walked over to Mama, who had put little John on a quilt on the floor. "See this Sadie," she said as she patted her stomach and then Mama's—this is happiness right here—this is…"

Suddenly Edgar came running through the front door with a horrified expression on his face, "Lizzie, you need to come quick, there's been an accident—it's your John. He's…"

Lizzie paled as she stood quickly, spilling her cup of tea on the floor. "What happened, Edgar? Is he alright? How do you know this? Where is he now?"

Edgar, who, at twenty–one still carried his boyish bulk, was red–faced and out of breath and seemed at a loss as to how relate this bad news to his older sister. "Well, uh, a man came into the blacksmith shop at the end of the lane and told Papa, who was there getting Prince shod, because, you know, he really needed it and…"

"Edgar," Lizzie shrieked her eyes wide and her face laced with fear. "Get to the point, for Pete's sake, what happened to John?"

Mama intervened trying to help Edgar find his tongue, "Edgar, just slow down, take a deep breath and tell us what you know."

"Well, it seems John fell off the tractor out in the field where he was seeding and he must have hit his head or something," he finally related. "They've taken him to the hospital in Harrisonburg and that's all I know. Papa says he'll be glad to take you wherever you need to go."

"Thank you, Edgar," said Mama, patting him on the shoulder, then turning to Lizzie who seemed unable to move, "Lizzie, Sarah and I will keep the boys, you go on with Edgar and Papa."

I had never seen Lizzie in anything less than complete control of a situation and the way she was acting unnerved me. She stood, wringing her hands, as her body shook with fear, yet she could not seem to take any action forward. Mama finally took Lizzie's shaking hands in her own and said quietly, "Lizzie, you need to go to John now—it may not be as bad as it sounds and he'll need you with him. Now just go. The boys will be fine. Let us know something as soon as you do, alright?" She walked calmly over to little John and picked him up off the floor.

Lizzie numbly shook her head like a little girl and did what her mother told her. As she walked out of the door with Edgar, she didn't' seem to notice her two older boys looking up at her with questioning eyes that showed they too had never seen their mother behave in this way and they too were very afraid.

CHAPTER FOUR
November 1891

Lizzie's husband, John, had died that day out in the fields seeding winter rye. He had fallen from the tractor, broken his neck and died on the way to the hospital. Lizzie was now, at twenty-three, a widow and mother of three little boys with another on the way. She was devastated, of course, but Brethren/Mennonite farm folk are a stoic breed and she continued bravely on with her life, though her dream had been altered considerably. At my age then, I couldn't imagine being the least bit happy and going forward with my life when the dream you had always dreamed was ruined. It was the first time I had been this close to death in my family—it would not be nearly the last.

I was nine years old when my brother, Michael Robert Zigler, was born two months prematurely, weighing less than three pounds. I don't know for sure when my sister Lizzie decided that I was her "charge" after I was born but I remember the very moment I knew this new brother of mine was "My Robert."

"He's the puniest little thing I ever saw, Mama," I said, looking down at my baby brother, who was only three days old. He was lying in a makeshift cradle of quilts in one of the drawers of my parent's pine bedroom chest. Every one of us had been born in this downstairs room and laid in a walnut cradle Grandfather Zigler had made – this new baby required something different.

"Sarah, he was born too early and his lungs aren't developed well enough for him to breathe right. I haven't been able to nurse him because he's too weak which means he will stay weak unless we find a way to get some milk in him. Here, I'll put him on this little pillow and you sit down over on that chair."

I went to the chair and watched as she carefully scooped up the tiny creature that barely looked like a baby at all. He was all shriveled and red and looked more like a newborn hairless kitten than a child. She put him on a little flat pillow, brought him over to me and laid him in my lap. I was a little fearful at first, having only handled healthy babies – this one was so fragile and I was wary.

"Now, Sarah, take this medicine dropper and put it in his mouth and try to get him to swallow the milk – every drop is important," she said as she handed me the medicine dropper full of goat's milk. Noticing my hesitation she smiled and said, "Not to worry, Sarah, he won't break."

I did as she said using the method I had developed for the orphaned animals I dragged in off the farm from time to time. Robert stared intently up at me with those piercing blue eyes and I just knew he was begging me to save him.

"Robert, you simply must swallow this milk," I ordered him as the milk drooled down his chin onto the pillow, very little of it actually being taken in. "You don't have to worry, Sister Sadie will take care of you, I will always take care of you, always, but you have to do your part. Do you understand me?"

Just then he began to choke and wheeze, his face turning from red to blue to purple.

"Mama, help me – something's wrong with him!" I said completely panicked.

Mama gazed worriedly down at her newest child, pondering what to do next. Suddenly, she commanded anxiously, "Sarah, go tell Alice I'm going to need her for a while yet – I'm not sure Robert is going to make it!"

"What do you mean he's not going to make it?" I said, "Of course he's going to make it." Having just laid claim to this sibling and vowed to be his protector, I was not about to give up on him that easily.

"Just do as I say, Sarah, find Alice and bring her in here right now!" she said firmly, picking Robert up from my lap and sitting down the rocking chair in the corner of the room.

Alice Madden and her husband Ned lived in an old log cabin down the road from us. Papa had lived there as a boy and now rented it to the Madden's for one dollar a month. Alice had been born a free Negro in 1843, the same year as my father. Like all of the Brethren, my parents had always been opposed to slavery and continued after the war to treat Negroes with dignity and respect. As a child, I grew up knowing no other way of doing things—only gradually did I learn that this was not an attitude shared by many folks around us. Once I had gone to the store with Alice to buy some things and Mr. Wimer who owned the store said to her in a not so nice voice, "We only allow people in here that can pay for their goods. You make sure you do." I felt so bad for her knowing that there was no more honest person around. I gave him a dirty look which he ignored as he turned and said under his breath, "Lord save us from these nigger loving Dunkards."

I found Alice out puttering in the garden. She was petite and very dark-skinned. She wore a long, homespun dress and around her neck was a white neckerchief. She was singing a hymn in her silky voice.

"Alice, Mama says please come in right now – something is wrong with Robert, but I don't know what and she said something about him not going to make it and I…." I couldn't finish as feelings of fear raced through my whole body.

"I'm coming, I'm coming," she said, taking my hand and running with me into the house and to the bedroom.

She snatched Robert and his pillow from Mama and sat down on the bed. Carefully she pulled aside the little undershirt that swamped is emaciated body and announced with authority, "This baby's not going to make it lest he gets more milk than you got, Ms. Mary. He's no bigger than a minute and you gotta keep up your strength to take care of things around here."

"Thanks for coming, Alice. I'm about at wits end over this baby. He has terrible colic and isn't breathing well at all. I've tried everything in my cabinet. Nothing works."

"He just can't die, Alice, he just can't. What are we going to do? What can I do?" I cried, pulling his shirt back over his protruding ribs, not wanting to see how bad he really looked.

"Well, there's something I can do," she said, opening the front of her dress. Several months before Robert was born, Alice had had a baby boy they named Sam.

"But Alice, you have enough to do to take care of Sam," said Mama.

"Lordy, Ms. Mary, I'm full as Bessy the cow – I've got plenty milk for the both of these boys and some to spare. Don't you worry yourself one bit – I don't have much in this world, but what I have, I'm glad to share."

I was a bit taken aback with her total lack of propriety since we Brethren women kept every personal body part out of sight. Our long dresses were designed to cover us from neck to toe and to diminish any curves we might have – the black stockings we wore made extra sure that an ankle would not be seen by the kick of a heel. We dressed privately even among the women in the family and I had never even seen my sister Lizzie naked. I had seen other women nursing babies, but they kept themselves modestly covered with a large flap in the front of their dresses that hid both their breast and the baby.

Alice, on the other hand, sat down, exposing her full brown breast and somehow coaxed Robert to attach his tiny mouth and he began to suckle. I was mesmerized. Here was this very white baby and this very black woman, locked together in a life – line that would ultimately save his life.

CHAPTER FIVE
Summer, 1894

That it was God who had saved my brother's life and that all the praying my family did over him had worked, I had no doubt whatsoever. Such is the faith of a nine–year–old who gets the result she prays for. As with all child–like faith, the years ahead would test that belief many times. I was twelve years old now and three years had passed since I had committed myself to being "my brother's keeper."

And in those three years, I was confident I had done my part in assuring Robert's fragile survival. During the first year after his birth and Alice Madden's life–line of breast milk, he slowly began to gain weight. His lungs, however, were still weak and he developed asthma at a very early age. He would wake in the middle of the night, unable to breathe and Mama or Alice, if she had stayed over, would hold him over steam from a pot on the wood stove in the kitchen to clear him up. I would hear them from my bedroom upstairs and before long, I moved a palate to the floor outside Mama and Papa's room. At the first sound of Robert in trouble, I would rush in, even before Mama was full awake, grab up my wheezing brother and head out to the kitchen to do what eventually became my job – Mama was grateful since she was tired all the time. I would hold that tiny baby over the steam, begging him to breath, begging God to help him breathe, and after the crisis had passed, I carried him over to my palate and sang hymns until we both fell asleep.

In the tradition of the Church of the Brethren, I, as a twelve–year–old, prepared for my baptism. That morning, I viewed myself in the mirror at the end of the upstairs hall after dressing for this sacred and singular ceremony. To have a mirror at all was unusual for a Brethren home and what I was doing would be considered vain. I observed that even in the loose dress that Mama had made for the occasion, I could see the outline of my developing breasts. I pulled the material tighter over them – yes, I was definitely growing up. Instead of that fat little–girl pigtail snaking down my back, we had unbraided my still very curly hair and pulled it back in a ribbon that also gave me a more mature look. I liked way I looked – I liked the way I felt, even though this was certainly what the Bible called "vanity." As I gazed at my reflection I thought about what this day meant to me. We went to church every Sunday and I was exposed to the preaching of many men of faith, both there as well as eavesdropping on the long conversations of traveling preachers from my perch on the back stairs. We were a religious, church–centered Brethren family, yet I observed from time to time that both Mama and Papa were not cut from the same drab cloth as many with whom I attended Church each Sunday. Strict doctrine was less important to them than living out their faith in the way they lived, the way they treated people, and sometimes that meant pushing the boundaries of that faith and acting in surprising ways. I also read religious books and other fine literature that John Flory left here on his trips home to the Valley from school in Ohio. He seemed to take a particular interest in my education and I suppose I'd had a crush on him ever since that visit to our home when I was five and he had tried to encourage Lizzie to continue her education, to no avail. I had also run across a word definition at school that perfectly described that special quality he had; "A strong feeling of enthusiasm or excitement for something or about doing something." The word was "passion." I had heard that John was home after graduation from Morris College and half–hoped that he might show up at my baptism. Perhaps God would give me some of that passion on this special day.

As I walked down the steps into the living room, Papa greeted me with a big smile, "Well, now, don't you clean up right nice yet?" He was already dressed in his church clothes, ready to go. He sat at the dining room table with an open Bible in front of him. He motioned for me to sit down opposite him at the table.

"Do you understand, Sarah, what you are about to do today at Baptism – what it means?" I adjusted the dress that had been fashioned by Mama so as not to float to the surface as I was being dunked. As an added precaution, we clipped a wooden clothes–pin at the hem of the skirt between my legs.

"Yes, Papa, I think that I do," I said, taking my seat, preparing for the serious questioning I knew was about to begin. I knew he always expected something deeper and more thoughtful than a yes or no answer.

"Could you be more specific, please? We Dunkards believe that this is a personal decision you make as a young person, able to understand its meaning—what does this mean to you?" The term "Dunkard" had come from the baptismal ritual itself. Instead of sprinkling drops of water over an infant's head, the person taking his or her baptismal vows was "dunked" head–first three times into waters that reached their waist.

I was torn between an answer that I thought my father wanted or expected to hear and what I was really thinking at the time, which could often be very different things.

"I am accepting all the doctrines of the Church of the Brethren," I began, taking the safe route, "and joining the adult congregation. I am saying I believe what the Church fathers have set as rules for our behavior and…."

"Sarah Edna Rebecca Zigler," Papa said firmly, and it was clear to me I had chosen the wrong approach. "I asked about *your* beliefs – what does this mean to *you?*"

"Well, Papa, I do believe most of what the Church teaches. I believe in God, I believe that Jesus is his only Son, although sometimes I'm not really sure exactly what that means. I also believe that there is something born in each of us called the Holy Spirit that guides us to do the right things and to be the person God created us to be. I believe we are born with a mission in this life."

Papa smiled knowingly, his eyes twinkling, "And my dearest, Sarah, just who and what do you think God wants you to be – exactly what is your mission?"

I knew exactly what he was up to. He was waiting for me to declare that I was being guided by the Holy Spirit to go to college one day and become a teacher. I wasn't about to fall for that today. I didn't want to argue with him about an issue he had made perfectly clear to my sister years ago.

So I just replied, "God wants me to be the best person I can be. To serve others just like you and Mama have done all my life – to respect everyone, like the Negroes and tramps that stop by here all the time."

Papa wasn't fooled but accepted my answer on good faith. He would most certainly take the subject up again at another time.

There were four of us, three girls and one boy, who were to be baptized that day. We were all twelve years old and had grown up together at Linville Creek Brethren Church: Grace Shenk, one of my cousins, Susanah Miller, Henry Blosser and me. This was usually a family affair, but Mama had decided to stay at home with my new sister, Mary Ruth, born earlier in the year. Papa was to be the only member of my family who would come that day. Robert had followed me around all morning, knowing something was going on. He was still very small but his intellect was already sharp. His clear blue eyes looked up at me and he asked, "Sadie going bye–bye?"

I knelt down to his level and said, "Yes, Robert, Sadie is going to be baptized today down at the creek."

"Wobert want to go see Sadie dunked," he said and I was amazed that he seemed to know exactly what this meant. It would not be the last time I would be amazed at this incredible brother of mine. His miraculous survival had only been the beginning of his amazing journey.

"Papa, can Robert go too?" I asked, knowing he would not refuse. With everyone in the family, Robert usually got his way.

Mama stood on the porch waving goodbye with Mary Ruth, my baby sister in her arms as the three of us piled into the wagon and drove down the lane. "Sadie gonna git dunked. Sadie gonna git dunked," chanted Robert as his little bottom bounced on the seat beside me. How I loved this little boy. Our bond was extraordinary and would continue to be as the years passed.

Like the early baptisms of Christians, ours were performed in a river, or in our case, Linville Creek. The congregation gathered at a place on the creek that was deep enough to dunk us for this rite of passage. The day was warm but overcast and the creek had warmed enough that stepping in wouldn't take our breath away. I looked around at the crowd and felt a pang of disappointment when I didn't see John Flory, but I pushed it aside.

"Would the candidates for baptism please step forward?" said Pastor Glick. The four of us moved away from our families and took our places in front of the pastor who stood at the very edge of the creek. I hadn't known until that moment, but somehow the symbolism of leaving our parents space and moving into our own gave me a feeling of anticipation and awe. What I was about to do was important and though I might not know its full implications, I knew that it was a sacred step into my adulthood.

We each repeated our Baptismal vows with great solemnity—or at least as solemn as a twelve–year–old can manage to be.

Pastor Glick then waded into the water until he was almost up to his waist. He motioned Henry to come in. We all knew Henry couldn't swim so he was very hesitant. He also wasn't very tall so the water was a bit deep for him to stand.

"I baptize you in the name of the Father," said Pastor Glick, pushing Henry's head forward for the "God the Father" dunk. Like a fishing pole bob, his backside floated to the top. Pastor Glick took his hand and pushed it back down. The same thing happened with "God the Son" and "God the Holy Spirit." The three of us twelve–year–old girls, waiting our turn, were starting to get tickled. Trying to retain our composure, we made sure we didn't look at one another or we would be lost.

But Henry wasn't finished. As he came up for his final breath, he wailed, "Can't see – can't see!"

The pastor calmly and quietly said, "Henry, just open your eyes!"

That was it – we could hold our mirth no longer. As Henry exited the creek, Pastor Glick glared at the three of us, unsuccessfully trying to stifle our girlish giggles. Getting tickled in a church situation, particularly a baptism is always the worst. Susanah and Grace went next to be dunked and all went smoothly as long as we didn't look at each other. I looked at Papa, expecting him to be giving me "the look," and was relieved when I saw he was occupied with three–year–old Robert, trying to keep him out of the creek.

With the name Zigler, I was as always last when we went in alphabetical order. I tried my best to bring myself to a place of appropriate seriousness for the moment but Henry's "Can't see, Can't see," and his bobbing backside, threatened to break through.

Pastor Glick reached out his hand and gave me a stern look that said, "This needs to stop!" I took a deep breath and said a little prayer as I walked into the water up to my waist. "Sarah Edna Rebecca Zigler, I baptize you in the name of the Father," the pastor said as he placed his hand behind my head and dunked me full under the water of Linville Creek. "And of the Son." I took another breath as I was dunked the second time. "And of the Holy Spirit," he announced loudly, finishing the third dunk. At that moment, the sun came out from behind a cloud and shone brightly as if to sanctify the events of the day – I had an unexpected feeling of reverence come over me. And then I heard a little boy's voice cheering, "Yay, Sadie," as he applauded excitedly.

On the way home Robert was full of questions. "Did you see God, Sadie? Was the water cold? How long before Wobert can do dat?"

Later at home I wondered what God might have thought of our irreverence of that day. Would our baptism be somehow tainted due to our lack of proper behavior?

At dinner I asked Papa, "Papa, did you see what happened tonight?"

"You mean when Henry yelled out he couldn't see?" he said with a slight smirk on his face.

"Well, yes, and did you hear us girls?"

"To be honest, I was trying to keep from laughing out loud myself," he said non-chalantly.

Astounded, I said, "Really, Papa, do you think God would have minded us laughing at such a religious moment? Would it count anyways?"

"Oh, Sarah, we're made in the image of God—I'm sure God was laughing too."

S.J.W.

CHAPTER SIX
Christmas, 1895

I had spied the large box with my name on it under the Christmas tree the night before. Christmases were a festive time in our household and most likely more elaborate than most Brethren homes. We gathered greens from pine, spruce, cedar and holly trees on the property and the fresh odor of them assaulted your nostrils the moment you walked in the front door.

The large cedar tree was cut from the woods and decorated with homemade ornaments that had been handed down from Mama's family, the Knupps, who now lived in Ohio. There were even a few glass ornaments that had been store bought.

Christmas morning I woke very early. Mary Ruth, the newest Zigler, was crying to be picked up and fed. I had not taken to her as I had to Robert – perhaps it was that I wasn't pulled into a crisis of life and death the way I was with Robert, who seemed to have chosen me as part of the solution. There was, of course, the fact that he had reminded me of the pathetic baby animals I saved from the farm. Ruth, as we called her, was born stronger than Robert and Mama had been able to nurse her. She slept in the handmade crib by the stove in the kitchen and I left her care to Mama and Alice. Robert had a room right next to mine upstairs and many times at night he still needed assistance breathing.

"Mama," I said, coming down the stairs in my night-gown, "Ruth is crying – I think she's ready to eat."

Mama came out of her bedroom looking as if she hadn't slept at all. Ever since Ruth had been born I had noticed that she was moving slower and always looked tired. She was forty–four years old and had borne seven children, which, for a farmer's wife, wasn't particularly unusual, but even at thirteen I took note of it. Was this what I wanted for myself? Since John Flory's first visit, an idea had been forming in my mind: is there another path for me?

"Mama, when can we open presents?" I asked hopefully, looking at that package for me.

"As soon as everyone gets up, does chores, and I've nursed Ruth," she answered, picking up the baby and going into her bedroom. "Lizzie and the children are coming over later this afternoon."

"Everyone" this Christmas was just John, Robert, Ruth and me. Edgar and Ben, like Lizzie, had married and left home. Lizzie continued to live on the farm where she and John had lived with her four children. In March of 1892, Lizzie had a little girl she name Elsie Maude. Help for maintaining the farm came from other Mennonites who have a long tradition of stepping in when needed.

After chores, John and Papa came in, the bitter cold of the December day rushing into the house.

"Shut that door, John," Mama scolded, "We don't live in a barn, yet!"

We settled around the tree in the living room. Robert, still a puny, sickly child, was four and very excited this year about Christmas. With all of his problems he had a sunny disposition and a curious and extremely sharp mind. I had started to read with him and he soaked up every word. He had already begun memorizing Bible verses and the poetry of hymns. He followed me around like a puppy and was easy to handle unless he thought I was getting too bossy. Then he'd straighten up his tiny frame, squinch his eyes and say firmly, "Sadie not the boss of Wobert." And of course, he got his way with me. Our gifts were always simple; an orange and a little candy were a delight in our family where every penny went to maintain our large household and the many guests who flowed in and out. This fact made the box under the tree that had my name on even more an oddity.

"Here, Robert, this is for you," said Papa, handing him a small sack tied up with bright ribbon. Robert struggled with untying the ribbon as he frantically tried to see what was inside.

"Sadie, help Wobert – I can't get dis open!" he said, coming over to me shaking the bag.

I untied the ribbon and handed it back to him. He opened it and squealed with delight as an orange, a tangerine and a handful of candy fell out.

For John and Papa there were socks we had made. As with all the clothing we wore, we had spun the wool from our sheep, woven the cloth on looms in the upstairs of the smoke house and sewn them by hand. They would do well in this cold winter weather for outside chores.

Then it was my turn.

Ceremoniously, my father handed me the box from under the tree.

"Sarah," he said, "This year your mother and I have a special gift for you. You have been such a help to your mother with Lizzie gone and Robert and Ruth were born. You are also excelling in your studies in school – so..."

He handed me the box – it was very heavy and, not expecting the weight, I almost dropped it on the floor. I recovered quickly and unwrapped the present.

Inside, carefully wrapped in tissue paper was a large book. I gasped when I saw the title, "Pilgrim's Progress" written in fancy gold lettering on a maroon, red–leather cover. Etched in the leather were two figures, a young man with a staff and an older bearded man pointing the way.

I opened the book to a page, ornately decorated with the words "Presented to" and under that, in Mama's beautiful script, "Sarah E.R.Zigler," by "Her parents, December 25th 1895."

I was speechless. How had they afforded this extravagant gift? I had received a few small books as gifts from others in the family through the years but nothing as amazing as this.

I flipped through the book, as my parents and siblings looked on. There were pages and pages of beautifully engraved illustrations. The one at the beginning of the book was full–colored, the rest were either in black and white or a sort of green ink.

"Well, Sadie," said Papa, expectantly, "Aren't you going to say something?"

I finally found my voice, "This is the most wonderful gift I have ever received. Thank you, Mama, thank you Papa—it's so beautiful, where did you find it and how could you have…?"

"One of our guests who traveled through was selling them door to door. He had lost everything after the war. You remember Mr. Plougher from New York City – he's stayed here a time or two? We negotiated a trade for some goods he needed from the farm. We both were pleased with the deal. And he mentioned how impressed he was with your interest in literature. When he comes back through here you'll have to thank him also."

I remembered Mr. Plougher very well. He had made a great impression on us all whenever he stopped at our home for a meal and a night's rest. He was obviously well–educated, cultured, and always had a tale to tell about some new discovery or idea. Sometimes he even brought a small gift for Robert.

As we went into the kitchen to fix our Christmas breakfast I looked at the book again. Was I wrong to think this might mean that my parents were warming up to the dreams I was beginning to have for my future? Was it premature to believe that I had a life to lead that would not hold me to marriage and year after year of childbearing as had my mother?

Only time would tell.

CHAPTER SEVEN

June, 1896

That my brother, Robert, had a doll he carried around constantly might be less of an oddity than the fact that the doll was a Negro like his best friend Sam.

From the get–go he and Sam were literally inseparable. Since his mother, Alice, nursed both of them and then continued to be an integral part of Robert's life, it was little wonder none of us thought a thing about it.

Alice had made the rag doll and placed it in Robert's crib when he was first born to comfort him. It was a little black boy in overalls and a plaid shirt. She had painted on the face and sewn black yarn on its head that she had twisted into curly tufts. It was very soft and as soon as Robert could grab anything, he latched onto that doll and you rarely saw him without it from then on. She had made Sam a similar one.

Robert's other best friend early on was Lizzie's daughter, Maude. That he was only six months older than she and yet, her uncle, was an embarrassment to Robert. Since Lizzie's husband John Shank had died before Maude was born she spent a lot of time at our home. Maude, as her father had been, was a Mennonite. She also had a doll, a white one, and when the three of them got together with those dolls they were a sight to behold. They insisted that if they were required to go through the many church activities, so did the dolls.

"We're going to baptize today," declared Robert, a five-year-old self-proclaimed pastor one sunny day, and off they went to Linville Creek, clutching their converts, with me tagging a safe distance behind.

I hid behind a bush as the little congregation arrived at the creek. Each presented his or her doll to be baptized in the religious tradition of that "parent."

"I'll go first," announced Maude who was always very bossy. It was the middle of June so all three "pastors" were already barefooted. Maude hiked up her long, calico-feed-sack dress, took her doll into the creek, and scooped up a little water in a cup she had brought for the occasion.

"Esther, I baptize you in the name of the Father, The Son, and the Holy Ghost, AMEN!" she proclaimed, pouring the cup of water over the doll's head in the tradition of the Mennonites.

Sam, as was his custom, lingered back, waiting his turn.

"Me next," said Robert, stepping into the creek with his doll.

"Joshua, I baptize you in the name of the Father," plunging the black doll head first into the water.

"And of the Son," down again into the watery depths, "And of the Holy Spirit." The final plunge was deep and long. "Now that's how we do it in the Brethren Church!"

"OK, Maude and Sam now let me baptize Elijah and Esther into the Brethren Church," Robert said, boldly taking over the proceedings as a Brethren Pastor. Maude glared at him but handed over her "Esther."

Robert took the two other dolls, dunked them three times and pronounced them officially members of the Brethren Church.

"Now you Sam," said Robert, becoming more confident in his role every minute, especially since he knew it was needling his "niece."

Sam came cautiously forward with his doll and murmured something under his breath as he dunked black Elijah quickly once in the creek.

"Now do Joshua into your church," said Robert, handing over his black doll to Sam who performed the sacred ritual once again.

"Good, now Maude," he ordered, completely forgetting that she usually ran the show when they played, "Let Sam baptize Esther into his church and then you can baptize Elijah and Joshua into the Mennonite Church."

Maude, surprised and not at all happy at Robert's new found voice, hesitated a moment and stepped back away from the creek and the rest of the little congregation.

"I don't think that would be appropriate – I have to get home now," she stated bluntly, glancing at the two black dolls, then turned with Esther and ran back to the house, leaving black Joshua and Elijah apparently unwelcome to join the Mennonite Church.

Robert stood, gazing after her, with a puzzled expression, wondering just why that was.

Sam understood why.

And so did I.

CHAPTER EIGHT

Fall, 1896

T here comes and age when a child begins to view her parents in a different light. Sometimes it comes on gradually and sometimes it happens, as it did with me, due to a particular and memorable event.

From my birth, my parents had been caretakers, rule makers, spiritual guides and teachers of the practical life. I didn't see them as individuals who had any significance, thoughts or purpose outside the perimeters of taking care of my wellbeing and the wellbeing of our family.

That all changed for me in the fall of 1896, at the age of 14, when we had a visitor named George Holsinger who stayed at our home for a full three weeks. I became aware that my father was not only a unique individual but was, in fact, a bit of a radical.

Professor Holsinger had been head of the music department of Bridgewater College, the Brethren College in Bridgewater, Virginia, for 16 years. He taught vocal, organ, piano, music history, harmony and composition. He also directed large choirs, composed a vast number of hymns and edited many music books. He had stayed in our home before while he traveled up and down the Shenandoah Valley teaching in singing schools and at churches like ours in Broadway. For weeks, in his upstairs room at our home, he composed music. His voice was a beautiful, sweet, tenor and every time I had a chance I would go to where he was teaching music lessons and holding church "sings."

"Come out to the wagon, Michael," said our guest after supper, "I've something I want you to see. Sarah, you and Robert come, too."

The four of us walked out to his wagon that sat under the overhang at the barn. This evening, for some reason, he had not unhitched the horse for the night. In the wagon was a large, covered object that took up most of the area rear of the driver's seat.

"I brought this over from Singers Glen from a man who had ordered it but decided against keeping it in his home. Been over there working with the singers and the latest edition of the Harmonia Sacra, an amazing work, that – I understand you've been trying to get it reprinted for your own people here at Linville Creek Church. Good for you Michael, we need forward thinkers in our congregation – The Dunkers can be so stiff-necked sometimes."

My father, a forward thinker? This was the first time I had ever heard anyone apply this trait to him. To me, he had always seemed to fit in the category of "Stiff–necked Dunkers" Professor Holsinger had mentioned.

The professor walked slowly over to the wagon, teasing us with the suspense of the moment, and then, ceremoniously pulled back the tarp that covered the...

"It's an organ," I screamed, "A real organ." I had seen one before in a catalogue but since the Brethren Church considered any musical instrument as too worldly, they did not allow them in the sanctuary so I had never seen an actual one.

"This is technically called a 'harmonium,' Sarah, or sometimes a 'reed organ.' Michael, with all your interest in the singing schools and the like, I thought you might want to purchase this one – it would make a wonderful addition to your musical family. I can give you a good price."

I looked over at Papa, expecting him to immediately shun the idea. Our family adhered to most all of the Brethren rulings to avoid fairs, carnivals, and other such frivolity, and although there was music in our home, the only instrument we had was a harmonica or mouth harp. I was stunned when Papa said, "Let's hear what it sounds like."

Professor Holsinger climbed up on the wagon and sat down on the bench. He began pulling out the white knobs that were set above the keyboard, put his feet on the two foot–boards and began pumping alternately with each foot. He lifted his hands and began playing one of his own familiar hymns, "Purer in Heart, Oh God–Help me to be." We all began singing along with the reedy tones of the harmonium and even the cows were transfixed – they stopped eating the hay in the manger, started moving their heads from side to side, rolling their large brown eyes, and, every so often, came out with a tuneful "Moo," as if joining our hymn–sing.

"How about we bring that beauty into the house right now?" said Papa.

"But Papa, the church says…"

"Never you mind, Sarah, the Lord and I will work this out between us and I feel certain everything will be just fine."

I was shocked and delighted all at the same time. Here was my father, an elder and leader in our church, outright defying a church rule.

"Robert, go fetch Ned and Henry from the barn and ask them to come over and get this thing in the house," said Papa after they had driven the wagon over to the back porch.

The four men hoisted the rather cumbersome piece of furniture off the wagon and onto the porch, where we were met by Mama, lugging Ruth on her hip, and exhibiting a look of utter astonishment and disapproval on her face.

"Michael Robert Zigler, what on earth do you think you are doing? You can't bring that thing into our home," she scolded, as if she were talking to one of us.

"Now, Mother," Papa said, in a tone he used when he knew he had some convincing to do, "Let's just see – you may decide you really like it."

"But the elders, they'll never approve of such a thing and what kind of example does that send to the children, to go against church rules?"

Papa was, in almost all situations, mild–mannered and non–combative, especially with Mama. In this case, however, he had already made up his mind and in a firm, preacher–like voice, he said, "Mother, the Good Book says again and again there ought be praising the Lord with all manner of instruments and singing. Why Psalm 150 talks about praising with lutes, harps, trumpets, strings, pipes, and loud, clanging cymbals. Never have understood why the church is so cranky about this anyway. And this is our home, not the church sanctuary. Now where do you want to put it?"

Under her breath I heard Mama say, "How about up in the attic?" She turned briskly and went into the house murmuring, "I have an awful headache," knowing the matter had been settled.

The organ, besides being a musical instrument, was an elegant piece of furniture made of polished oak wood with detailed carvings. It was placed along the wall in the large living room/dining room which had, in years past, indeed been a church meeting place. This fact was not lost on Robert and me who knew well the history of our home.

Papa's rebellious act of that evening would be a touchstone for me in years to come. I had always respected him as a good man, a good Christian, a good Brethren. Now, I could see that those things need not be false about him just because he had decided to do something he truly believed God would have approved, even if the church would not. I would appreciate him and respect him in an entirely new way and would weigh some of my own decisions based on the events of this day.

Roberts's asthma had flared up with all the excitement and he was sitting in the kitchen behind the wood stove, wheezing and trying to catch his breath.

"What seems to be the problem, young man?" asked the professor kindly.

"He has had difficulty breathing ever since he was born months too early. I've tried all my remedies and herbs and nothing works," said Mama, apparently resigned to the new resident of our home.

"May I?" he said, as he walked over to Robert.

Mama nodded.

"Close your eyes, son," he said and began rubbing Robert's head and chest with his hands. He continued this for quite some time as my brother's breathing evened out and became regular and clear. Robert opened his eyes for a moment, and then sleepily declared, "I think I'll go up to bed now," and we didn't hear a peep out of him until the next morning.

"Now, Mrs. Zigler, you mentioned you have a head-ache. Would you allow me?"

As Mama nodded her permission, he began skillfully massaging my mother's brow, head and neck. As he did this, the lines in her forehead softened and she began to relax in the chair. She smiled and said, "I thank you, sir," and all resistance to the new acquisition was completely gone.

For the rest of the evening we sang around that beautiful instrument and there was harmony in my family in more ways than one.

CHAPTER NINE

Spring, 1897

I'm not positive when the tradition of welcoming tramps began here in the Valley of Virginia, but the travel of men, women and children probably had existed after the War of Independence and blossomed after the Civil War. Wars had always produced soldiers who came home afterward to no livelihood. Many became migrants who rode the railroads and sought work, food and lodging along the way. There were also those who had lost lucrative jobs due to changes in economic conditions. These travelers were guided to safe houses by secret signs on buildings and posts, not unlike the early Christians in the days of Roman persecution or runaway slaves during the Civil War.

The sign of safety for the Zigler household was on the blacksmith shop down the road from our house. Years before I was born, the family had hosted at least two guests a week during the spring and fall harvesting seasons. Fearing a fire in the barn, Papa invited our guests to sleep upstairs in our house. Since Robert and I both slept in rooms there too, we were never quite comfortable until we heard the men snoring from the room where there was a cord bed set up for them. Mama and Papa called it "The Tramp's Room" but Robert and I called it "Plougher's Room," named after a frequent visitor to our home, Mr. Plougher. This unique man was an exception to our snoring rule because he had become our friend and we were certain he would do us no harm.

"Welcome back, Mr. Plougher," said Papa, extending his hand in welcome. "Good to see you again – heading to Florida this year?"

"Yes sir, Mr. Zigler," he answered, taking off his black, shiny top–hat as he came into the living room. He sat down a large tapestry–like bag on the floor. "Seems there's a good fruit season for picking this year. Hello, Robert," he smiled, seeing my brother anxiously waiting for him to open his bag of treasures.

"Hello, Mr. Plougher, did you bring a puzzle for me?" said Robert, who loved the unusual gifts this man brought from his travels.

"Now Robert, don't be rude, Mr...."

"No, no, that's just fine. I like a young man with curiosity and a good mind for puzzles. I have something even more special for you this trip." He pulled out a seemingly average rock from his bag and began to spin his tale about its significance. "Now Robert, this is no ordinary rock. This rock is a small piece of a gigantic boulder that fell from far out in the universe down to earth. Do you know what that boulder is called?"

"No sir," answered Robert in awe, turning the rock over in his hands then bringing it up to his eyes to look more closely.

"It's called a meteor and…"

I listened to his astronomy lesson from the kitchen, waiting my turn to thank him for the wonderful book he had made possible for my last Christmas. Though I found it difficult reading at first, I had come to treasure the beauty of the illustrations and gradually began to comprehend some of the deep meaning of Bunyan's writing.

I observed this fascinating visitor to our home with great curiosity. We rarely heard these traveler's personal stories. Most were very quiet and answered only questions they were asked. Mr. Plougher was different in both appearance and behavior—the top hat he wore was only the beginning. Even in his worn clothes, he somehow presented as someone who had once been considered a gentleman. His speech was cultured like John Flory and he always brought news of interesting places and scientific discoveries.

After Robert was sufficiently entertained by the tale of the magical rock, I came into the living room. "Mr. Plougher, I want to thank you for the book you sold to my Papa for me. I had heard the name of it at school, but never imagined I would ever own one," I said as I held out my hand to shake his. I noticed it was smooth and un–weathered, unlike most of the men around here.

"You are most welcome, Miss Sarah. I had noted seeing some of the books you already read and thought this classic was one you might enjoy over the years. Have you had any trouble with Bunyan's style of writing?"

"A little," I admitted, "but I look at the illustrations and get an idea what the chapter is about and then just read – it's so beautiful the way he puts his words together to tell the story."

"Well, don't give up – you'll get into the flow the more you read it."

"Come on to supper," ordered Mama, and we sat down to yet another feast at the Zigler dining room table. As always, Mr. Plougher shared news of his travels and people he had met. I always marveled at his knowledge of politics and happenings from around the world; the way he expressed himself was like hearing an aristocratic intellectual speak.

After supper we all gathered in the living room. Both Robert and I were sometimes allowed in on the discussions, and always invited when the guest was Mr. Plougher. Others who came were often too rough in their speech and sometimes talked about subjects Mama and Papa thought inappropriate for us.

"I see you have a new acquisition," he said glancing at the organ, "Does anyone play?" The presence of the harmonium had now been accepted by everyone in the family, and even Mama loved to gather us all around the instrument for hymn singing. I suppose that as long as we were praising the Lord, she decided God wouldn't object.

"I do – a little," I said. "Dr. Holsinger has been giving me lessons on the organ and singing too." My skill at the harmonium had improved considerably with the lessons and though I had a pretty good natural voice, Dr. Holsinger had taught me much about using it properly.

"Would you do me the honor of a little music? It's one of the things I miss from my youth," he said, sighing and looking a bit melancholy.

I was shy about playing for anyone except family – a Brethren girl was expected not to appear to be a show off. But Mr. Plougher seemed to have a need to hear some music. I looked toward Papa and he nodded.

"Sarah," said Papa, "why don't you and Robert sing that hymn you were practicing the other day – I think it was number 56 in the Hymnal."

I walked to the organ and sat down on the pine bench. This particular harmonium had one manual or set of keys— some more elaborate ones had two. The black and white keys were exactly like a piano but there were fewer of them. Immediately above the keyboard were fourteen white porcelain knobs called "stops" which, when pulled out, determined the different sounds that were produced when the organ was pumped. Air from the pumping of the two foot boards filled bellows which flowed past a vibrating thin piece of metal called a reed. I pulled out several stops as Dr. Holsinger had taught me and began pumping with my feet.

"Which hymn is that?" asked Robert, who loved to sing, but unlike the rest of the family, had trouble staying on pitch, which may have been due to a slight defect in his hearing – this never dulled his enthusiasm.

"Come Thou Fount of Every Blessing," I answered as I continued pumping and the organ filled with air.

Mr. Plougher walked to the organ and gently caressed the dark wood of the instrument, running his hand over the ornate carvings. "Exquisite," he said, almost prayerfully.

As we began to sing, he closed his eyes.

Come thou fount of every blessing,
Tune my heart to sing Thy praise.
Streams of mercy, never ceasing,
Call for songs of loudest praise.
Teach me some melodious sonnet,
Sung by flaming tongues above
Praise the Mount, I'm fixed upon it,
Mount of God's redeeming love.

The organ's reedy chords blended with our voices; mine, a high soprano and Robert's child–like, a little off–key alto.

We paused, waiting to see if we should continue.

"Oh, my, how wonderful. Miss Sarah, you have a beautiful voice. I can hear that you have had some fine vocal training."

"How about me?" said Robert, not to be ignored.

"A very fine voice also – how about another verse?" he said, patting Robert on the head, a kind but patronizing gesture this five year old boy did not appreciate.

"The next one is my favorite," said Robert, shrugging and moving away. "It goes, '*Here I raise my Ebenezer*,' and I don't know what an Ebenezer is or how to raise one, but I like to say it."

We all laughed as Robert began raising his Ebenezer. His boyish voice was a monotone consisting of about four notes total, but this fervent rendering of his favorite verse made up for his lack of pitch. He stood beside me, his small body erect, his head thrown back, and his eyes fiery as he sang:

Here I raise my Ebenezer,
Hither by Thy help I'm come,
And I hope, by Thy good pleasure
Safely to arrive at home…

Even before Robert finished the verse, his asthma flared up due to his deep breathing and Mama quickly took him into the kitchen where she would heat up some water for steam.

Mr. Plougher looked longingly at the organ and said, "Might I?"

I looked at Papa who raised his eyebrows – though we knew Mr. Plougher was not your average tramp, we were still surprised at his request.

I slid off the bench and stood beside the harmonium. Mr. Plougher stepped up and took his place on the empty bench. He ran his hands over the surface of the keys then reached up to pull out and push in the stops he preferred – this was certainly not the first time he had been exposed to this instrument. He took a big breath and began pumping with his feet and then began to play.

The music that flowed from our harmonium that evening was like none I had ever heard. Mr. Plougher's right hand began playing a pattern of notes that stated a theme or tune. When he completed that theme, he began to play the same sequence of notes again. Several measures into the first theme, his left hand began the original theme again, resulting in intricate harmonies. I closed my eyes, letting the music sink in. Winding in and out, in and out, like the weaving of different colors of cloth on the loom in the smoke house, ultimately coming together to make something of beauty. The simple four–part harmonies of the hymns we sang at church, though lovely and satisfying, paled to this cacophony of sound coming from the harmonium. I had always been inspired by the poetry of the sacred music at church but this music certainly came from God Himself and it touched my very soul. Was there more music like this out in the world – and where on earth would have Mr. Plougher been exposed to it? Why hadn't I heard it before? I promised myself that the next time Dr. Holsinger came by, I would ask him.

Little by little Mr. Plougher began to be frustrated as he struggled to play the piece faster and faster. He finally stopped abruptly, raised his hands off the keys and said with a smile and shake of his head, "I guess a Bach Invention needs a pianoforte rather than a harmonium, but thank you for letting me try it."

"Sarah, how about another verse of that hymn?" he said, motioning me to sit beside him on the bench. "I'll play and you sing."

"*Oh, to grace, how great a debtor…*" I sang in my full soprano voice as Dr. Holsinger had taught me, taking deep breaths. This was an example of the poetry of hymns that touched my heart and soul.

> *Prone to wander, Lord I feel it,*
> *Prone to leave the God I love,*
> *Here's my heart now take and seal it,*
> *Seal it for the courts above.*

Mr. Plougher dropped his head and I saw tears streaming down his face.

Quietly he said, "Your voice reminds me of Jenny Lind. I heard her in New York city when…"

He stopped to gain his composure, cleared his voice and continued, "You must develop that voice of yours – you have a God-given gift."

He sighed, got up from the organ and announced quietly, "I think I'll turn in now."

Later that night in my bed, with Mr. Plougher snoring in the next room, I wondered about this man's journey— what had happened to bring him to this life he was leading? Certainly Mr. Plougher didn't know when he went to a concert in New York City and heard a world–famous singer, that one day he would be a Knight of the Road, a tramp living on the generosity of others.

I wondered about my own journey ahead. Perhaps I could also be a famous singer like Jenny Lind. One more dream to add to my lengthening list.

Unfortunately, a series of events would be set in motion that fall that would change the course of my life.

CHAPTER TEN
August, 1897

The summer and fall of my fifteenth year, we did what we always did to prepare for the winter ahead. We canned vegetables and fruit, sweating over jars and jars of steaming food that would sustain our family and all of the visitors who ate at our table. That day we had put up fifty jars of tomatoes and thirty jars of green beans. As they sat on the counter cooling, we waited for the "pop" of the metal lids that signaled a perfect seal.

"Well, that was a good day's work," said Mama, grabbing three–year–old Ruth who was trying to steal one of the jars of tomatoes off the counter.

"Give that youngin' to me," said Alice, who, as always, was right in the middle of all of the workings of our household and noted instinctively the exhaustion on her face, "you needs to rest some now."

"Thank you, Alice; I'm just plain tuckered out all the time these days. Don't know what I'd do without you and Sarah." She paused, deciding whether to approach the subject, "Which reminds me, are you planning to go back to school this fall, Sarah?"

My heart stopped. My education plan had been moving forward nicely. Robert had started school early at five so my care of him had eased considerably.

"I'm planning to, Mama," I said, cautiously, "I still want to go to Bridgewater College and become a teacher someday." I would graduate from high school in two years and then apply to Bridgewater College where John Flory now was a professor teaching German and English. I had done very well in school all along, though in recent years it had been a challenge with frequent absences to be at home with Mama and little Ruth. I was determined not to complain so as not to arouse Papa's objections to some of my plans. I did my work, seeing it as God's will for me at the time.

"Well, you know what your father thinks about that," she said, looking me in the eye to make her point. Papa had finally, after many years, convinced Linville Creek to have a Sunday school. Once again he had broken with Brethren tradition and I was very proud to be his daughter. It also gave me an opportunity, with his blessing, to teach the children there. I bought and borrowed books that specifically trained teachers of Sunday school. After all, I rationalized, teaching was teaching and I could apply what I was learning in other settings. My star pupil was Robert, who analyzed every Bible story we studied – I took a great deal of pleasure that he already was willing to challenge the details of some of the wilder tales like Jonah and the Whale. "I know God can do anything he wants but somebody living the belly of a giant fish is just a little hard to swallow," he said giggling at his own attempt at humor. I did the best I could to explain that plain that I believed "God's Truth" was sometimes learned through outrageous stories that needn't be completely factual to be true. Of course, these explanations were given in the safety of our home, not at church where some would have seen me as blasphemous.

"Yes, Mama, I do," I said, pausing to form the next important question, "And what do you think about it?"

Mama collected her thoughts as she viewed the fruits of our labor, and then said, "You know I've always wanted to support your decision about that, but lately, I'm not so sure we can do without you here at home. I can't do much anymore and Mary Ruth takes a lot of care. I just don't know—we'll see."

"We'll see," in our family, usually meant that my family's needs would come before my own. I felt a knot in my stomach and foreboding in my heart. I knew arguing about it would have no effect. Family loyalties came first and foremost and I was bound by birth to these loyalties. Sacrifice was required and expected.

"I think all the jars are sealed," said Alice tapping each jar top with her finger, "Are we ready to take them to the cellar?"

"Let me go get Robert," I said, "He can hand the jars to us."

Alice and I stood at the top of the stairs while Mama and Robert handed us the jars, one by one, to be carried to the wooden shelves in the basement. We had been canning all summer and they were laden with jars of every fruit and vegetable we had grown in the garden. There were also jars of meats, pork tenderloin and sausage from the butchering of the pigs as well as sauerkraut made early in the season from cabbage. There was always a feeling of great satisfaction as we looked at the rows and rows of glass Mason jars holding the summer's bounty.

After endless trips down the stairs, Alice and I were finally getting to the finish line.

"The last one, Ta Dah!" said Robert ceremoniously, as he handed me the jar of tomatoes.

"Thank you, Robert, you've been a great help—would you like to come down and see?" I asked as I started down the steps cautiously

Robert bounded, much less cautiously, down the steps behind me.

Suddenly, we heard the creaking of wood. In an old house, not an unusual sound, but this was different. I screamed, "No stop, no please stop," as if my pleas would somehow have an effect on the avalanche that was happening before me. The sound became louder and louder, and I watched in horror as the shelves, one by one, buckled and fell to the floor. The shattering of the glass jars was deafening and the odor of the mingled foods accosted our senses. In particular, the smell of the sauerkraut, which is nothing anyway but rotten cabbage, was nauseating. I had started toward the breaking shelves, hoping to do something but Alice immediately pulled me back as glass shards flew through the air. I decided it better to shield Robert from the destruction and covered him with my apron.

Mama came running down the steps to join us. Brethren women are not known for their expressions of emotion, but we all looked around at the destruction and back at each other and everyone burst into tears. Robert looked at us with awe and wonder. "It's alright, Mama, Sadie, we can get some more," he said trying to console us. Of course, there was nothing to be done.

When we were finished with grieving our loss, we called Papa and the other men. They came in with shovels and we watched as all of our season's labors were taken out to the dump pile to be buried. Full of glass, they couldn't even be salvaged for the livestock.

Looking back, the events of that fall seemed a foreshadowing of the shattering of my dreams. The cellar fiasco was only the beginning.

To this day I have no idea why Mama decided to take Robert with her on a trip to see her parents in Ohio that October. The trip itself had been Papa's idea—he could see that Mama was tired and needed to get away for a while. I was happy to stay at home and continue going to school and Robert, ideally, would have too. Instead, Mama left me at home with Mary Ruth, so both Robert and I would miss a whole month of school. And that turned out to be the least of it.

Perhaps it was our conversation that day when Mama realized I still hadn't given up my plan to go to college and be a teacher. Whatever the reason, she, John and Robert left on a train from Staunton and went to Ohio for a month's visit. I had no choice in the matter so I tried to swallow my resentment and bide my time until they came back and I could return to my studies. In the meantime, I could read and perhaps get some of my homework from the teachers and do it at home. Alice and Liz Canody, another Negro woman who had come to work for us that fall, were both around to help with Ruth and pitch in with the household chores.

About ten days into their trip, Ruth became ill with what we thought was a simple chest cold. With Mama away, I wasn't sure which of her remedies would help her. We were in touch by letter but that was very slow and by the time I got an answer, Ruth's chest cold had quickly turned into what the doctor diagnosed as pneumonia. I was frantic, feeling the responsibility of her care and wondering why in the world Mama would leave me, a fifteen–year–old, practically in charge of a three–year–old and an entire household. I felt completely overwhelmed, not to mention that I missed Robert and resented Ruth as a substitute charge.

I did all of the things doctor suggested and drew on my experience with Robert's breathing problems through the years. Liz or Alice, one or the other, did stay in the house at night with us which gave me a little more sense of security. Sister Lizzie came over once in a while to check on us, but she had her own family to look after and didn't stay long. She had looked after me when she was the same age as I was now and I felt she expected me to do the same without complaint. Since she had left home, we hadn't been particularly close – our interests and goals were so different that we had little to share with each other.

I prayed on my own and I prayed along with the rest of the family, as I had done with Robert and fully expected the same result – that was not to be.

It was decided that Ruth would sleep in Robert's room next to me upstairs so I would be near her if she wakened in the night. I had become a very light sleeper when I had begun helping with Robert so I was always ready if Ruth needed something.

That night I put Ruth into Robert's bed about eight o'clock. She seemed to be fine, even a little better, with less coughing and her temperature had gone down a bit. I was so tired, I didn't even kiss her good–night and went immediately to my room where I read a little of "Pilgrim's Progress" until I fell soundly asleep with the lamp still burning and the book open on my chest.

At 5 AM I heard Papa moving downstairs getting ready to go out and do morning chores. I had slept really well and was refreshed and ready for the day. I closed my book, blew out the gaslight and put my feet down on the cold, October floor. I was a little surprised that I hadn't heard Ruth but took it as a good sign that she had had an uneventful night.

I went into her room where she lay, I assumed, still fast asleep, just as I had left her the night before. I don't know how long it was before I realized something was very wrong. Ruth chest was not moving and there was an unnatural stillness about her and she was very pale. I went to her and touched her little hands – they were as cold as ice.

"Papa, Alice, come quick, I think Ruth is d…." I screamed, but couldn't say the word. Both of them came bounding up the stairs and into the room. Alice went directly to Ruth, touched her gently and declared with a solemn voice, "This baby gone to Jesus."

How could this have happened? She didn't even call for help or cough or maybe she did and I was just too fast asleep and didn't hear her. I was a complete wreck with grief and guilt and nobody even noticed as they began making preparations for what would come next. I felt so alone. Not even God seemed present.

Lizzie came home as soon as she heard as did Edgar and Benjamin. We wrapped Ruth's tiny body in a blanket and waited for the doctor to come, though we knew there was nothing to be done.

Papa immediately turned off his emotions and moved directly into the practicalities of the situation.

"We must let your mother know right away. She'll want to come home as soon as possible. Edgar, go to the telegraph office and send a wire. Lizzie, go over to the church and tell Pastor Glick that we will be needing a service there. Sarah, there will be people coming by, you and Alice start fixing something for people to eat and drink…"

On and on he went while I stood there beside my dead sister wondering what I had done wrong. Certainly this was my fault in some way, although no one suggested this might be so. And why had God not saved Ruth the way he had saved Robert? This made absolutely no sense. I was a bundle of mixed emotions; grief, guilt, sadness and creeping in without warning, resentment and anger; anger at God and anger at my mother, which only left me feeling even more guilt.

Mama, Robert and John were to arrive on the train in Staunton the next day but an early October snowstorm held them up there for three days. I was almost relieved. I didn't know how I was going to face my Mother after such a terrible failure of duty. She had trusted me and now Ruth was dead.

When they finally arrived, Robert ran into the house first and into my open arms. Such a sensitive little boy, he wept and wept, but strangely, I did not. When Mama walked in I didn't know what to do – would she blame me, hold me responsible somehow? She came to me first, put her hands on my shoulders and said, "Oh, Sarah, I'm so very sorry." She took me in her arms where she wept and I stood like a plank board, unable to shed a tear or feel anything.

As was tradition, the funeral was held three days after Ruth's death. We huddled as a family around Ruth's tiny casket in the cemetery at Linville Creek Brethren Church. The snow from the early October storm had practically melted and the fall sun shone brightly on the turning leaves. I kept

Robert near to console him as well as give me something to do to avoid my mixed feelings about the whole situation. People offered their condolences in soft voices as they passed by the family – I wanted to scream. Just when I thought things couldn't get worse, I looked up at the next person in line. There was John Flory and on his arm was a lovely girl. "Sadie, I'm so sorry for your loss. I know how hard this must be for you." He looked fondly at the girl on his arm, "Sadie, I'd like you to meet my fiancé, Nannie Coppock. Nannie, this is a dear young friend of mine, Sadie Zigler."

CHAPTER ELEVEN

Spring, 1898

Something had changed in Mama's behavior towards me in the months after she came home from Ohio last October. She was more attentive and seemed to be watching me all the time. Truth be told, my behavior warranted some watching. In the weeks after Ruth died, I had become sullen and difficult to have around. I was a tangle of emotions I could neither understand nor control. I kept asking myself what I could have done differently. I always woke up for Robert every time he needed me. I knew I had never loved Mary Ruth in the way I had Robert and wondered if that had anything to do with my not attending her as well. Though I grieved her passing, I knew full well that I would have been devastated if it had been Robert instead.

And then there was the matter of John Flory getting married – something that really shouldn't have mattered at all. I had never had fantasies of actually marrying John, who was 15 years older than I. Yet, his attention to me had been so supportive to my plans that the thought of my having to share this attention bothered me more than I wanted to admit. He probably wouldn't even visit us anymore. I was on my own now planning my future and I didn't need him or any other man. "And I'm not ever going to get married," I vowed silently. "I will be my own woman from now on."

I went about my chores mechanically, avoiding conversation with Papa, Mama or John. My one ally was, of course, Robert and I tried to remain the same as always for him. I probably was even more attentive to him trying somehow to make up for my failure to save Ruth.

Robert returned immediately to school but I did not. I had already missed almost a month of school and had been too busy with the chores at home to do much reading or homework that the teacher was kind enough to send. I resented this interruption of my educational plan. At the same time, my feelings of resentment were compounded with guilt over my part in Ruth's death.

Papa and John were occupied with the running of the farm and left Mama, Robert and me to grieve in our own way, as they did theirs. Mama continued to be extra–loving to me as I sulked around the house and often rebuffed her attempts at affection, still blaming her so I could be mad at someone besides myself.

"Sarah, would you please come in here for a moment?" she called one day. She was in her bedroom where she lay ridden with debilitating rheumatism which had developed soon after Ruth's death.

"Yes, Mama, may I help you?" I replied stiffly, walking into the room and waiting for some request from her to run an errand or such.

"Please sit down," she said, painfully trying to prop herself up on the pillow. I helped her adjust her position and went to sit across the room on a chair, avoiding her gaze.

"Here," she said, patting the space beside her on the bed, "Please, sit here."

Again, I was surprised at her wanting me so close to her for some reason.

"Look at me, Sarah," she said as she took my hand. "Look at me!"

Hesitantly, I looked into Mama's sad eyes.

"It wasn't your fault, Sarah. Little Ruth's death was not your fault and it was not God's fault."

"But Mama, I…"

"Please listen to me carefully. I have watched you these past months, moping around, angry and so very sad because you blame yourself. I know this because I've felt the same way about my part in it." She shifted around again, uncomfortable in one position for very long.

"I also feel very badly that I went off and left you with such a responsibility at your age. That was…"

"But Lizzie was my age when she took care of me," I said, still holding on to what had become a comfortable way of seeing myself in a negative light.

"I never went far away when you were little under Lizzie's care and I realize it was unfair to do that to you. Will you please forgive me and most of all, forgive yourself for whatever you believe you did or didn't do?"

"But why didn't God save her like He did Robert? I prayed and prayed and He…"

"Sarah, this is what I believe about God and His presence in our day to day lives. Nothing was ever promised us anywhere in the Bible that every prayer we pray gets answered the way we want it. What is promised is that no matter what happens, God is with us to help get us through the things that are painful and that we don't understand. I have no doubt that God was with you and Ruth the whole time she was sick, and she is with Him now in some way or another. And God is with you right now, seeing your unhappiness and grieving with you."

I wanted to believe what she was saying but I wasn't ready to let go of beating myself up.

"But I've been so mad at God, and haven't even prayed lately. What must God think of my acting so disrespectful?"

She smiled at me and her eyes twinkled.

"I feel sure that God can handle your being mad at Him, Sarah."

For some reason, her giving me permission to be mad a God allowed me to move into a different place. I began to feel a huge weight start to lift from my body and my spirit.

"What should I do now?" I asked, hesitantly, beginning to trust this "new" Mama. "Where should I go from here?"

"My dearest Sarah, God has blessed you with gifts unique to our family. You are probably the smartest one of the bunch—only don't tell Robert I said that," she said with an unexpected sparkle in her tired eyes. "You have a curious mind that never stops asking questions, you have a beautiful voice and play the organ; you read literature that is far beyond your years. You ask where to go from here? This is what I think." She paused and then said the words I had been waiting to hear from my parents my whole life.

"Go back to school in the fall and concentrate on your studies. Keep asking questions, read everything you can get your hands on, sing, play the organ and never stop believing in yourself and God. And someday, if you still want that, go to college and become a teacher. God, I am positive, would like that very much."

CHAPTER TWELVE
Fall 1898

I n September I went back to school in Broadway and dived joyfully into my studies. I had been away from school for more than a year, helping out at home. I had kept up with my reading so they let me start as a rising junior meaning I would graduate with my class. With John Flory's endless stream of reading material out of the picture I sought out books from the library. I had been right about him not coming by to visit us anymore. Between his new marriage to "what's her name" and his duties as professor at Bridgewater College, I supposed he was just too busy. I kept telling myself that it was silly to miss him as much as I obviously did. Apparently, my feelings for him were stronger and maybe even a little different than I had thought. I still looked on him as a mentor, but at sixteen found myself fanaticizing about him. Of course, I shared this with no one, particularly Lizzie, who had started pushing me to find a boyfriend. After John Shank had died, she remained a widow with four small children but was already looking to marry again.

Lizzie and I were drying dishes after Sunday dinner as she picked up a lecture she had begun on the way home from church. "If you can't find a boy you like at school, how about the ones at church?" she said in a motherly tone. "You've grown up with all those boys and they're from good Brethren homes – they'd all make good husbands. Don't tell me you haven't noticed the way they look at you." She stopped and looked me up and down with a leering smile. "What about that boy I saw you talking with after church – he certainly looked interested."

Uncomfortable with the conversation and her rude staring, I said firmly, "Lizzie, I've told you before, I'm not interested in a husband right now, maybe never," I said, weary of her constant nagging. "For heaven's sake, I'm only sixteen and I still want to go to college when I graduate. With all this in and out of school the past couple of years, I haven't had time for boys."

"My point exactly – when I was sixteen, I was dating John F…"

"And we know how that turned out," I said with sass in my voice. Lizzie looked as if she had been slapped and I quickly realized that what I had said was really unkind. "I'm sorry, Lizzie, that wasn't nice at all. I'm…"

She recovered with a shrug, used to my moods and my occasional sharp tongue, and continued right on, "Well, at least I had some dates and some experience before I settled down with my John and I'm hoping to marry again someday. Companionship is so important for a woman. Even if you become a teacher or something, wouldn't you want to get married?"

I went to Mama's cabinet and took out some tea and two cups. "How about we go out on the porch and have some tea?" I said, trying to move the conversation away from me and my love–life, or lack thereof. "By the way, how are you getting along with your in–laws?" When it became too difficult to keep up John Shank's farm after he died, Lizzie and her children had moved in with his parents on another Mennonite farm.

After I boiled the water for the tea, we walked out to the front porch where two rocking chairs waited for us. The fall breeze felt refreshing and the wonderful aroma of the lavender tea and the gentle motion of the chairs back and forth seemed to clear the air between Lizzie and me.

"They've really been wonderful. We always got along but I wasn't sure about living with them under the same roof. Mennonites have such a wonderful way of stepping up when they're needed. The children love them and feel very much at home as I do." She smiled contentedly and sipped her tea.

I was always impressed that even as a widow Lizzie was happy with her life and she just could not understand why I wouldn't want the same.

A few days after my conversation with Lizzie, I stood at the end of the hall upstairs, staring at my reflection in the mirror. I supposed I wasn't ugly, but I had never considered myself much of a beauty either. I had continued to develop early and like a good Brethren girl hid my ample breasts and full hips under my plain homespun dresses. I fiddled with my hair, which I suppose was probably my best feature. I hadn't cut it for years and after my childhood pigtails, I had begun either pulling it back where it hung almost to my waist, or piling it up on the top of my head in a large bun. My hair was dark brown and quite wavy and had a sheen about it. My features were plain, and I had always thought my nose seemed too big for my face.

Looking back at me from the mirror was a sixteen–year–old girl who had big dreams for herself. I had gotten over my guilt of Mary Ruth's death though the grief of it still haunted me and reminded me that life was indeed fragile. I vowed I would not waste mine. Teachers at school were encouraging about my plans to attend college and be a teacher. There was nothing to stop me from being able to fulfill every purpose that God intended for me.

"You look just beautiful, Sarah," said Mama as she climbed the stairs. She was still suffering from debilitating rheumatism, but was able to get around pretty well now. "Who is this boy you're sitting with at church – do I know him – who are his parents?" She fiddled with my hair and arranged my dress.

"His name is Daniel Miller, they just moved here from Pennsylvania so you probably don't know them," I answered, annoyed at her interrogation – she was far too excited about this – certainly more excited than I was. "I met him last week at church and he asked me to sit with him this Sunday for service. It's no big deal, I barely know him."

"Well, it's good to see you getting away from all the studying you do and…"

"Mama, are you going to church today?" I said, hoping divert her away from what I assumed was Lizzie's influence and constant talk about my lack of social life.

"I don't think I will. I'm a little tired from the company last evening for supper. They stayed the night and didn't leave until about thirty minutes ago. Robert and your father will just have to go it alone today. I'll have my service right down in the living room like they used to in the old days. I might even get your Papa to pull down the partition for atmosphere," she laughed, and I marveled at her positive attitude with all she had to deal with.

I waited outside on the porch, watching for Daniel and his family's wagon that would carry us to church. I was mad at myself for even agreeing to sit with Daniel, but I couldn't seem to get rid of him. Oh well, it would all be over in a few hours.

At about ten, the large wagon, pulled by a beautiful black stallion, drove up to the gate. Mr. Miller "whoa–ed" the horse and the wagon full of Daniel's entire family stopped. I counted – besides Daniel, his mother and father there were five children from the ages of toddler to teen lined up on the bench–like seats. Dressed conservatively, they were a typical Brethren farm family and they all stared at me curiously as Daniel helped me into the rig. He shyly introduced me to his parents and siblings. We drove the short distance to the church without anyone saying a word to each other. When we reached the parking area outside the church, Mr. Miller tied the horse to the railing.

The Linville Creek Church of the Brethren had been built in 1830 on land donated by John Kline, Mama's medical mentor and a Civil War Martyr. The huge hall, which was bigger than a barn, could seat one thousand people when a Love Feast was held twice a year. Inside and out the church was built of plain, unpainted wood.

"May I?" Daniel said as he jumped from the wagon and held out his hand to help me down.

"Thank you, Daniel," I said as I hopped off, immediately releasing my hand from his. He was a nice looking boy, blond, taller than I and obviously had been taught good manners. I started walking toward the church heading toward the women's entrance. "You know that the women go in a different door, don't you? We go in there," I said pointing to a little side landing with wide steps to accommodate the women's skirts and allow for them to gather and visit before the service. "You go over there where the men are going in—I'll meet you inside at the back where you'll see some raised seats—the young people usually sit there." I don't know why I felt the need to tell him this. The protocol was probably the same at his former church. He did seem a little taken aback by my telling him what to do which only egged me on.

I approached the women already gathered outside in their Sunday dresses and bonnets. One of them even wore a fashionable hat with a bow.

"Good morning, Sadie," I heard Lizzie, who had come that day to spy on me, call gaily and with entirely too

I walked by her without a glance and into the church where I looked for Daniel. He had already come in and found us a seat on the bleacher–like benches.

"This place is huge, do they ever fill it up?" he whispered as he looked around at the half-full church.

"Only when they have the Love Feast – people come from miles around for that and the place is packed. Really something to see," I answered, as the congregation settled and began to quiet down.

The Love Feast, as the Brethren called communion, was held once a year and was the high point of the Church's life. It incorporated the entire Biblical account of the last supper, including the meal and foot washing and was open to anyone who had been baptized. As a teenager, the foot washing was not a particular favorite of mine. I always seemed to get beside some old lady with stinky feet, which didn't put me in a particularly spiritual mood even if I knew the deeper meaning of it. The meaning of the ritual was quite simple, really. At the Last Supper, when Jesus washed his disciple's feet, he was showing that we must all serve each other and all mankind equally. There were to be no masters, no one above another and each of us is required to be humble enough to wash another's feet, which in Jesus' time was an act of great humility. `

Pastor Glick and the other deacons and elders filed into the front pews in the order of the time they had been elected to the ministry. They all wore the high–collared jacket with no buttons, befitting a Brethren man, and had beards of various lengths.

"Let us all stand and sing our opening hymn, Holy, Holy, Holy," he announced as the song leader took his place at the front of the congregation. The custom of congregational singing with a leader had been handed down for many years in our denomination. Hymn singing was a vital part of the service and of the spiritual life of every Brethren Church member. Since the men and women sat on separate sides of the church, we were divided naturally into parts; soprano, alto, tenor, bass. From the time we were little we had begun learning every verse of every hymn so congregational singing was like participating in a large chorus.

After the hymns there were several scriptures read by some of the lay ministers and a sermon by Pastor Glick. I was not particularly fond of our preacher as he fit into that category of "stiff-necked Brethren" Papa talked about. Instead of preaching about love in the church, his sermons were more about whether or not people were following the doctrinal rules and what would happen to them if they chose not to obey them. Today was no exception as he finished his sermon with, "Brothers and Sisters in Christ, we must follow the path of our ancestors who strictly adhered to plain living and abstinence from all lusts of the flesh," He looked sternly at the woman with the fancy hat, "There is no room in the Church for those who would wander from that path. AMEN!"

I leaned over to Daniel and whispered, "I thought the whole point of the church was to welcome sinners in the first place."

Daniel looked at me as if I had blasphemed the Holy Spirit and I knew this would be the last time I would sit in church with him.

As I walked out the women's entrance after the service, the ladies were huddled in a group engaged in a spirited conversation about something. I overheard Pastor Glick's wife say, "And you know, they were married less than a year when she died. He met her in Ohio while he was at Morris College and she was a lovely girl. I'm not sure what she died of but I sure do feel sorry for John – he's such a wonderful man."

I felt badly that this particular news did not make me feel particularly bad.

CHAPTER THIRTEEN

June, 1899

I graduated first in my class at Broadway High School at the age of seventeen in the June, 1899. My next step would be to apply to Bridgewater College where John Flory was now a professor and single once more. After I had heard the news about his wife, I kept hoping he might pay us a visit but that didn't happen. I supposed that he looked on me as any one of his former students who weren't particularly unique. If he saw me that way, I wouldn't give him another thought.

"Sarah," Papa said when we arrived home after the graduation ceremony, "Let's go for a little walk, we need to talk about something."

Mama had not been able to go to the graduation which saddened me. She had been so supportive of my education and goals these past few years and I know how proud she would have been to see me in my graduation dress that she had made. This had not been an easy task with her rheumatism but she was determined that I have something special to wear. Though the dress conformed to the Brethren style of plainness, there were several features that Mama had added that made it unique and even a little bold. It was made of dark blue muslin that we had woven on looms in the smoke house. The full blouse was made with tucks from shoulders to waist and she added buttons in two rows down the front, something that was frowned upon. The sleeves were puffed at the shoulders and the waistband fit tightly around my waist. I filled out the blouse on top but didn't have a tiny waist as was the worldly fashion; however, the style of the dress became my figure. Tucked in at the waist was my graduation present from Mama and Papa – a gold watch on a black silk cord that had been Mama's from the Knupp side of the family.

"This dress is a little hot for walking around in this weather. May I go change first?" I asked, not wanting to ruin my new dress with perspiration.

"Well, then, let's just sit on the porch a while," he answered, and I sensed he was in a hurry to get whatever he wanted to say, said. I was not surprised when he began, "You know your mother hasn't been well lately and something has come up that needs immediate attention."

"What do you mean, Papa?" I said, fearing the worst. "It's just her rheumatism isn't it?"

"The doctor has discovered something else and has strongly suggested that she go to Johns Hopkins Hospital in Maryland for some tests. He's not sure what's going on but the hospital in Harrisonburg is not equipped to do what needs to be done." He was trying to be calm and relay the facts he thought I should know, but his voice broke. He cleared his throat and looked directly at me and I knew what was coming.

"I know you had planned to apply to go to college in the fall, but Sarah, I will need you here to help with Robert and the rest of the household duties," he said, not really expecting any response except, "Of course, Papa."

"Of course, Papa," I said, quietly, a lump in my throat and a sinking feeling taking hold of my stomach. I looked away and fixed my gaze on the smoke house so that he could not see the tears in my eyes, as he continued.

"I want you to know that even though I'm not as keen as your mother about your going on to school, I will support you in it when the time is right. I am very proud of what you've accomplished and I know this is not what you planned but your mother is…" He stopped and I quickly looked back at him as I suddenly realized that he had tears in his eyes. He was frightened, something I had never seen in my father, and this alarmed me. Was Mama going to die, too? Was it ever going to end, this constant loss in our family? I wanted to comfort him in some way, but held back, not quite knowing what to do.

All I could do was say, "Papa, I will do anything I can to help. College can wait – I can wait. We must take care of Mama, that's what's important." And I realized that, in that moment, I meant what I was saying.

CHAPTER FOURTEEN
JUNE, 1903

S oon after my graduation from high school in June, 1899, Mama had gone to John's Hopkins Hospital for the tests that were recommended and the news was not good. She had several malignant tumors in her pelvic area and before they sent her home, the doctors surgically removed them. She came home to recover and seemed to be doing fairly well.

I had resigned myself to my duties at home where, in addition to caring for Mama and Robert, I took over the preparation for the many guests that still frequented here. Mr. Plougher continued to bring interesting stories and books and we always had a wonderful music session when he came. Dr. Holsinger also continued giving me organ and voice lessons and encouraged me to come as soon as I could to Bridgewater College where I could formally study music. John Flory had decided to continue his studies at the University of Virginia in Charlottesville and left Bridgewater and the area in 1902. He had never visited us once after his wife died. I was disappointed but accepted the reality that I was not as special to him as he had been to me. What I had learned from him would just have to be enough to sustain me in my journey ahead.

In 1902 Mama had another flare–up of pain and other familiar symptoms and was sent back to John's Hopkins where more malignant tumors were found and removed. We all tried to remain optimistic, including Mama, but the doctors were not. The cancer continued to spread, and they gave her, at the most, another year.

We moved her bed into the living room and lowered the partitions that were used for the Brethren meeting house in the past. The early summer sun shone brightly through the opened window where we had placed a multitude of flowers. African Violets in clay pots were set away from the direct sunlight, their velvety green leaves and blossoms of pink, purple and lavender brightening up the room where Mama lay, day and night. She was weak and pale, but her spirits were good and the red geraniums in full bloom on the wide window sill seemed to give her the extra color she lacked. Robert sat at her bedside, reading to her from the Bible. At twelve, he was still puny and could do little hard labor on the farm so he rose to the occasion and was a great help with her. She encouraged him to memorize long passages at which he was extremely adept. I worried that he was skipping school on a regular basis to be with her but understood that he needed to do this, just as I did.

I was still waiting for the right time to apply to Bridge-water College. Neither of my parents had mentioned the subject during the past three years. I was now twenty–one years old, praying the time would come soon, but as each year passed, I began losing hope that it would ever happen for me.

"Sarah, would you please come in here for a moment, I'd like to talk with you about something," I heard Mama call from her bed. I was in the kitchen with Alice, washing the fresh spinach from the garden. She had taken over the maintenance of the garden for which I was very grateful.

"Robert, will you give us a little time alone please?" Mama said, patting him on the knee gently.

Robert, who was having difficulty understanding all that was going on with Mama, hesitated a moment before he sighed and moved to the couch by the fireplace.

As I approached her bed I could smell the lavender Alice had grown in the garden and put in a bowl of water to lessen the odor of sickness in the house.

"What can I do for you, Mama?" I asked, fluffing her pillows. I had put on her pink flowered nightgown that gave color to her sunken cheeks and put up her hair – she looked almost pretty.

"You can stop fussing over me to begin with," she frowned, as if talking to a little girl. "And you can pull up that chair and listen to me." And like a little girl, I did exactly what she said.

Robert, who had picked up my skill of eavesdropping, sat in the living room waiting for us to begin.

"Robert," Mama said in a stronger voice than usual, "Would you please give Sarah and me a little time alone? Thank you as always for your reading. Why don't you go out on the porch and memorize that passage in John you were just reading?"

"But…"

"No buts, Robert," she said firmly.

Robert ducked his head, obviously a little hurt, and obeyed. As he walked by my chair I patted him on the arm and smiled. "Thank you Robert, I'm sure we won't be long."

Mama cleared her throat and began.

"Sarah, I'm feeling much stronger since my last surgery and really feel good about what lies ahead for me. You've been a wonderful daughter, taking such good care of me these past couple of years."

"Mama, I was happy to do it and I…"

"Sarah, please, I want you to listen to me and listen well. You have given up what you wanted to do after you graduated from high school. You were about to be accepted at Bridgewater College and you've stayed home with me…"

"But Mama, I…"

"Just be quiet yet!" she said falling back into her Pennsylvania Dutch.

She took a deep breath.

"I need to tell you something important and you must do as I say."

"Anything, Mama," I said.

"Throughout my own life, I have been content and fulfilled as a woman. I chose the life I have led and I have been blessed. I honestly have not quite understood your dreams and plans for yourself, but I want you to know that I have always respected them. Lizzie is more like me, and is happy with her choice of having a husband and family – she'll be marrying again this year. You, on the other hand, are a lot like your father. Because you are a woman, it seems odd to both of us that you have always wanted to do things differently. But that being said, there is no reason why we should not support you."

I sat, wondering where this was leading. Even though Mama and I had become very close since Ruth died, she rarely sat down with me like this.

"This is what I want you to do." She adjusted her pillow so that she could sit very erect. Her face took on a shining glow and her eyes blazed with a determination I hadn't seen for a long, long time. She paused as she looked out the window through the bank of flowers and then, looking directly at me, she became a preacher, and her sermon began thusly:

"This fall, I want you to enroll for classes at Bridgewater…"

I gasped, hardly believing what I was hearing.

"Your father and I have discussed this and agree that you have put this off for too long. And I, for one, never want to think that I have stood in the way of your future happiness. Times for women are changing. We may well have the chance to vote in your lifetime. Do you understand what I'm saying?"

I was speechless. When I found my voice, I said, "But do we have the money to do this?"

"Your father has spoken with John Flory and he's been in touch with the college; they have made arrangements. We are just fine. Robert won't be going to college for years and we can save up for that."

I ran to Mama's bed and embraced her, which was still not something we ordinarily did, even with our new closer relationship.

"Oh, Mama, thank you – thank you."

"Now, now, that'll do – I'm happy you're pleased," she said, pulling away quickly.

"Pleased. I can't believe it," I said. "Where's Papa, I want to thank him, too."

I went into the kitchen where Papa sat, drinking a cup of coffee. He looked up. I started over to him but thought better of it—his stern expression let me know he was not nearly as enthusiastic as Mama had been.

"Papa, how can I thank you, I just talked with…"

"You have mainly to thank your mother for this decision," he said matter-of-factly. "She convinced me it was the right thing to do. I have always pushed for the things that were most important to me. I suppose I shouldn't be surprised that you might have inherited that trait from me, even though you are a woman." He suddenly broke into a wide grin. "I wish you well, my dear daughter. I wish you very well."

I went to my room where I dug out the application to Bridgewater that had been in my desk drawer for four years. And it had certainly not escaped my awareness the mention of John Flory and his part in this new development.

CHAPTER FIFTEEN

September, 1903

"Listen to that, Sadie," said Mollie, as we walked down the stairs from our room in Founder's Hall, the new residence hall for female students. "That's the sound of our future."

The daily trip from Broadway to Bridgewater would have been difficult so I was staying in the new dorm with my cousin, Mollie Zigler, as my roommate. She was younger than I by several years, more the age of most of the freshmen there, and we had known each other through family, but were not that close. She was planning to study science and become a nurse. How refreshing it was to be with Brethren women who had a vision for themselves.

From atop Memorial Hall, one of the red brick buildings that made up Bridgewater College came the sound of the large bell that hung in an imposing bell tower. The tradition was that this bell was rung the first day of classes of your freshman year and again on the day of your graduation. Thus, at twenty–one–years of age, I began my first day as a college student.

That year, the fall of 1903, Mollie and I were among the largest student body ever at Bridgewater College. Even at its founding in 1880 there had been five women enrolled in a student body of 129 and this year there were 251 students and many more women. Besides the obvious thrust of being a Brethren school which stressed biblical tenants, Bridgewater had a strong belief in the importance of co–ed education. In their information about the school it was stated, "… in regard to co–education of the sexes the only true method of education. Their reciprocal influence will be beneficial in the Chapel, Dining room and Recitations rooms."

"I can't believe I'm finally here," I said, feeling like a child on Christmas morning. I looked around me, taking in my new surroundings. The campus was beginning to show signs of autumn – the grass was still green but the trees were showing some color, particularly the Dogwood, which were a rich red. Bridgewater College was situated in the little town of Bridgewater on several acres of land. All of the buildings were plain, box–like and made of red brick and trimmed with white woodwork. Several had white columns out front. Cement walkways led from one building to another and were lined with some large old trees, left there when the land was cleared and other smaller trees that had been planted over the years. As students came out of their respective residence halls, the atmosphere was a mix of anticipation and friendly exchange of greetings – everyone spoke though we, as yet, knew not a soul.

Each day before classes began there was Chapel, at which we sang hymns of praise, had scripture reading and a sermon. Services were held during the week as well as three or four on Sunday.

"What classes do you have today?" asked Mollie as we neared the Chapel.

"I have a literature class with a professor I never heard of, a Dr. Norris," I answered, pulling my sweater around my shoulders to ward off the nip in the air. "I had hoped John Flory would still be teaching but he took off to University of Virginia last year for further study, I…" I could have kicked myself for mentioning his name because Mollie immediately picked up on my interest.

"OOO, Sadie," she said with a twinkle in her eye, "You're a little sweet on him, yes? The look you get on your face whenever you mention him…"

"Come on, Mollie he's way too old for me. He's just been such a huge influence on my education and if it weren't for him, I wouldn't be here in the first place," I defended myself, knowing I was lying to her and to me.

"Why, Sadie, you're blushing!"

"I am not!" I said, indeed feeling my face getting warm. Good heavens, what was that all about? I remembered my sister Lizzie doing the same thing the first time John came to the house.

"Are you taking any music courses, I know how much you enjoy that?" she said, changing the subject, for which I was grateful.

"I'm taking harmony, piano and voice from Dr. Hildebrand who took over Dr. Holsinger's position when he retired. He studied under him so I think he'll continue what I learned before," I answered, feeling my heart beat faster just saying the words that meant I was on the path I had hoped. I wasn't sure what kind of teacher I wanted to be, regular school or music, so I was taking a Classical curriculum that would cover both.

This day was the beginning of a dream that had begun so many years ago and I was more than ready.

* * * *

My first semester went even better than I had expected. My worries about being older and less prepared than the other students turned out to be unfounded. In many ways, I was more prepared because I had done so much reading on my own all those years at home. My musical training under Dr. Holsinger proved to be a firm foundation for my classes in the music department. In my literature courses, I was actually a bit ahead of most of the younger students who had read in high school only for grades and because they had to, not as I had, for the love of learning and the literature itself. When we studied *Pilgrim's Progress*, and I was required to write a paper, I received my first "A" grade from the professor as well as an invitation to his office on a clear, cold winter day near the end of the semester.

Dr. Norris' office was in the administration building on the third floor. As I climbed the stairs I wondered why in the world I had been summoned. Had I done something wrong?

His secretary let me into the tiny office that contained a desk and two wooden chairs. The entire four walls were lined with books from floor to ceiling except for the entrance door; there was one tiny window and the only open space on the wall displayed the professor's doctoral degree from Harvard. He had been hired as soon as he graduated and appeared to be only slightly older than I, even though his dark hair was thinning on top.

"Miss Zigler, please sit down," said Dr. Norris, graciously rising from his desk chair to shake my hand, "I have been quite impressed with your work in my class this semester – a pleasant surprise, though Dr. Flory did recommend you very highly before he left for Charlottesville."

"Thank you, sir," I said, sitting in the pine chair across from him, "If it weren't for John Flory, my zeal for education would probably not have been. His encouragement has been invaluable, especially since I've had to wait so long to get here." Again, I felt the slight warmth as I talked about him. "Stop it," I said to myself, "Just stop it!"

"Your paper on John Bunyan was outstanding and your grasp of his deep religious journey showed great maturity and insight. Had you read it before?"

"My parents gave me a copy when I was twelve – I have read it several times since then," I said, feeling quite pleased as I watched his bushy eyebrows rise in surprise.

"Twelve years old? That's quite an accomplishment for that age – I am amazed that you had any idea what it was all about."

"Actually," I admitted with a smile, "I had little idea of the depth of the stories then – that has only come with age, and as you know, I am quite a bit older than most of those in my class." I waited for a negative response to this information.

"Which is actually why I have asked you here today," he paused and looked around his study and then shuffled some papers on his extremely tidy desk.

I waited as he lifted up a copy of some sort of publication and handed it to me. "This is the monthly put out by the Philomathean Society. Have you seen it?"

I was aware that there were several literary societies that were invitation only membership. Both men and women who excelled in the field of literature were asked to belong after they proved themselves in class – most of them were juniors or seniors.

"Yes sir, I saw a copy the other day in the library," I said, taking the small, printed copy from his hand and flipping through the pages. "I wondered what it was."

"We have been very pleased with the response since we began its publication in the '96-'97 session." Dr. Norris rose from his chair and began walking around the cramped office. He wasn't a tall man but had an imposing stature, almost too big for what felt a little like a closet. He ran his hand through his dark hair and suddenly turned toward me. "I'll get right to the point—you have been recommended as a candidate for membership in the Victorian Literary Society and I would like you also to consider working on the Philomathean Monthly, at a beginning level, of course."

I was stunned, "But I am only a freshman, I…"

"But your work is far above that level," he said, his face becoming animated. "And I feel that as long as you've waited to begin this part of your education, you should be encouraged to move forward as quickly as we can make possible. Would you consider this when you come back for next semester in January?"

I could barely sit still in my chair and took a deep breath before I answered. Dr. Norris had sat back down at his desk and leaned forward waiting for my response.

"Yes sir, of course, I would be honored, thank you so much, this is more than I could ever have imagined. Thank you, again," I said, beginning to feel like a babbling, excited school girl.

"Well then, that's settled," he said standing and offering his hand again, "Someone from Victoria will be in touch right after the first of the year. We will look forward to your association with what we consider one of the best programs in the state. Have a wonderful Christmas vacation."

I walked to the door, which he opened for me and gave me a slight bow. It was all I could do not to giggle.

I supposed that Boston must be a little more formal than Bridgewater.

I ran to tell Mollie my news. She met me at the door of our room with a mournful expression.

"Sadie, you have a note from home that just came from the office – I'm sorry, I couldn't help but read it. It's your mother."

CHAPTER SIXTEEN

December, 1903 – January, 1904

Papa picked me up in the wagon and I returned home from Bridgewater College. He barely said a word the whole ride, his thoughts at home with Mama. I, on the other hand was thinking back to the hours before he arrived, when, instead of packing up essentials for the Christmas holidays, I had packed up everything I owned from my dorm room. I knew what was coming.

He let me off at the porch and I walked into the living room where Mama still lay at her place in front of the window. I knew immediately that she would not survive this latest crisis. Her color was grey and she barely opened her eyes when I made my presence known.

"Hello, Mama, it's me Sarah – I've come home," I said, feeling the weight of that statement and what it might mean for my future, sink in.

Mama reached out her hand and I took it. It was clammy–cold and limp in mine and I just wanted to cry. This strong vibrant woman I had known and loved for twenty-one years was no more and the awareness that this was the beginning of the end was almost more than I could bear.

Christmas was a sad occasion with no decorations or gifts as Robert and I tended our mother the best way we could. We didn't even go to church on Christmas morning. I had not seen my family since Thanksgiving when Mama seemed to be doing much better. Her turn for the worse had been sudden and dramatic.

For the week after Christmas we watched and waited as Mama began to slip away. On the morning of January 11, 1904 the entire family was called.

That bitter January day I stood in the living room by Mama's bed, along with Papa and Robert. Lizzie and the others had not, as yet, arrived.

The room smelled medicinal and stale with illness and something else I didn't recognize immediately. I looked at Mama and I knew what it was – it was the odor of death. Robert, who was just thirteen, got up from the bedside and came over to me, tears streaming down his face. He had already experienced the death of his baby sister, but he couldn't seem to comprehend that he was about to lose his mother. I embraced his teenage body awkwardly, this boy, who in my arms, was still "My Robert."

Papa looked at me as he sat, holding the hand of this woman with whom he had spent almost forty years. He nodded his head as I disentangled myself from Robert and approached Mama's bed.

I looked at her face, so thin and drawn. Her eyes were closed and she seemed to be barely breathing. I wondered if she had already died and leaned over to kiss her, measuring the sound of what was still a shallow breath of life.

I touched Papa's shoulder gently and he patted my hand with his free one. I was struck with the reality that these two people, who had been so strong in my life all these years, were not indestructible; they were older, frail and vulnerable.

The flowering plants that Mama so loved sat wilted in their clay pots – no one had watered them for weeks. They added to the atmosphere of death in the room.

I went into the kitchen where I looked for something to do; if I could make myself busy or do something for Papa or Robert, I could escape the grim reality of what was happening in the living room. I looked for some of Mama's chamomile tea to brew. There was none because there had been no Mama to grow or harvest it for some time – another loss to grieve.

Suddenly, Papa called, "Sarah, you need to come in here!" I knew that this was the sound of a man who was about to lose his stoic composure. His voice whispered, "She is leaving us."

He took both of her hands in his and kissed them tenderly, then kissed her forehead.

I came to stand by Robert who was openly weeping and pleading, "Please don't go, Mama, please."

I looked down as mama's eyes suddenly opened widely, but she was not looking at any of us, she was looking toward the winter sunlight coming in the window which seemed to be particularly bright all of a sudden.

"Mary Ruth, Mary Ruth!" she said in the direction she was looking and then her eyes went blank and her breathing stopped with a sort of gasp.

Robert, who didn't seem to realize what had just happened said, "Why did she say Mary Ruth? Mary Ruth is dead."

As Papa closed Mama's eyes with his hand he said, "I think, Robert, that your sister just welcomed your mother into paradise."

There was so much comfort in that statement, and as we all wept, I felt that there was truth in what he said.

Robert went outside on the porch, uncomfortable with the open show of emotion, not knowing exactly what might be expected of him.

As I moved to join Robert on the porch, I saw Papa adjusting the homemade quilt around Mama, as if tucking her in for the night. I remembered all the times she had tucked her own children in for the night and imagined her now tucking in little Ruth to whom she had not even gotten the chance to say good–bye.

On the porch, Robert and I were quiet and looked out over the snow–covered farm. The scene was so full of Christmas, yet the joy had gone out of the season.

I began thinking of all the preparations that would need to be made in the coming days, immediately switching from the deep grief of the moment to the practical things that had to be done.

Robert, wanting to change the subject suddenly said, "Hey Sadie, when are you supposed to go back to Bridge-water?"

My grief was suddenly compounded by a sense of despair that was so deep that I could hardly bear it. I stayed with the thought for only a moment as I answered Robert's question, "College was a wonderful experience that I will always cherish. Now, Robert, we must let your brothers and sister know about Mama and make plans – there is much to do."

Later that month I received a manila envelope in the mail from Bridgewater College. Inside was a copy of the January issue of The Philomathean Monthly, Volume VIII, No.4. Listed on the front page were the names of the Editorial Staff: W.A Meyers, Editor-in Chief, Virginia Lee Society, Associate Editors, J.H. Cline and H.K Wright-Virginia Lee Society, W.H. Sanger, Flora Good-Victorian Society and W. B. Norris.

Also on the front page was a poem called "Hope."

Hope sleeps deep in the heart like dew in a lily's cup;

Hope comes forth like the heaven's blue when the storm clouds have flown:

Hope shines under the tears like a diamond in the stream.

O, poor faint human heart, forsaken a thousand times,

Ever turn thyself heavenward, hoping and
trusting anew.

Just as Arachne, unwearied, spun each day a
new web

When at evening the threads were torn by the
hand of Fate. C.F.

I turned to the back page where, in the last paragraph
were written these words. "Mr. I.N. Zigler attended the funeral of his cousin, Mrs. Michael Zigler, January 13. Mrs. Zigler was the mother of Miss Sadie Zigler, who until Christmas was a student at the College. Her friends express their
deep sympathy in her sorrow."

S.J.W.

CHAPTER SEVENTEEN

April, 1905

During the year after Mama died, Robert was inconsolable. He had in the time leading up to her death, been her companion, her entertainment, her nurse. These two had, from his birth and fragile beginnings, formed a bond that was unusually close. This had become even stronger after Mary Ruth's death.

"Robert, you really need to go to school today — you've missed all week," I said as I picked up a pile of his dirty clothes on the floor. Once a tidy boy, he had become messy as well as sullen.

"I don't feel well enough," Robert whined as he sat in his usual spot in front of the window where Mama's bed had been, still in his pajamas and clutching a tattered black Joshua. He looked like a four–year–old.

"Your teacher called to say you're falling behind and it's getting close to the end of the school year. She says you are one of her best students and she wants you to finish up strong. Mama wouldn't want you to sit around moping like this."

"I'm not moping, I'm sick. You know how puny I've always been," he said faking a wheezing cough he had perfected over the years for getting his way.

"Robert, enough of that," I said sharply, "You're going to school – now get dressed!"

Robert stood up, walked to the stairs, turned and flung black Joshua across the room right at me.

It was rare that I ever raised my voice, especially to Robert, but lately I found myself irritable, frustrated and experiencing feelings that were similar to those after Ruth's death – only these feelings were deeper and much more complicated. Only very gradually did I become aware that the emotion I was experiencing was not only grief, but a smoldering anger. My natural even temperament and quiet demeanor hid this rising resentment and only once in a while did it come to the surface. I would feel guilty when I took it out on Robert who was my only safe target. I had no resources to help me sort out my feelings and no one to tell who I thought would understand. Mama had been there to help when Mary Ruth died and I felt angry at God, but she was gone and this anger felt more dangerous.

I was now the only adult female living in the house. I had taken up the duties required by the traditions of hospitality in our home, to feed and house the stream of humanity that flowed through it. Liz Canody and Alice Madden, bless them, were my saving grace, helping to prepare meals, do laundry and the myriad of other chores.

Papa worked out his grief by throwing himself into farm work. Almost sixty years old, he was still healthy and strong and along with the farm hands, managed to keep everything going.

"Have it your way, I'll go," Robert pouted as he came down the stairs dressed and ready, "But if I get sick at school you'll have to come get me," he said feigning his cough.

"Sam's out front in the wagon ready to take you. You'll be fine. Mama is proud of you," I said.

"Mama's dead," he said flatly and walked out the door.

Yes, Mama was dead, as was my dream of going to college. That bell in the tower on the Bridgewater College campus would never ring again for me.

When September drew near, I was confronted with the reality that my cousin Mollie was preparing to go back to Bridgewater along with all the other students, and I was not. She had known, probably more than anyone, how I must be feeling and for Christmas had given me a book on prayer, Throne of Grace, she hoped would help – it did not. I was twenty–three years old, unmarried, high school educated, living at home taking care of my father and my younger brother. Mama had been my champion and the main reason I was permitted to enroll in Bridgewater College last year. Now that she was gone and everyone in the family was grieving and adjusting, the possibility of my returning wasn't even discussed. Duty to family came first and foremost and I was expected to accept it without complaint—my family, my church, my community, and yes, God expected this of me – I expected this of me.

And for a time, I was too busy to consider the alternative life I had left behind and if the thought did creep in, I pushed it away. The choice had been made by the circumstance of time, gender and a loyalty to family which I accepted without asking why or what if. I pulled out the little book by Henry Altemus that Mollie had given me for comfort. "The writer has felt, (oh, how often!) that in times of weakness and weariness – of suffering and sorrow – there is no refuge – no place of rest, which can, for a moment, be compared with the heavenly mercy–seat. There, the burdened soul may cast itself on the bosom of infinite love – there anxieties, doubts, and fears may be freely disclosed…" I had always I believed this was true, but I could not seem to shake my negative feelings. Sometimes in my daily prayers I did ask God if there were still the possibility of my becoming a teacher – God was mute on this point. I was angry with God once again but Mama had assured me He could handle my anger just fine!

One day when we were doing some canning of the late summer vegetables, Lizzie came over to help Liz, Alice and me. She had tended to stay away, avoiding the gloom of the household after Mama's death. She and I were not estranged, but we were certainly not close enough for me to ask her about the way I was feeling. I doubted she would understand but I was desperate to talk with someone and she was my only sister.

"Lizzie, let's go outside a minute, I need to talk to you about something," I said, cautiously. "Alice, why don't you and Liz take a break while the jars cool?" The bread and butter pickles we had made and canned sat on the counter waiting to seal.

"I'll make us a cup of tea for good measure," I said sadly looking at Mama's medicine/tea cabinet. Alice had taken over the growing of herbs and teas and the shelves were beginning to fill up again. Little consolation.

"Of course," she said, her eyebrows rising in surprise at my request. She fussed with her apron over her pregnant belly—this would be her first child with Charles Myers, her new husband.

We walked outside where the fall air felt refreshing after the day in the hot kitchen. We sat down in the two rocking chairs on the porch and began to sip our tea and rock.

Lizzie jumped right in, eager to know why I had sought her out. "I knew something was bothering you – too much work around here I imagine," she said with what I took as judgment in her voice.

"No, that's not it," I said, irritated at her implication that I might not be as much of a worker as she had always been and still was. "The work has always been here." I felt myself increase the intensity of my rocking and my breath was getting shallow.

"Then what – do you miss Mama so much?" She was trying, she really was, but the gulf between us had grown over the years after she left when I was only ten and she acted more like a parent towards me than a sister. I was already sorry I had opened this can of worms with her.

"Of course I miss her," I said, feeling myself getting frustrated and knowing that before I even started to express the depth of my true feelings, Lizzie would not understand. "It's just that – oh, never mind."

"You aren't upset about college are you? I just don't think that was ever meant to be, Sadie. If it was, God would have made it possible. You just have to accept the will of God and move on with your…"

"Just stop it with the God talk, Lizzie, I'm not in the mood," I snapped, slamming my hand down on the arm of the chair and spilling tea all over my dress.

"Well excuuuuse me, Miss High and Mighty," she said, her expression incredulous at my perceived blasphemy. "If you hadn't read all those darn books and gotten so blessed educated, you wouldn't be so uppity. Just accept the way things are. You know, if you had just gotten married like I did, you…"

"Enough, Lizzie, enough," I shouted, feeling my face getting flushed and standing up from my chair. It was all I could do to not throw my cup at her as I stomped through the screen door, slamming it behind me with great force.

"Sadie, my advice as your older sister is to go see Pastor Glick and talk to him" I heard her voice rise, her sage advice fading as I stomped upstairs. "This is not healthy –

that comment about God is awful – you need spiritual help!" she yelled.

I really didn't have much confidence that Pastor Glick could help me but I felt badly that I had been so out of control with Lizzie during our conversation, so a few days later, I went to go see him after apologizing to my sister. I could only hope that he was a better counselor than preacher.

His office was as plain and stark as the rest of the church but had even less character and warmth than the sanctuary. Unlike the offices of professors at Bridgewater, there were no shelves full of books suggesting a man interested in much of anything. There were no degrees on the walls because ministers in the Brethren Church were not required to go to a seminary or college. Some ministers, like John Flory, chose to do that, but not Pastor Glick or most of the deacons and elders at Linville Creek Church of the Brethren. The only thing on his desk was an open Bible – that was it. There were no plants or anything to brighten up this room that clearly reflected the man who worked there.

He asked me if I'd lost faith in God.

"No, Pastor Glick, I have not lost faith in God, I think I have lost faith in my life and its purpose," I said, sitting in his office at the church. I was already sorry I had come, but I listened for his response.

"Isn't your purpose to serve God, no matter what He requires of you?" he said, thumbing through his Bible, looking for something to quote.

"I always believed that, and I also believe that God gave me the desire to get more education and be a teacher. It seems that every time I get close to furthering my goal, something happens at home and I'm required to wait again."

"Ah, but Sarah, patience is a God–given virtue that must be cultivated over time and your duty to your parents outweighs any plans you might have for yourself," he offered, very pleased with himself that he had honed in on a Biblical concept.

I tried once more to help him understand that I was trying to live a Godly life. "But why would God put that desire on my heart and then make it impossible to do that very thing?"

His expression took on a sinister look. "Maybe it wasn't God that put that desire in your mind," he said knowingly. "Maybe it was the evil one leading you astray."

It was the Devil talk that finally alerted me to the fact I would get nowhere with this conversation. I was certainly well aware of evil in the world but the existence of an actual Devil with a forked tail was a belief I did not share and I certainly was not going to debate that point with Pastor Glick.

I was feeling more and more frustrated so I said, as nicely as I could, "Pastor Glick, I appreciate your time and wanting to help. I think what I will do is go home and pray some more about it."

I started to leave but Pastor Glick stopped me as suddenly, he knelt on the floor, grabbed me by the arm and pulled me down on my knees beside him. "Let us pray," he said in his most preacher-like voice. "Dear Lord, we ask that you cast out any prideful or wayward sprits that the Devil has put in this young woman's mind. Keep her safe from the Evil One and lead her to pray unceasingly for your will. In Jesus Name we pray. AMEN."

I got up from my knees and practically ran out the door.

Though I did not pray the prayer that Pastor Glick had prayed, I did pray — and I prayed and I prayed until one day, my prayers were answered, though not perhaps as Pastor Glick might have wished.

CHAPTER EIGHTEEN

May, 1907

"Guess who's coming for the weekend!" said Papa, coming into the kitchen where I was preparing yet another meal for yet another group of guests. I tried to keep my resentment in check each time I was expected to entertain our constant company but I rudely grunted, "Who?"

"John S. Flory," Papa said, giving me a stern look. "Now get that scowl off your face—I'm getting a little tired of that attitude of yours."

I ducked my head, guiltily, regretting that I had let my feelings show.

"Sorry, Papa," I said and suddenly absorbed what he had just said. I felt my heart leap with a joy that I hadn't felt for a long time. "Is he really coming here? I thought that he was studying at the University of Virginia."

"He's back at Bridgewater now and coming to preach at church this Sunday. He'll be staying here Friday and Saturday nights."

"That's wonderful, Papa," I exclaimed. "Will he be here for supper on Friday?"

"Probably not until a little later in the evening. He has classes on Friday and has to get here after that."

For the first time in months I was excited about something. I dived into preparations with great purpose and anticipation. Even though Papa had said he wouldn't be here for supper I fixed some of the dishes I knew John loved and even made a mince–meat pie from what we had put up last year.

At supper on Friday night, I could barely contain my excitement and just picked at my food. As Papa had predicted, John wouldn't arrive until about nine o'clock. As I cleaned up from our early supper I began to hatch a plan for my first meeting with my mentor since I had seen him and his fiancé at Mary Ruth's funeral ten years before. I went upstairs to get dressed.

At the mirror in the hall I thought of that Sunday when Mama declared me "beautiful" before I went to church with Daniel Miller. I realized what I was feeling today was exactly what Mama and Lizzie had hoped I felt that day with Daniel.

John had remained a widower since he lost his wife in 1898. I felt almost giddy as I saw myself in the dress I had carefully pulled out for the occasion. Lizzie had made this one for me, hoping I would wear it for courting a beau, which she still hadn't given up harping upon. The dress was a deep maroon and styled much like the one Mama had made for my graduation from high school. The collar was still high but had a bit of lace trim and Lizzie had also added some buttons down the front. I pulled the dress over my head and adjusted the waist. My figure hadn't changed very much in the past few years, and if anything, I had lost a bit of my youthful weight. I piled my long hair on top of my head in a bun and as I carefully pulled my gold watch on the cord, the final touch, over my head, I said to my image in the mirror, "Just calm down, Sadie, he's just an old friend who looks at you as a little girl."

About eight o'clock our guest walked into our living room as he had so many times before. He was still strikingly handsome at 37 and still had that confidence and poise about him.

"Good evening, Sadie, so happy to see you again," he said, taking my hand in his and looking into my eyes. I felt my heart leap and I knew I must be blushing.

"Thank you, John, I appreciate that," I said, pulling my hand away and trying not to sound like a smitten school girl, which is exactly the way I felt.

"It's been quite a while. So sorry to hear about your mother and that I couldn't be here for her service. I know this has not been easy on you, especially having to drop out of college. I do hope that you haven't given up that goal for yourself."

There it was, right out in the open at the get–go. One of the things I had always loved about John Flory was that he never minced words or avoided an uncomfortable subject.

"So good to have you here again, you've certainly been a busy man these past few years," said Papa, quickly changing the subject. "Sarah's been invaluable here at home since Mary passed – we couldn't have managed without her, especially helping take care of Robert."

I ducked into the kitchen before I might say something I regretted. As I began brewing the coffee and preparing the mince–meat pie and ice cream, I suddenly had a surge of something that had eluded me for the past year – HOPE!

John was tired so our conversation over pie and ice cream didn't last long. We exchanged pleasantries and caught up on his studies at University of Virginia and his returning to Bridgewater College as a professor. He didn't mention his short marriage or his wife's death and I chose not to ask. It was as if ten years had never passed and I once again felt completely at ease with this dear friend to whom I could confide anything. As I showed him to his room, I began to go over in my mind what I would confide this time around.

The next morning I woke at 5 A.M. after hardly sleeping, too excited about the plan I had hatched for the day.

I set the long rectangular table at one end for four: Papa, Robert, John and me. I still couldn't get used to Mama's empty space at the table and I looked over to the window where her bed had been and where she finally died over three years ago. There were no flowers in the window, as their presence was a painful reminder of her absence and our loss, not to mention, my own.

On the kitchen counter sat bowls full of ingredients for our country breakfast. In one were the scrambled eggs I would cook last in the large iron skillet on the stove. I had already cooked pork sausage patties and the odor of them wafted through the house. Bread was made yesterday in the outside oven. Already on the table was a bowl of smearcase and a jar of strawberry preserves.

I knew that John also arose very early and that he would stay in the house while my father went out to do the morning chores before breakfast. Since Robert had no school today he would be sleeping in and that time would provide me an opportunity to approach John and ask him about my feelings of grief, frustration and guilt. I knew without doubt he would be the one Brethren minister who would understand.

"Good morning, Sadie," John said as he came down the stairs into the kitchen. "Something sure does smell delicious." He was casually dressed in trousers and a blue starched shirt open at the collar, very un–preacher–like and I felt myself blush at the thoughts that were going through my mind. I turned back to the sink where I had been washing a dish.

When I had recovered my composure I turned to face him, wiping my hands on my apron. "Good morning, John,

I hope you slept well and that you have a good appetite – I'm so used to fixing for farmhands, I have enough to feed a crowd."

"I did and I am," he answered going over to where I had laid out the sausages on a piece of cloth to drain. "Ah, this is what I smelled upstairs – may I?" he asked as he picked up a piece of sausage and popped it in his mouth, reminding me of a little child sneaking food when the cook wasn't looking.

I laughed, already feeling better than I had for a long time.

"I certainly understand why folks come from far and near to eat at the Zigler household," he said, and I felt a twinge of resentment that I had spent my life in this kitchen preparing food for everyone who came down the pike.

I must have worn my feelings on my face because John said quietly, "And you have not had much choice in the matter, have you Sadie?"

My eyes welled with tears and I turned away, "How did you know?" I said dabbing my tears with my apron.

"Dearest Sadie," he said gently as he placed his hands on my shoulders, turned me towards him and looked deeply into my eyes. "I have known you since you were in grade school – you hold a special place in my heart. I am also a pastor and teacher and I know pain when I see it. Please tell…"

I had always been aware that when he talked to me, I felt that I was the only person in the room and his eyes always seemed to look deeply into my very soul. I had been so grateful for his constant support and encouragement through my years as a child and a young woman. But now, looking into those intense eyes, I was feeling something new and a little dangerous. With so little experience with men, I wasn't sure exactly what it was. But suddenly I was also aware that John had a strange look on his face. His eyes widened and he quickly dropped both his gaze and his hands from my shoulders.

There was an awkward silence between us before he cleared his throat and continued in a kind, but professional tone, "Sadie, please tell me more about this. Have you talked with anyone about how you are feeling? Why don't we go outside a walk a bit—it's such a beautiful spring day."

I recovered my composure, relieved that we were back to a more familiar kind of conversation. We walked outside into the yard where the early morning briskness cooled the heat that I had felt only moments ago.

"I tried to talk to Lizzie about it, but, of course she didn't begin to understand. The only thing she did was suggest that I was in deep spiritual trouble and sent me off to see Pastor Glick," I began, relaxing into the walk and the familiar surroundings. This way, I didn't have to look into those eyes.

"Of course Lizzie doesn't understand. She chose her dream and has lived it out. She never understood my encouraging her to get more education way back in high school. She would support Robert in that because he's male, as would Pastor Glick. Unfortunately for you, we live in a time when women choosing a path of education is the exception not the rule. So did you go see Pastor Glick?"

"Oh, indeed I did," I said, chuckling at the memory of us kneeling on the floor of his study and my subsequent escape. "And all I got from him was an attempt at exorcism for the evil spirit that inhabited me and gave me terrible ambitions for myself."

"Oh for Pete's sake" John said, shaking his head, trying his best not to laugh at a fellow pastor. We walked in silence as he seemed to be preparing carefully what he wanted to say in response. We had walked almost to the barn where we saw Papa tossing hay to the cows. He waved at us and as John waved back he stopped and said in a serious voice, "Sadie, there are certain lay ministers in the Brethren Church who have not been well–schooled in Biblical history, translation and interpretation and often take scripture and make it conform to their own personal beliefs about God and God's working in our lives. They mean well, but can do more harm than good when it comes to someone like you who can think for themselves. But the Church of the Brethren also has a rather progressive side that allows us radicals to expand and explore new ideas. Just take your father for instance." He glanced toward the barn.

"But Papa hasn't encouraged me to go back to school," I answered with the little anger I allowed myself.

"Even though he went along with Mama back before she died and told me to enroll."

"Sadie, the truth of it is, right now your father does need you and so does Robert," he stated bluntly and I knew that he spoke a truth I didn't want to hear.

"But what choice do I have?" I said as tears began to roll down my cheeks and I began to weep as I had not done since Mary Ruth and Mama had died. I turned away, embarrassed at my show of emotion and lack of control. I was suddenly in his arms crying on his shoulder like a little girl. He held me as a father would until I had cried myself out. He became uncomfortable before I did and pulled away. I became aware that I wanted to stay there forever, but I was no longer a little girl and apparently John Flory had sensed that in me.

We walked back to the house in an awkward silence.

We reached the front porch and as we stood there, I thought about the time when John and Lizzie stood there so many years before as I eavesdropped inside the door.

After a moment he began, "Sadie, I'm a preacher, so I'm going to preach to you a little. Is that alright?"

I nodded.

John's face relaxed into an expression with which I had become familiar through the years. It was kind, gentle and understanding, but firm. His voice settled into what I was sure he had perfected as his Pastor/counselor mode of communication. "Let me tell you about the God in whom I believe and how that God works with us to fulfill what we were created to be – to use the gifts we were given at birth. How old are you now, if you don't mind my asking?"

"Twenty–five," I said, thinking, 'am I really that old?'

"Twenty–five?" he gasped, seeming to be surprised himself. "Why you're just getting started! I've observed you all these years. First of all, you are a voracious reader. Everything I brought by for you, you not only read but absorbed like a sponge. You were reading Pilgrim's Progress when you were twelve and even comprehending it to a degree. Dr. Norris told me about that paper you wrote and how he had invited you to join the Literary Society." He began pacing up and down the porch gesturing with his hands in the air as I had seen him do when was preaching in the pulpit. "The God I believe in gave you a passion for learning and a brain to use. That doesn't simply go away just because right at this particular time you are otherwise needed. You've always worked hard here at this home – it's a requirement."

I felt that familiar resentment rise until he continued, "Yet, you always found the time and inclination to broaden your horizons. That needn't stop now. I don't believe God has a timeline for any of us. I don't know whether you will go back to college or not, but I do know you must never abandon your education. As to your dream of being a teacher, there are other ways of your teaching besides in a school. You teach Sunday school don't you?" He stopped his pacing and finally looked at me.

"Well, yes, but that's different," I answered, but was wary of meeting his gaze again.

"Why is it different? At least for now. You are using your gift of being an educator. You've always been a teacher – look at what you did for Sam Madden. At that time there would have been no place around here for a little black boy to go to regular school and yet you taught him to read. You opened up a whole new world for him."

I had never thought much about teaching Sam to read although I do remember some of the neighbors had spoken to my parents about whether it was a good idea for a Negro to get too educated.

"And what about your music?" he continued, getting more and more animated, the way I had always loved. "You have a beautiful voice, you play the organ. You could go out to Singers Glen and I'm sure George Holsinger would buck the system and might even let you become involved in the Harmonia Sacra training there."

"But that's just for m…"

"Sadie, for heaven's sake, where's your spunk?" he said, once again looking me right in the eye, his eyes blazing. "Just ask him. He knows how hard your father is working to get the Harmonia Sacra back in the Brethren Church again. He won't say no, I promise you."

"What do you think Papa will say?" I said, mustering the courage to meet his eyes.

"You're a grown woman, Sadie; you have some right to live at least part of your life without your father's approval. He loves you and wants you to be happy and so does God. Don't let anyone make you feel ashamed of wanting to be happy – of wanting to pursue your dreams."

He hesitated as we looked at each other as two adults who weren't quite sure exactly what this relationship had become.

The spell was quickly broken as he continued softly, "Who knows what God has in store for you? Sometimes we must wait; sometimes we must alter our plans. Make the best of what you have right now in the present. Read, teach, sing, laugh, enjoy your life – the future will take care of itself – end of sermon!"

We both smiled.

"Thank you, John."

And then, there was Robert, coming out from behind the door where he had been eavesdropping.

"What's all the ruckus out here?" he said, pretending he hadn't heard every word. "Sounded like we were having a revival meeting."

"We were," both of us said, laughing.

CHAPTER NINETEEN
August, 1908

After our little morning "Revival" that Saturday the family spent the rest of the day and evening reviewing all that had happened during the past ten years since we had seen John. He and Papa talked theology and though John tended to be a little more liberal than Papa, they always seemed to come to an agreement after a spirited debate.

Robert, now seventeen, hung on to every word that John said and was particularly taken with his passionate view of the pacifist doctrine of the Brethren Church. Robert's rather unusual interest in the whole idea had come at an early age. In many of the Old Testament passages, stories related God's tendency to "smite" the enemies of the Jewish people, even to the brutal killing of women and children. Each time I had taught these stories in Sunday School, Robert had simply refused to believe that a loving God would do such a thing and since I tended to agree with him, he grew more and more to believe that war or violence toward others was fundamentally wrong. He was torn between believing the Holy Bible as God's word and deciding something was in error. I was never able to come up with a satisfying answer and, in truth John didn't either. In his way, however, he guided Robert away from throwing up his hands and rejecting the lot of it, rather suggesting an alternate approach.

"Robert," he said, as we came to the end of a long discussion about the subject, "People like you and me told these stories and sometimes they told them to justify their own human tendency toward violence. You must remember that Jesus never said a word about condoning war or enslavement, just the opposite actually, but people in today's world use these terrible ancient stories to support their own views on both. Love is the answer – always. Keep being horrified at what you read and decide what you must do about it NOW." Once again I marveled at his simple, yet eloquent way of bringing clarity to difficult issues. And what he said that day helped form the man my brother would become.

I had noted that the remainder of Saturday through Sunday morning, John's attention to me seemed altered in some way. He was not distant, but was careful that we were not alone and made a concerted effort to make our conversations communal. I am convinced it was not my imagination that something had shifted between us after our encounter in the yard that day. I had no idea whatsoever what any of it meant.

John Flory had left immediately after he preached his usual outstanding sermon at church. Since he had been with us Friday and Saturday he thought it appropriate that he accept a Sunday dinner invitation from another family in the congregation. And then he was gone, but not without leaving me changed.

During the year after my "revival" with John Flory, I gradually came out from under the black cloud that had hovered over me since Mama's death. I followed John's suggestions about reading more and with a new eye for what I chose to read. Most of my previous choices in religious literature had held closely with the Christian beliefs as taught by my own church. I soon realized that I was reading more books that challenged some of those dogmas. John had mentioned that there was a progressive wing of the church that allowed for questioning and exploring. I didn't put it together until later that my shift had much to do with my encounter with Pastor Glick and his approach to the problems I was facing at the time. I observed that his sermons centered more on criticism and judgement than support and understanding.

Besides the black cloud lifting from my life, there was another cloud that had formed in its place that surprised even me. It was a cloud that buoyed my spirits and, were I a poet, would have said I was floating upon. On that cloud I relived that day with John Flory, every word, every glance, every touch. I knew I was being silly but I didn't care. I had never felt this way and I liked it.

I had also discovered a new fiction author who was becoming very popular at that time, Harold Bell Wright. In his first book, "The Printer of Udell," he openly criticized the popular church citing that they cared more for doctrine and dogma than serving people in need – I was beginning to agree. This new approach to my belief system was exciting, yet a little frightening. The concept of hell, fire and brimstone had also been a part of my early Christian formation. The roots of that brand of teaching are difficult to dislodge. And this author also had a romantic streak which he wove into the characters of his serious stories and I reveled in them.

There were many times I found excuses to miss church on Sunday mornings. I think Papa was so relieved that I was in a better frame of mind that he allowed me the benefit of the doubt. On one of these Sunday mornings I had told Papa I needed to take some bread that we had baked yesterday to a family down the road. "I need to take it while it's fresh so I think I won't go to church today," I said, avoiding his knowing smile.

"I suppose it will turn to stone if you wait until after, but you're the cook!" he chuckled. "Sadie, you're a grown woman, it's between you and God. I'm a little tired of Pastor Glick myself."

He turned back to a paper he had been reading, "Did you see this, Sadie? Seems John Flory has gotten married again. Sure am glad to hear that – a man like that needs a good woman by his side."

"What did you say, Papa?" I said, walking back to the kitchen with his plate.

"John Flory – he's gotten married again, here, read for yourself," he said as I came back into the living room, barely able to maintain my composure.

He handed me the latest issue of the *Philamathean Monthly.*

"Really? Well, isn't that nice," I said, taking the paper from his hand, knowing full well that I didn't think it was nice at all.

I read the notice, "John S. Flory, acting President of Bridgewater College and professor of English announced his marriage to Vinnie Mikesell on August 18, 1908..." My heart sank.

Since our meeting last year, John had come back from Charlottesville to Bridgewater College as acting president, so I wasn't surprised that he hadn't come to visit – I assumed he was very busy. Over and over in my mind, I replayed the events of that day and the feelings associated with it. Had I been so foolish as to expect that there was more to our relationship than a deep and abiding friendship? Certainly, he had not said anything that would suggest that there was any future for us in any other capacity. Yet, as I thought back, I couldn't put out of my mind the electricity that I felt went both ways when we had looked into each other's eyes.

"Silly girl," I said under my breath as I sat down on the couch.

"What did you say?" asked Papa looking over my shoulder at the book I had picked up and begun reading.

"Nothing, Papa, I hope he will be very happy," I said tossing aside the *Monthly* with more force than I intended. It landed on the floor where Papa picked it up, and giving me a questioning look, placed it on the table.

"What is that book you've been reading?" asked Papa, "You never put it down."

"It's called "Shepherd of the Hills" by a preacher named Harold Bell Wright,"

I said quickly, hoping that if I mentioned his profession, Papa might not ask too many questions. I was also anxious to move away from the John Flory conversation.

"Never heard of him – is he a Brethren minister?"

"No," I said, "the Disciples of Christ Church. He's in California right now at a church there."

What I didn't tell him was that I had heard this particular preacher was getting ready to leave the ministry to devote full time to his writing—I also withheld the nature of his writing concerning criticism of the church. Papa did not do too much outside reading but I found myself making sure that my books were tucked safely under my mattress when not in use.

"Papa, you said you were going over to Singers Glen tomorrow. May I go with you?" I asked, starting a conversation I had been planning for weeks. After the news of John's marriage I decided I would take to heart the things that John had suggested for me. If he was not to be a part of my future, my future would still, in part, have him to thank.

"Of course, I would love the company and George Holsinger himself will be there teaching. You remember he used to come by here a lot and taught you and Robert to play the organ? I know he'd love to see you again. What about Robert—we'll be staying overnight?"

"He'll be fine, Papa, he's seventeen; he can fend for himself. I've asked Alice to check in on him."

"Oh you have, have you – pretty sure I'd say yes?" he teased.

I just smiled, knowing if he had said no, I would have stood up for myself. This newly developed independence, like my new ideas of faith, was also a little uncomfortable at first. My mother and Lizzie had modeled a submission to men's authority that was comfortable for them. They really knew no other way. I had to learn to approach my father in a firm but gentle way and, little by little, he seemed to adjust to it. Again, Papa's liberal approach to life in general helped him to accept this new daughter of his. And as for me, I felt more confident than I had in years.

The next morning after I had gotten Robert off to school, we hitched up and loaded the wagon and headed over to Singers Glen, about ten miles away.

"The Singing School has already been in session a week so we'll be going in right in the middle of it. I think you'll enjoy observing the process of teaching the men to use the hymnal and read music."

Observing was not exactly what I had in mind, but I didn't share that with Papa.

The view of the Shenandoah Valley on the ride over to Singers Glen was spectacular that August day. The wagon bumped along the gravel roads in view of the Allegheny Mountains on one side and the Blue Ridge on the other. Fall had just begun to make its presence known with a few Dogwoods beginning to turn red. The weather was still quite warm and the sun shone brightly on the cornfields where the stalks had begun to turn brown and would soon be ready for harvesting and storing in silos on the many farms along the way.

"You're awfully quiet – you up to something?" he said, pretending he was teasing, but, in truth, wondering if it were true.

"Just enjoying the scenery," I said gaily, knowing that I had indeed been rehearsing exactly what I would say to Dr. Holsinger and how I would say it.

We pulled up to the small white frame Mennonite church and tied up the horse alongside the many others there. The sound of music floated through the air as the morning session had already begun. We quietly opened the door and saw a room full of men whose voices filled the room.

Long before I was born, Joseph Funk had begun these singing schools, training musicians and singers to be Master teachers who would teach others to read music from hymnals. As a young boy, Joseph and his Mennonite family moved from Pennsylvania to Rockingham County. As an adult he settled in what was then called Mountain Valley, now Singers Glen, where he worked as a printer. He found great success in the music business, doing translation and compilation as well as printing music. His greatest contribution was the development of shaped note hymnal originally called A Compilation of Genuine Church Music, which he published in 1832 in Winchester, Virginia. This unique notation system consisted of different shaped notes to denote pitch. It was a combination of music textbook and a hymnal with harmonizations of tunes into three voices. In 1847 he printed the fourth edition of his original work and renamed it Harmonia Sacra. In this edition he would use seven rather than four shaped notes and would later add another voice part. He then organized a method of training when he realized rural churches like the Church of the Brethren and Mennonite relied on their memories for hymn singing and even when hymnals became available, they did not know how to use them. Papa was still trying to get the people at Linville Creek to use the Harmonia Sacra without much success.

We took our seats at the back of the church and listened. Well, I listened, Papa sang along with the other men. He had a rich bass voice and I relaxed into the beauty of the

When the morning session ended, Dr. George Holsinger, who had aged considerably since I had seen him, approached us with a warm smile.

"What a pleasure to see you, Michael, Sarah," he said, extending his hand to Papa and nodding to me.

Firmly shaking Dr. Holsinger's hand, Papa said, "It's so good to see you up there doing what you do so well. It's been a while since I've seen you."

"I think this may be my last Singing School. I'm getting too old for this," he said feigning the bent frame of an old man, "but I do so love it. Sarah, how's that beautiful voice of yours?"

"A bit out of practice, I'm afraid, but I intend to remedy that soon," I said, laughing at his gesture, "and you'll never be too old!"

Papa looked at me as if to say, "What are you up to now?" Recently, I seem to have prompted that look more and more frequently.

"Let's go have some dinner. The ladies of the church have prepared a feast over at the Miller's. Please join us," said Dr. Holsinger, starting toward the door of the church.

"Are you sure we won't be two too many?" Papa asked, as we followed Dr. Holsinger out to the lawn.

"Are you joking, Michael, the ladies aid society always prepares enough for a small army!" he said as he led us to a large white frame home across from the church.

He was right, of course. Outside the house on the freshly mown grass were long rectangular tables covered with white tablecloths, holding every country delicacy known in this rural Shenandoah Valley community. Platters of home–fried chicken, bowls full of potato salad, macaroni salad, fruit salad and cole slaw, plates of deviled eggs, pickled eggs, pickled beets and three kinds of pickles, homemade yeast rolls and churned butter as well as fruit pies and cakes for dessert.

The women serving the large group of men were obviously mystified by my presence and I received more than my share of glances from both them and the men there.

I waited until Papa got up to go get seconds, and then approached Dr. Holsinger.

I took a deep breath and said, "Dr. Holsinger, may I have a word with you, please? I have a question."

"Of course, Sarah, what is it?" he answered with that, still sonorous tenor voice of his.

"This may seem rather out of order but John S. Flory put me up to it so…"

"That John, he's a real pistol – what's he up to now?"

I ignored the question, feeling that stab of pain even bringing up his name. I really needed to put thoughts of John behind me. If there had been any hope of a future with him, there was definitely none now – he was married and that was that. This "new Sadie" needed to move on.

Watching to be sure Papa wasn't on his way back to our table, I began to make my case.

"I know the Singing Schools have always been for men, but I was wondering if you might be open to… I mean would it be possible for me to…?"

His smile twinkled. "Why don't you just come out and say it, Sarah – you'd like to be trained at Singing School."

"Well, yes, I…I" I sputtered, delighted that he wasn't surprised or offended by my request.

"Of course," he smiled a conspirital grin and leaned toward me, "I've sneaked in a few women in the past few years. I've become a little more radical in my old age. We can talk about…"

"I've never seen so much food in one place. Sarah, what are you grinning about?" said Papa as he came back from the food table with yet another full plate.

"Just happy to be talking music with my teacher, that's all," I answered, stealing a glance at Dr. Holsinger who was grinning like a Cheshire cat.

We stayed for the afternoon session where I took in every nuance of the training with renewed interest. Papa, who didn't miss a trick, sensed that something had changed. As we walked to where we were going to stay for the night he asked, "You and Dr. Holsinger were having quite a discussion at dinner today. Anything you want to share?"

"Papa, what would you think about my training to be a song leader and teacher of *Harmonia Sacra*?" I asked, hoping to get his approval, but now, not depending upon it.

He paused and smiled. "Sarah, I think that would be just wonderful. I sort of figured out that's what you and Dr. Holsinger were up to and he hinted to me after the last session that I might have a nice surprise." He took my hand as we walked and said wistfully, "Mama would have been so pleased and proud and I am too, I am too. When do you plan to train?"

"As soon as the next singing school is held here in Singers Glenn. I'm hoping it won't be too long. I really want to train under Dr. Holsinger before he retires."

We spent the night with one of the members of the church. I could hardly fall asleep with excitement and anticipation. We awoke early the next morning and left for home.

When I heard later that year Dr. Holsinger had died, I was sure my chances for being included in the next Singing School were slim to none. But soon after, I received a letter from one of the teachers at Singers Glen.

Dear Miss Zigler,

I would like to invite you to join us for the next Singing School in Dayton, Virginia, to be held in the fall of 1909. Although you well know this is unusual, Dr. Holsinger made it clear before he died that you would be welcome here at any time. He vouched for your musicianship and your character and mentioned your father's efforts in the Brethren Church to reinstate the Harmonia Sacra there. We will be in touch about specific dates. You may find it difficult to be here for the entire two weeks, but we welcome you for any time you are able to come.

In Christ, James

CHAPTER TWENTY
April, 1909

"I t means hope, my name means hope," she said as we sat on the porch after supper on a lovely early spring day. It was the season when the vagabonds began to come down from the north to find work on the farms in our area. She and her family had come onto our property the way most of our guests had all through the years, by reading the code sign painted on the blacksmith shop down the lane.

"It's a beautiful name, Nadya," I said, looking into those dark, mysterious eyes. I guessed she was about sixteen years old. Her beautiful, olive skin identified her as what we called "gypsies." They traveled from place to place like the tramps we entertained, to find work to support themselves. Their reputations were not as solid as the tramps and there was a general mistrust of them. One of the particular objections was their practice of fortune telling which Brethren church people considered evil. They traveled as families and we had never had any trouble with them. We rarely asked questions of our guests, allowing them their anonymity, but Nadya seemed to want to talk, so I listened.

"We came down the river on our houseboat – I think it's called the Shenandoah River. We were going to float on down a little but we needed to stop and sell some of our wares for money for food. Would you like to see?" she said, taking out a cloth bag from the large pocket in her brightly colored dress.

As most Brethren families, we lived simply, but these people lived from hand to mouth and with great uncertainty as they traveled, their only homes, houseboats or the charity of others. And yet they seemed to be quite happy with their lives. What freedom they must feel having no ties, no responsibilities, except to each other – this kind of life was intriguing to me and I was surprised that I almost felt a little envious.

"Of course, I would love to see," I said, noticing, draped at her neck, several necklaces. Her ears were pierced with long dangling earrings hanging almost to her shoulders. The only piece of jewelry I owned was my neck–watch which was functional enough that it wasn't considered "adornment" by the church. Her gaily bedecked body was a real contrast to the plain surroundings of our home and I must admit I was drawn to the dazzle.

"Did you make these?" I asked, holding a bracelet of brightly colored crystal beads.

"Oh yes, we all learn to do beadwork when we're real little. Here, try this one on – it will look pretty," she said, proudly, handing me a necklace of blue and white beads.

I hesitated. "Well, Nadya, we don't wear much jewelry because...Oh well, let me try it on." I slipped it over my head and it lay sparkling on my drab housedress.

"How much for this one?" I asked, really wanting to support her and her family. Later, I could give it to Mollie as a gift.

"Oh, nothing," she said, her dark eyes sparkling, "I want to give it to you for being so nice to us."

"Why thank you, Nadya, I will always remember you when I wear it," I said with a twinge of guilt at my little white lie.

We didn't have room for the whole family in the house so we set up bedding on the two porches for the mother, father, and two little boys. Nadya would sleep in my room on a palate.

Nadya continued to talk on and on into the night about their life on the road and the river before finally falling asleep. I think I must have gone to sleep as she was babbling on.

The next morning as I went down to prepare breakfast, I left Nadya sleeping on the floor. She had slept in her dress and her dark tosseled hair spread out on the white pillow – she looked angelic. I felt a tug of affection for this beautiful gypsy girl.

As I began setting the table, Papa came in from his early morning chores.

"They're gone!" he said, motioning toward the porch.

"Who's gone?" I asked, wiping my hands on my apron.

"The gypsies – they've flown the coop!"

"But Nadya is still upstairs asleep," I said, alarmed and getting a very bad feeling about this.

"Well, they seem to have abandoned her for some reason. You'd better get her up and see if she knows anything about this."

Just then, Nadya, rubbing her sleepy eyes, came walking down the stairs. "They've gone, haven't they?" she said matter–of–factly, sitting down on the bottom step like a little child who was already feeling quite at home.

"Did you know?" I asked, amazed at her calm demeanor.

"Not for sure, but my mother said I should bring all my clothes in here just in case I needed them. Guess I'm going to need them," she sighed, showing no sign of any distress that her parents had left her in a strange home with people she didn't know.

"You don't think there's been a mistake?" I said trying to make some sense of the situation. "Maybe they'll come back when they realize you're not with them."

"Probably not," she said flatly, "This happens sometimes when girls get in trouble and we can't travel for a while. They'll be back after…"

She then pulled her large dress tightly over what was obviously a very pregnant belly. How in the world had I missed it?

And so it was that Nadya became our long–term house guest.

Out–of–wedlock pregnancies were rare in our community both within our church and in the general conservative community of Broadway. Sexual activity outside of marriage was frowned upon to the extent that "bad girls" who did get pregnant were shunned if they stayed around or were sent away to relatives. For Papa and me, taking her in was just another gesture of Christian charity and we accepted it with no fanfare or judgement. Nadya needed help – she had been left in our care and we would take care of her.

She and Robert were about the same age so became fast friends. Even though Robert had friends from high school in Broadway, his best friend was still Sam Madden. Robert was fascinated with the jewelry Nadya had made and thought some of our non–Brethren neighbors might want to buy some of it. He had always had such a kind heart and wanted to help. Occasionally the three of them would walk into town for a soda at the country store. This took them past neighbor's houses both church people and others. Once, when Robert knocked on the door of one of his school chums, the boy's mother came to the door. When she saw a white boy, a Negro boy and a pregnant gypsy girl on her porch, she quickly slammed the door. Word spread and soon everyone began locking their doors, even the church ladies. Our open door policy was tolerated but we were looked upon by the rest of the community as a little peculiar.

"I'm taking Nadya to church this Sunday," I said as Papa finished up his morning Bible reading. "She's probably never been and I think she'll especially like the hymn singing. I've been teaching her some of the hymns at the organ for the past few weeks. She's loved that and really has a nice voice." The truth was, her voice was nice but a little loud – I guessed she would not blend all that well in more ways than one.

"You might get a few comments, you know," he said, merely stating a fact rather than an objection. He was getting used to my new independent behavior and actually seemed to be enjoying treating me as an equal adult in the house. "This particular situation is a little different from these folks just coming here to stay and night or two and I'm sure you heard about that lady slamming the door in Robert's face. That story has gotten around and even the church people are a little uneasy about Nadya. I won't say not to go, but be prepared for some 'looks'."

"Let them look," I said defiantly, feeling that surge of confidence that continued to grow in me as each day passed and felt more natural all the time.

On the next Sunday, I picked out a dress for Nadya that I had fashioned to cover her condition a bit more than her own clothes.

As we walked into the church, I began to move to our place on the women's side of the church. Robert and Papa took their seats on the men's side. There were a few Negro members of our church but they always sat on one of the back pews. I never knew whether it was their choice or they had been told to sit there. They had their customs of inter-action with the white folks in the community – even at our home, when invited to join us for a meal, they would choose to eat in the kitchen or back porch, never at the dining room table.

I had already made up my mind that I was not go-ing to let Nadya sit in the back so I walked, guiding her by the arm, to my usual pew near the front. Papa had been right; there were looks and titters of conversation among the congregation as we walked down the center aisle. On the women's side, young girls were whispering to each oth-er while their mothers, in prayer veils, tried to quiet their giggles. On the men's side, the men struggled to keep their eyes straight ahead as their young sons elbowed each other, smirking. When we began singing the first hymn, Nadya got even more attention as she sang every word, every note per-fectly in tune, in her lusty young voice. I beamed at her and she smiled shyly back as I took more than a little pleasure my act of defiance.

I was little worried that Pastor Glick might use Nadya's presence as an opportunity for making a point in his sermon, but he refrained from what could have been an awkward situation. I was relieved and had to give him credit for this – it would be only a matter of time before he showed his true feelings.

Since Nadya had attended church regularly for several months, when time came for the Love Feast, I approached Papa and asked if he thought it would be appropriate to take her.

"I'm not so sure about that," said Papa, "you know church policy has always been that if there is dissension within the membership, the Love Feast is not held until things are sorted out – and my dear Sarah, you have caused a bit of dissension by taking her to church on Sundays."

"Exactly what dissension is that?" I asked, with a little too much challenge in my voice.

"Sarah, please," he said firmly. "You have become your own person and I have accepted this, even admired what I see as my own liberal leanings being developed in my adult daughter, but you know very well what I'm talking about."

And, of course, I did, though I had to stop and absorb the fact that my father was praising me in a way that he had never done – and how good that felt.

"Yes, Papa, I know that what they see as a sin of her being pregnant and not being married plus the fact that she is not a baptized Christian, makes her participating in communion inappropriate. Not to mention, they think she's a little heathen!" I smiled as I realized this "little heathen" was becoming like a daughter to me, and I wanted to protect her from being hurt by anyone.

Suddenly, I had an idea. "What if you asked Pastor Glick for special permission? He hasn't said anything yet has he?"

"No, not yet, but sometimes it takes a while for him to get worked up to it. I'll ask him and see if he's got the nerve to say 'no' outright," he said, scratching his beard as he did when he was about to come up with an idea. "I know what we can do. Let's invite him to Sunday dinner after the service this week. He might be more likely to say 'yes' after one of your home–cooked meals."

Feeling particularly good about the fact that my father and I were plotting something together, especially against Pastor Glick, I stuck out my right hand to him and as we shook hands, I said, with a smile, "Deal."

On Sunday, Pastor Glick came to dinner after church. I fixed all of his favorite dishes. Robert had gone home after church with a friend so there were just the four of us. Conversation at the meal was sparse; Nadya sat across from Pastor Glick and this seemed to make him uncomfortable. He never said a word to her and kept his gaze on his plate. When we had eaten, Papa rose from his chair and said, "Pastor, could I speak with you a moment out on the porch about an issue of some importance."

"Certainly, Brother Zigler. Sarah, thank you for this outstanding meal. Your mother taught you well," he said, getting up from his chair and extending his hand to me.

"Thank you, Pastor Glick – I'm happy you enjoyed it," I responded with an especially gracious smile that was less than sincere.

The two men walked out onto the porch as Nadya and I cleared the table. I so wanted to take my eavesdropping place but since Nadya was within earshot, I refrained – I didn't want her to hear anything that might make her feel badly. As I heard the men's voices rising, I said, "Nadya, would you please go out and start washing the dishes, I'll be there in just a few minutes."

As she went into the kitchen I moved closer to the porch door.

"Under no circumstances will I give you permission to let that little heathen gypsy come to the Love Feast. I've said nothing about her coming to church because I want to be a good Christian but she isn't even baptized!"

"She's been abandoned by her parents, for goodness sake…"

"And for good reason, it appears more every day," he said, his neck starting to turn red above his high priestly collar. "The church since John Kline's day has held that the unity of the church as a whole takes precedence over everything – this means we go as far as we can to advocate for the right, but not if it would break the church. We don't even let our Negro members come to the Love Feast," he finished with satisfaction in his voice and the red rising from his collar full up to his face. His eyes were blazing with religious fervor as if he were preaching to a congregation.

"I'm quite aware of that fact and staunchly disagree with the policy," Papa retorted, taking a step toward the Pastor and looking him full in the eye. He took a moment and lowered his voice to a firm but gentle tone. "Jesus commanded us to love one another and take care of widows and orphans – I don't recall that it says anywhere in the Bible that He mentions that color or race or being a pregnant gypsy girl have any bearing on the matter."

Pastor Glick's red face turned pale and he seemed, for once, to have no response.

"And that is my final word, Brother Glick," said Papa, and then, smiling a proper Christian smile, walked through the porch door into the house.

"Always right inside the door listening aren't you, Sarah?" he teased, not in the least surprised at my presence there.

"Good for you, Papa," I said proudly as he walked into his bedroom and slammed the door.

He stayed there for some time and then came out with a grin.

"You know what your Mama did about the Negro members of the Church and the Love Feast don't you?" he said, choking up a little.

"I think I remember a story about that," I said. "Tell me again, Papa."

He sat down on the couch and motioned me to sit beside him. I saw Nadya out of the corner of my eye come to the kitchen door and stand there where she listened to my father's story.

"Well, part of the problem with Negroes coming to communion soon after slaves were free was the issue of the Holy Kiss after the feet washing. Even though the Brethren had always opposed slavery and welcomed some of them as members of the church, the idea of kissing a black person on the face would have broken the whole fabric of the Brethren community during that time. So they made the decision that they could participate in the feet washing, but could only be kissed on the hand. It wasn't so much the way the Brethren felt, as it was what it did to other people who might be looking on. It might even cause somebody to shoot you in those tense days."

"So what did Mama do?" I said, knowing it was still difficult to talk about her without emotions overflowing.

He sighed and then burst out in a devilish grin. "Your Mama, bless her soul, used to take Liz and Alice to the kitchen of the church early before the women came to prepare the communion meal and had her own private foot washing with them. She never told me where she kissed them, but I have a pretty good idea, knowing her." He laughed and looked back at Nadya, who stood with wide eyes in the doorway. "And I know you, Sarah Edna Rebecca Zigler – you're your mother's daughter – give it a try!"

During her pregnancy, Nadya was a great help with the chores. I was grateful for one more hand to help and came to feel like a mother to her. And as her mother, I defended her against the cruel gossip of the community and the unkind treatment she sometimes endured.

On one occasion the two of us had walked into Broadway to pick up a few supplies at the country store there. Nadya wandered off as I was shopping and as I went to the cash register to check out, I saw her at the candy counter, looking at the large display of sweets. I noticed two young girls about her age whispering to each other and pointing at her. I'm sure Nadya noticed but was used to this. Suddenly one of the girls walked to the counter where Claude Smith, the owner was checking someone out, and she said loudly, "Mr. Smith, that gypsy girl over there is stealing your candy, you'd better stop her."

Nadya had not even picked up a piece of candy but Claude quickly walked over to her and said roughly, "Shame on you, don't you know better than to take something that doesn't belong to you – no, I suppose you don't. Miss Zigler please take her out of here and don't bring her back. You people may take in every person that walks down the pike or floats down the river, but the good folks of Broadway shouldn't have to put up with it."

I left my groceries on the counter, took Nadya's hand and walked past the two girls who were giggling and quite proud of themselves. I gave them a stern look and we began walking home.

"You shouldn't be upset, Sadie, this happens to us all the time. Everybody knows we're just trash anyways – I'm used to it."

"Well, I'm not," I said, putting my arm around her, "You are worth more than either one of those nasty girls and don't you ever forget it."

During the afternoon before the Love Feast, women of the church prepared the food for the event in the church kitchen. We made ground meat sandwiches and "sop" which was chicken broth with chunks of bread floating in it. This would be eaten on tables that had been converted from the wooden pews on either side of the church. After the foot washing, the meal was eaten in complete silence and then the sacrament of bread and wine. The wine was grape juice made from the grapes from arbors in some of the congregation's yards – the bread was unleavened, baked flat on large cookie sheets and cut into long strips that would be passed down the rows and broken into pieces for each person.

"Come on Nadya, we're going to the church to fix some food for tonight's service," I said.

"They eat at your church too?" she asked.

"This is a special service," I replied.

I purposely went early to carry out my plan. The men had already set up the tables. Along with the food preparation, the women would distribute the towels and basins for hand and foot washing at either end of the pews. I went into the kitchen – no one had arrived.

"Nadya, I want to show you what we will be doing tonight at the service. Since you haven't been baptized into our church you won't be able to come with us."

"O.K.," she said warily, as if she were afraid we would be doing something strange.

"Come over here and sit down," I said, taking one of the basins and filling it with water.

"Now, in the Bible there is a story about Jesus washing his disciple's feet. He showed us by doing this that we are all equal under God, that there are no masters, that we are all each other's servants. So…"

She was already barefoot so I took her brown feet into the warm water and splashed the water over them, then dried them off with my apron.

"Now we stand up and give each other the fellowship kiss to show our love for each other," I said and kissed her on each cheek.

Just about that time several of the ladies came into the kitchen. I smiled at them and said, "I brought a helper for us today. Are we ready to get to work?"

As I moved toward the sink I heard one woman say in a whisper, "She's worse than her mother."

It was soon after the Love Feast that Nadya went into labor and gave birth to a stillborn baby girl on Mama's bed where we all had been born. I assisted Liz Canody with the delivery and afterward held the tiny dead child in my arms. I had mixed feelings about it. On one hand, a new life had been lost; on the other, what kind of life would this baby have had with a child–mother living from day to day on a boat? Might she even have left a living child with me to rear?

We wrapped the child in a pillow case and Papa buried it out near the old tannery building. Nadya showed little emotion over the loss and wasn't even interested in participating in the little service we had. I supposed this was the way her people handled life on the road. Nadya stayed with us until one day, the next season, her family returned, thanked us profusely with words and many of their wares. They left with their daughter, whom they never intended to abandon forever. They knew that she would be well cared for in our home.

I considered asking about the circumstances of her pregnancy but thought better of it. It didn't matter anyway. She was back with her family and we would never see her or them again.

In the days after Nadya left, there was another emotion that I recalled having as I had held that tiny baby in my hands, wondering if she might have left a living child with me to rear. I was now twenty–seven years old – my Robert was practically a man. Perhaps my motherly instincts had come to the surface taking care of Nadya. Perhaps there was something missing in my life after all.

CHAPTER TWENTY-ONE
September, 1909

The small town of Dayton, Virginia lay almost equi-distant between Harrisonburg and Bridgewater on the Valley Pike. There were several commercial stores, a few churches, a residential area of modest Victorian homes and right in the middle of the town, on a single street, was Shenandoah Collegiate Institute and School of Music, founded in 1902. The school, associated with the United Brethren Church, had grown through the years from being Shenandoah High School in 1875, then Shenandoah Seminary to its present status as a fine music conservatory. I had attended any number of student and teacher recitals there through the years.

"Good morning, Miss Zigler, I'm James Ruebush and I'd like to welcome you to singing school," said the rather in-teresting–looking man who greeted me that Saturday morn-ing in September. He had dark hair parted down the middle, dark eyes and very large ears. He was dressed in a striped suit and white shirt with a starched high collar folded over at the neck and sported a cravat tie that made him look very much the New York gentleman. He reminded me a little of our old friend, Mr. Plougher.

James Hott Ruebush, I had learned, was the great—grandson of Joseph Funk, the father of the singing schools in the Valley of Virginia. Joseph Funk's descendants had continued his work since the 1850's and Professor Ruebush was no exception. He had studied at Ottobein University and the Grand Conservatory in New York.

I had been a little disappointed when I was told the sessions I would attend would not be held in Singers Glen. I longed for the tradition of that place as well as knowing that traveling to Dayton would not be easy. The training for singing schools had been moved from Singers Glen some years ago. The entire course this time would be held on six successive Saturdays. I had arranged to go by train from Broadway to four of the six sessions. Papa was not only supportive when I told him about it, but very excited about my participation, "Sarah, this is something you were born to do. I'm very proud of you and Mama would be too," he said, his voice still catching on the mention of her name. My heart swelled at his praise and I smiled when I thought of Mama and what she might have thought. Perhaps music was my destiny after all.

"You come highly recommended by the folks up your way and of course, your father's efforts to bring back the Harmonia Sacra are well known here at the College," he said, stroking his full moustache.

"Thank you so much, sir," I answered as we mounted the stairs in Howe Memorial Hall. From practice rooms, where students played pianos and organs and sang arpeggios and scales, came a cacophony of sound.

We walked into the upstairs room which was a combination chapel and auditorium. In this room we would be taught the rudiments of Joseph Funk's singing method.

There were already many people milling around. "I'm surprised to see some other women here," I said, noting there were three other women besides myself. "I've always been under the impression this was mainly for men."

"That used to be the case, particularly up in Singers Glen and the more conservative areas where the Brethren and Mennonites are. Here at the Conservatory we are a bit more liberal in that regard, and I, for one, believe women like you are entirely capable and sometimes superior in talent for this training," he said with a twinkle in his dark eyes. "Let me introduce you to one of those women who is here today."

We walked over to a short, plump woman who looked to be several years younger than I.

"Pearl, I'd like you to meet Sarah Zigler from the Linville area. She's Michael Zigler's daughter and was taught music by Dr. George Holsinger. Sarah, this is Pearl Wampler."

"Hello Pearl, please call me Sadie. It is a pleasure to meet you," I said offering my hand to shake. I noted her very firm, almost masculine handshake.

"Welcome to the big Town of Dayton, Sadie," she said with a warm smile and a look of mischief on her face. "Glad to see another woman taking opportunities like this. High time, I'd say, wouldn't you?"

I was struck by this woman's confidence and straight forward manner. I felt immediately I was in the right place.

"Ladies and gentlemen, please take your seats and we will begin," said Professor Ruebush. I was thrilled that he, himself, would be conducting the sessions. "On your seats you will find a copy of the latest edition of Harmonia Sacra, as well as a hymnal and some printed material for use later in the day. Please remain standing and open your books to the opening page. I will read this quote from Isaiah, and printed in my great–grandfather's original edition, as a prayer for our opening session. Let us pray. 'And the ransomed of the Lord shall return and come to Zion with songs and everlasting joy upon their heads – they shall obtain joy and gladness and sorrow and sighing shall flee away.' Amen."

We took our seats as the professor continued, "My great–grandfather, Joseph Funk, knew the power of music to enhance the spiritual lives of God's people and it is for this reason we gather here today – to make available to all the joy of singing praises to the Lord and give them also tools to use the hymnals they have provided for them."

In all my years of being moved by the power of the poetry of hymns and singing them in church, I had never had such a succinct explanation of what I had been feeling since I was a child. In a few sentences this man had summarized what I knew to be true – music was the means by which I had come to know God.

"Let us begin with a little review of the theory of shaped notes. Some of you may already have a knowledge of these and may even read music, but to ensure that everyone is literally on the same page, please give your attention to the chart right here that has been used since Joseph Funk's day to teach this method," he said as he took a directing baton and pointed to a chart whereon were printed the black shaped notes on music staves.

The next hour was spent reviewing music theory. We practiced scales and intervals. After that came the practice of church psalmody in familiar hymns like "Old Hundred." Before the break, there was another hour of sacred music in general and how it applied to the singing school method.

At the break I turned to Pearl Wampler who had taken a seat beside me, "Have you always wanted to do this?" I asked.

"Not particularly. I just like to rock the boat a little. I'm already a school teacher at a one–room–school here in Dayton which is sort of breaking the mold anyway, she said as we rose and started for the stairs. "I do love men, but really, Sadie, we women need to show that we are just as capable to hold jobs outside the home."

"You are my kind of woman," I said as we left the building and began to walk into the beautiful fall day. "You must have had a liberal upbringing."

"I guess you might say that, although my mother never had any ideas of working outside the home and had a batch of kids. Maybe it's just that our generation is just beginning to have our own ideas about what it means to be a woman."

I thought about my own mother and how she had willingly given up her life to being a devoted wife and mother. And Pearl was right; I had developed my own ideas of what it meant to be a woman.

We continued walking around the campus that covered several blocks in the tiny village of Dayton. There were not yet many buildings at this school situated along Cooks Creek even though it had been growing since the late 1800's. The women's residence hall and dining room were next to the Howe building and down the street were several other brick buildings. Our conversation was lively and stimulating and we soon lost track of time.

"Oh, dear," I said, taking my watch from my waistband, "we need to get back – we don't want to embarrass our gender by being tardy." I almost regretted having to leave such wonderful conversation with someone I already counted as a fellow radical.

At the afternoon session we again practiced church music, this time learning to beat time as the song leader. Sometimes we sang as many as five stanzas of a hymn to make certain that we had learned what was required.

As we returned to our seats I picked up a sheet of paper that had been printed out. It was an essay that had been omitted from the original 1878 edition and summarized what we would be doing for the next six weeks and why.

"Funk provides a detailed course in musical notation, poetic feet, conducting, solminzation (fasola), rhythm, harmony, the distinctive sound of each major and minor key and tone production. Above all, he urges the singer to expressive clarity through hymns dynamics, diction and entering the emotion of the poetry."

That night, exhilarated and exhausted with the activities of the day, I tried to relax and rest on the train ride back to Broadway. My mind was too charged and my heart was too full to even begin to fall asleep. Instead, I thought back to the past five years since Mama's death. So many things had come together during those years. In my early twenties I had seen myself as a grown woman who was independent and self–reliant because I had always had so much responsibility placed on me – first with practically raising Robert, helping with Mary Ruth, nursing Mama during her illness and then taking care of the household and Papa after her death. But looking back on these recent years, I realized that I had only scratched the surface of who I was as a woman. I had never lived anywhere but home with my family and those close ties tended to blind my ability to see myself apart from them. My faith had never been tested, nor my strength of character. My experience with grief and all that came after left me with a great peace about my life. Even the dreams of college and a career as a teacher no longer haunted me. Perhaps there were other uses for my talents and gifts that I had not yet discovered.

I had continued to be active in the Linville Creek Church of the Brethren, teaching Sunday school and music, but my faith was not limited to the church's doctrine. I was more dedicated than ever to Christian principles which guided how I lived my life. My experience with Nadya had taught me to stand up for anyone I felt was being treated unfairly or unkindly in the Church or community. I was quickly becoming known as rather a radical – just like my father and mother.

Today, I had begun another phase of my life in the field of music teaching. I had met a woman who, like me, looked to new possibilities. I had no idea where this would lead but the possibilities were limitless. Just as John Flora had once told me, there are many ways to continue education besides college. And, just like that, there he was again in my thoughts. Though the sting of losing a man I never actually had was gone, I could still treasure the passion I had learned from him for education, for music, for life. I couldn't imagine any man ever knowing me the way he seemed to know me, so I held on the image of myself as seen through his eyes.

The train whistle woke me from a deep sleep, "Broadway, Virginia – please disembark passengers," said the conductor as he walked through my car.

Outside, Papa waited in the wagon. "Well, Miss Sarah, how was it?"

"Where do I begin…?"

PART TWO
BROADWAY TO SUNNY SLOPE

"…when, if you please, was ever a woman wholly unmoved by the knowledge that she holds first place in a man's heart?"

Shepherd of the Hills
(Harold Bell Wright)

CHAPTER ONE

New Year's Day, 1910

"Lizzie, I'm leading one of the hymns at the old folks sing at Weaver's Church on Saturday night," I said excitedly, "why don't you come with Papa and me? We've been asked to stay overnight at the Blosser home."

Lizzie had come over to visit us with her six-year-old daughter. After her marriage to Charles Meyers seven years ago, she had had a little girl they named Mary Ann. Like Mama, Lizzie had continued to have children after forty. The three older boys from her marriage to John Shank were all in their twenties and when Mary Ann was born there were twelve years between her and Maude, just as there had been between Lizzie and me. History seemed to be repeating itself.

"Oh Sadie, you know I can't leave Mary Ann overnight, Charles wouldn't like that at all," she said as she automatically headed for Mama's tea and medicine cabinet. She opened the door, sighed as she looked at the empty shelves and said sadly, "Oh, well."

"Sister, you need to get out of that house and have a little time for yourself," I answered, still mystified at how completely happy Lizzie was in spite of everything that had happened to her over the years. Why, I wondered was I so completely different from this woman who had raised me? I walked to another cabinet and took out a canister of tea that I had grown myself. "I'll talk to Charles or maybe I'll get Papa to do it. We'll work it out. Put on that pretty calico dress you just made and let's go sing a little. We'll pick you up early in time to get there for the evening service."

"Does sound like fun – I've loved the Mennonite sings since I've been going to Charles' church. Did you say you were leading a hymn? I thought that was just for men," she said, always ready to challenge the ideas I had that seemed so foreign to her.

As I put on the kettle of water on the stove for her tea I tried to explain. "I went to a singing school training in Dayton last fall and my instructor, James Ruebush recommended me so I could get some practice," I said, still giddy over the memory of that wonderful experience.

"Practice!" Lizzie said incredulously. "Practice for what exactly? Honestly Sadie, will you ever be satisfied just being a woman?"

"Here we go again," I thought, trying to maintain my composure. "I love being a woman, Lizzie, maybe not exactly your definition of one, but there are other things a woman can be and besides being a wife and mother."

I put some oatmeal raisin cookies I had just baked onto a plate and took them over to Mary Ann who was sitting on the couch with a book in her lap. "Would you like a cookie, Mary Ann?"

She looked up from the book she was flipping through and I suddenly realized it was my copy of Pilgrim's Progress. Her eyes shone as she said, "I like the pictures, Auntie Sadie," and it occurred to me it was possible that even Lizzie's child could choose another way.

Lizzie must have been thinking the same thing as she walked to her daughter, quickly snatched away the book and laid it aside. "Mary Ann, why don't you come with me into the kitchen and help me wash my cup."

As I stood in front of that familiar mirror the next morning, it reflected back a mature, confident woman of twenty–six who was about to do something she had dreamed about for years. I had chosen a conservative white starched blouse with long sleeves and a discreet over–flap that diminished my full breast. My long black wool skirt would satisfy the Mennonites need for plainness and I even took off my neck–watch on the chain so as not to appear decorated in any way. But those Mennonites and Brethren would not be able squelch the feeling of pure joy on my face that revealed a woman who could hardly believe she had an opportunity not many women were afforded in this day and time. No, I hadn't graduated from college and become a teacher as I had dreamed, but I had followed this particular dream and was about to have it come true. Who knew where it might lead?

On that fateful day, Papa and I drove the wagon over to pick up Lizzie on the way to Weaver's Church in Harrisonburg.

"You know Sarah, I've been thinking," said Papa as he flicked the reins to urge on Noir, his favorite horse. Papa had a love for beautiful horses, particularly the ones with speed and often bought retired race horses for the farm. Noir, a slick black stallion, was one of these and the look of glee on Papa's face when our wagon passed another on the road was good to see. He still missed mama dearly and these small pleasures were welcome. "Robert is getting old enough to take over the farm in a couple of years so…"

"But Papa, doesn't he want to go Bridgewater College when he graduates?" I said, alarmed at this turn of the conversation. Robert, under my tutelage, had become an excellent student and more than that, he had developed a deep faith and a passion for peace. With further education he could be a pastor, a teacher or a missionary, something he talked about frequently. I was determined to argue his case.

"Well, he talks about that some, but I'm sure hoping I can convince him his place is to stay here on the farm. If he doesn't, I may have to sell," he said, dismissing my argument quickly.

And there it was again, the pressure of farm and family weighed against education and a wider world. I had introduced Robert to that wider world. He was someone uniquely motivated who might change the world for the better and the thought of him being tied to the farm for the rest of his life was almost more than I could bear. It was one thing for me to give up the dream I had for myself, but quite another for my dear brother. Yet, I stopped short of continuing his defense, hoping Robert would plead his own case when the time came.

The conversation ended as we pulled up to Charles and Lizzie's farmhouse. Typical of all the Mennonite farms in the Valley of Virginia, this one was neat and pristine with nothing out of place.

Lizzie was waiting for us on her front porch wearing the bright calico dress I had suggested. Her face shone with an excitement I was happy to see.

"Hello, Sadie, Papa, I'm so glad you asked me to go and Papa, I don't know what you said to Charles, but it worked. I've been looking forward to this all week.

"I can be quite convincing at times," said Papa with a wink. "How are Charles and the boys?"

"Just fine," she said stepping into the back seat of the wagon, "Glad to say the boys have stuck around to help with the farm, although Ben has a girlfriend he's pretty serious about so I don't know."

Papa looked over at me and I knew he was thinking about Robert. "He's a good man, your Charles; think you might be able to find someone like him for your baby sister here?"

"Oh Papa, please I…"

"Sarah, high time you find yourself a good man," he said with fatherly concern. "Robert will be taking over the farm soon and I can get along just fine with Liz and the others."

"I'm fine Papa just the way I am, let's just drop it," I said a little more sharply than I meant to. I was growing weary of this topic which had come up frequently in the past few years since Mama's death. Papa seemed to have assumed that after I left college that winter, I had all but given up on my dreams, but if I couldn't live out all of them, I certainly did not want to give up the one thing left that I valued, my growing independence.

Papa shrugged as Lizzie sighed, both of them letting it go – for the time being.

The wagon trip from Broadway to Harrisonburg was a long one and the day was cold and clear. As we traveled along the Valley road, the Allegheny Mountains on one side and the Blue Ridge on the other, the peaks rose into the sparkling blue sky, some with patches of white left over from the last snow. Many houses along the way still had their Christmas wreaths on the door.

When we finally pulled up to the Limestone Church right outside Harrisonburg, there were already quite a few horses, wagons and buggies tied up and people were streaming into the building. Folks came from all over to attend these annual "sings," both trained musicians and regular church and community members.

I was nervous about leading the congregational singing since, as Lizzie had so graciously reminded me, this was an honor reserved only for men in the church. Most likely what prompted my invitation was Papa's connection to bringing back the Harmonia Sacra tradition to the Brethren Church in Broadway as well as the fact that today, they were honoring my teacher and mentor Dr. George Holsinger.

Inside the church, the people were separated into men and women as well as vocal parts. On one side were the men, tenors and basses, on the other, the women, sopranos and altos. Some would be using hymnals but most would know all of the hymns, every single verse, for memory. Papa took his seat with the basses at the back and Lizzie sat with a friend of hers, with the altos. I walked to the front of the church and took my place with the song leaders for the day. Weaver's Church is a Mennonite church and some of the members there gave me a few questioning looks as I sat down on the front row. Thankfully, Professor Ruebush came over to welcome me and I felt much better.

The first song leader got up when it was time for the service to start and announced the opening hymn. He struck his tuning fork on his hand and lifted it to his ear, then gave pitches to each of the parts. A hum went up from the congregation responding to each pitch. As I hummed my pitch I felt myself smile – in just a few moments, I would be up there myself, giving pitches. Then the leader raised his hands and began to conduct the church, full to the brim with singers, in a sound that rivaled the angels in heaven to my thinking. My stomach was churning with anticipation as each leader took his turn and then the last before me, nodded his head.

"Today we have a special leader, Sarah Zigler from Broadway, who will lead our final hymn. She studied under the man we honor today, Dr. George Holsinger, was trained at the Singing School in Dayton just this past year and her father, Michael Zigler was instrumental in bringing back the Harmonia Sacra, which we are using today, in the Linville Creek Church of the Brethren in Broadway. Welcome, Sarah."

I stood up nervously and cleared my throat. "Our last hymn is one of George Holsinger's compositions. For those of you using the hymnal it is number 51, 'Purer in Heart Oh God, Help Me to be.' Please stand."

I took out my tuning fork from the pocket of my dress, gave the pitches to each of the vocal parts and they were matched by the congregation. I raised my hands – every eye in the building was focused on me, waiting as I prepared to beat one measure to set the tempo. There was a hushed, expectant silence that I stayed with for a moment, feeling the power of it, the power of a dream realized. My hands moved beating, one, two, three four, a pause, an intake of breath and then on the downbeat of the next measure came the booming sound of full four part harmony. I was suspended in time and space as I led the congregation in all of the verses of the hymn that my dear friend had composed in the upstairs of my own home. The circle was complete and I felt a joy that I hadn't felt for a long time.

When the service was over and I walked to the back of the church, I was met with mixed reviews. Those who knew me and my family connection were gracious in their praise and I relished it, probably more than a good Brethren woman should. Others, particularly the Mennonites who disapproved of a woman taking any leadership role in the church, were dismissive and sometimes even rude with looks that showed their disapproval, which only served to make me more determined to continue my path.

Outside, on our way to the wagon, Lizzie's friend, Mary, came running over to me.

"Sadie, what a wonderful job you do with the song leading. It's so good to see a woman up there for a change," she said with a wink and a look of conspiracy on her face. "By the way, my sister Pearl says you are a pistol!"

"Oh for goodness sake, now I remember Lizzie telling me your last name was Wampler but I didn't realize you were related to Pearl," I said, marveling at the serendipity of this connection. "I loved being with her at singing school and was so disappointed when she didn't come to the last couple of training sessions."

Pearl had come to the first three sessions and then just disappeared. I had so enjoyed the stimulating conversations with her and her progressive ideas were refreshing and motivated me more than any woman I had ever met.

"She's quite a firecracker herself and thank you, Mary, not sure everyone feels the way you do about my being up there, but I appreciate your support."

"Are you going back to Broadway tonight?" she asked as we walked toward the wagons.

"No, Lizzie and I have been asked by the Henry Blossers to come to a late supper and stay the night. Papa is going over to the Glicks."

"Why," said Mary with a knowing twinkle in her eye, "the Blosser place is right down the path and across the field from us. Do you think it would be alright if we came by after supper?"

"I certainly think that would be just fine," I said, a little wary of such a late visit. It was already almost nine, we still had to eat supper and I was tired from the evening and the excitement. "We'll ask Mrs. Blosser what time would suit them."

"That sounds good, and I'll see if Pearl wants to come, too, I know she'd like see you again and meet Lizzie."

She gave me that strange smile again and walked to her wagon.

CHAPTER TWO
New Year's Night, 1910

L izzie and I watched from the porch as the three of them walked down the dirt road and neared the Blosser house, their flashlights bobbing in the dark winter night. Mary and Pearl led the way, walking quite briskly, while hanging back was a young man.

As they came up the porch steps Pearl broke into a wide smile and said when she saw me, "There's my partner in crime – how wonderful to see you again."

"What in the world happened to you?" I asked as Pearl gave me an unexpected hug.

"I decided that maybe leading music was not going to be something I wanted to do and there's just so much time in a woman's life to get involved in things. Obviously you finished the training – Mary tells me you were really something this evening at Weaver's Church."

"It really was quite an experience – I hope they'll ask me again," I said noticing that the young man with them was hanging back, looking as if he had been dragged here unwillingly.

"Charles, get on up here!" demanded Mary, motioning to him. "This is my brother Charles Owen Wampler – this is Sadie Zigler."

"Charles WELDON, not OWEN – I changed it a while back when I figured out my initials spelled COW!" he said, walking up on the porch with a grin – we all laughed and I could see he felt a little more comfortable after making his joke.

"It's very nice to meet you," I said, taking his outstretched hand, "I've so enjoyed being with your sister Pearl. Turns out we have a lot of ideas in common."

He held onto my hand with a firm handshake, much like I had remembered with Pearl the first time I met her. I looked at this man, who was not very tall and quite slender. In the light of the porch, he appeared pale and almost sickly, not at all like a hearty farmer. In fact, both of his sisters were larger than he. His eyes were a clear light blue and he looked at me intensely, almost making me feel uncomfortable with his gaze.

"Sadie, I'm pleased to meet you. I'm well aware of the Ziglers and their fine reputation in the area – good Brethren stock," he said, finally dropping my hand. "My great–grandfather John Wampler had a place up in Timberville early on, then two more generations of Wamplers lived there until my father came down here."

"And before there were church buildings, I understand services were held at his house, just like the Ziglers," said Pearl, sitting down on the porch swing. "Guess we have a lot in common, don't we," she stated, looking knowingly at Charles and me and then at Lizzie who sported a conspirital grin.

"Did they have the partitions that came down from the ceiling?" I said, walking over to the porch swing and sitting down – I joined the back and forth motion with Pearl. I couldn't shake the feeling that there was a purpose in this meeting that I was not party to.

"From the ceiling, yes," Mary replied, taking a seat on one of the rocking chairs on the front porch and rocking to the rhythm of the swing. Lizzie, Mary and Pearl continued to glance at each other, then at Charles, then back to me.

"Did they also entertain every preacher and traveler who came down the pike like the Ziglers have?" I said, trying to keep the conversation going and ignoring the slight tension that was beginning to build.

"Not sure about that," said Mary, "but I wouldn't be surprised."

I noticed Charles was staring at me, making me even more uncomfortable when Mary said, "Pearl, Lizzie, Mary, let's go inside and see our neighbors, you and Sadie get acquainted, Charles." She motioned Pearl off the swing and the three of them disappeared into the house, leaving Charles and me alone on the porch.

After an awkward silence, Charles finally said with a smile, "You know, Mary is always trying to fix me up with one girl or another. Tonight, you are that girl."

"I have the same problem with my own sister," I replied, feeling more at ease at his honesty.

"So let's make 'em all happy and go for a little walk to the top of the hill," he said stepping down to the lawn and offering his arm. "I'll show you Sunny Slope Farm."

Something about his forthright and humorous approach to our situation appealed to me. Perhaps he wasn't any more interested in being matched up with someone than I was. I felt a certain safety with this man.

"Sounds like a wonderful idea," I said, taking his arm as we walked up the hill, past the Blosser barn and silo up the dirt road to the rise where we could look down at the home where the Wampler family lived.

The full winter moon illuminated, on the left, a large white Pennsylvania Dutch bank barn just like the one we had on our farm. On the right, a little further down at the base of a green pasture that stretched up the hill, was a large white frame house with a raised porch on the front with steps on either end. Lattice work covered the space beneath the porch. To the left of the main house was a smaller log structure that I assumed was a wash house or summer kitchen.

"My father, John Wampler built the big house after the Civil War. When he and my grandmother bought the property from the Harshbarger's the barn was already here that he added to and put on a tin roof. The log house was also there and had been moved at some time from the back of the property. It was moved again to where you see it now because they couldn't find enough water for a well. So the family lived there until the big house was built about 1871. My father said, 'I'm going to build a good house if it costs me $1000. It was a modern house for its time – do you want to go down and see it?"

"I think not, I'm a little tired from the activities of today," I said, realizing that this was not just an excuse. All the excitement had taken its toll.

As we walked back to the Blosser house Charles continued to tell stories of his family and of the property. It reminded me so much of the times in my childhood when I was required to know the significance of everything about the place in which I was reared and its history. I was struck with how comfortable I felt with this man I had only just met.

I suddenly realized he had asked me a question. "I'm sorry," I said, "I sort of drifted away, what did you ask?"

"I was saying I understand you led the singing over at Weaver's. That's a pretty big deal for a woman – surprised those finicky old Mennonites let you do it."

I laughed, "I only led one of the hymns and that was because of Papa and my music teacher, Dr. Holsinger – I don't think some people were too pleased about it."

"I think it's a good thing for women to have a little more participation in the church. Even Jesus had women following him around everywhere and included them in his band of disciples – I don't think he'd object, do you?" he said, with just a twinge of challenge, as if he might think I would be shocked.

"I'm sure He would not," I replied, catching myself not to be drawn in by this man who seemed to think very much as I did. After all, I'd done just fine as an independent woman so far. No need to amend that status.

I fell asleep immediately after hitting the feather bed upstairs at the Blossser house. I hadn't even had time to go over in my mind this eventful day even though Lizzie had tried, lying there beside me in the bed as we had as little girls at home, to get me to give my impressions of Charles.

Papa picked us up in the wagon early the next morning and asked the minute I was in the wagon, "Well, how did it go last night?"

"How did what go?" I replied, again feeling I was on the outside of an inside plot.

"The meeting with the Wampler clan, of course," he said glancing at Lizzie.

"They are a very nice family," I said, with as much nonchalance as I could muster.

I knew they wanted to know what I thought of Charles but I refused to say anything regarding that. I thought he was an interesting person but I had no intention of continuing a relationship with him.

About a week later, the next time we picked up the mail at the post office, I received a letter from Charles. I really hadn't thought much about our meeting that New Year's evening. Papa and Lizzie, of course, were after me about it, but I just said it was a pleasant visit and that he was a very nice person. I had no intention of letting it go any further and made that clear to both of them. I noted the date on the letter—it was written the very evening we had met which gave me pause. I certainly hadn't led him to believe that I wanted to continue our conversation, had I?

January 1, 1910

Dear Sadie,

I enjoyed meeting you this evening at the Blosser's. Although our time was short, I thought our conversasion was a good one. I hope that you will allow me to rite you and maybe visit you at your home sometime.

Sincerelly. Charles W. Wampler (not Owen)

P.S. Sister Pearl was already asleep when I rote this so she wasn't able to check my spelling, which, as you can see, is awful. I will do better next time.

I sat on the front porch reading his letter, amused at his self-deprecating remarks. I was not quite sure why my response was as resistant as it was to his request to communicate further. Had I really become so used to being independent that all doors remained shut to the possibility of a relationship with a man? Had my experience with John Flory soured me on the whole idea of ever marrying and having a family? What about the feelings I had when I took care of Nadya and felt so motherly towards her? Perhaps I was just being stubborn as Lizzie frequently accused me. Whatever the resistance, it was there and I wrote a short note back to Charles with no encouragement whatsoever for a continued correspondence. I heard nothing more from him.

CHAPTER THREE
March, 1910

E arly the spring of that year, we received word that Charles and Pearl were planning to come to visit relatives in Timberville and asked Papa if they could come to visit. Of course, since we never turned anyone away, they were welcome to come and I was anxious to see Pearl again. We had begun a correspondence by letter and I loved sharing our mutual interests and ideas about life. As to Charles (not Owen) I had really never given him another thought. Well, maybe once in a while when Pearl mentioned him and what he was doing, which she did quite often and, I felt, intentionally and purposefully. After what Charles had said about his sisters trying to fix him up with someone, I was suspicious and wary. I made a vow that I would treat them as any other guest in our home.

This was not, I soon learned, Charles' intention at all.

"That is one fine looking animal," said Papa as the wagon pulled up to the barn. The magnificent black stallion, all slicked up with polished harnesses hitched to the buggy, carried Charles and his sister Pearl. He was obviously an expensive horse, spirited and a bit hard to handle, which, of course appealed to Papa. Charles had a way with him, however, and calmed him down, also impressing my father.

"I always say," said Charles looking at me with a sheepish smile, "that a beautiful girl is the only thing in the world more attractive than a beautiful horse."

"I need to go in and get supper on," I said turning quickly and starting into the house. He could be more of a challenge to discourage than I thought and again I pondered the reason behind my resistance to his attention.

"I'll give you a hand," said Pearl, hopping off the wagon leaving the men to unhitch the horse and bed him down for the night.

As we walked into the house, Pearl looked up at the partitions attached to the ceiling. "Now, that's what Mary was talking about. I'd never actually seen them before. Fascinating architecture."

"It appears our families have that history in common," I said, so excited about seeing Pearl again.

"Indeed we do," she agreed as we went into the kitchen. As always, I had spent the entire day preparing supper.

The men came into the living room and sat down, continuing a lively conversation that had already begun outside.

"...in the draft horse business?" Papa was asking Charles who also looked up at the wooden partitions in the living room.

"Well, my father sort of handed it over to me right before he died four years ago, and I took over the farm. He had done real well with the horse business even when it went to pot in the late 90's," he explained, gesturing with his hands and telling the tale as if he were giving a speech. "Said it was for two reasons: one, he always had better horses than anyone else because he didn't mind spending money for them and second, because he had a reputation for honest dealing." Papa was leaning in from his chair across from Charles and was taking in every word.

"Pap bought the stallion you saw, Gueriar, and asked me to take care of him. I've always been a little puny, as you can see," he laughed, standing up from his chair and pointing out his slight stature. "So to be asked to do that job when hardly grown was a real boost," he said as he returned to his seat, "I've never felt bigger."

"Your father sounds like a wise man encouraging you as he did," said Papa, shaking his head approvingly.

"Well, he was pretty right about most things but his confidence in the horse business was a little off when he said once, 'somebody will get something that will run over the ground without a horse pulling it, but it will never be of practical use.' Well, we both know how that's going to work out with Henry Ford working on that motor car of his," he quipped, obviously pleased that Papa was such a good audience.

Meanwhile, with my skills at eavesdropping having been honed to perfection all these years, I realized I was also listening to his every word to the point that I suddenly became aware that Pearl was waiting for an answer to a question she had posed.

"Excuse me, Pearl, what was that?" I said embarrassed at my rudeness.

"I was asking where you went to college," she said, "You never mentioned it when we were in Dayton last year."

"Well, unfortunately, my college experience was cut short when Mama died in 1904. I actually only went for one semester," I said, turning away from her to put a roast chicken on a platter and to hide the disappointment that I knew showed on my face.

"Really?" she said, appearing quite surprised, "I just assumed that with your obvious intelligence and the wide range of reading you've done, you had a degree from somewhere. And you didn't go back?"

"No," I said, matter–of–factly, and with a lingering touch of regret that I thought had been long buried. "I've been responsible for taking care of my younger brother, Robert, who was just 13 when she died; and, of course, taking care of visitors that come through our home on a regular basis. How about you?"

"I graduated from Shenandoah College in Dayton a while ago," she said, happily, not seeming to notice the look on my face. "I've been living at home with Mother, Mary and Charles and teaching school off and on since then."

"I envy you that," I said quietly, feeling emotions I hadn't felt since dropping out of Bridgewater.

Pearl looked at me, suddenly tuning into my feelings. "You can always go back," she said, encouragingly. "Education is so important, especially for a woman these days. We'll be getting the vote before too many years and I intend to be right there first in line."

"You really think so?" I said, astonished at the news and welcoming the change of subject. "Where in the world is this happening? Somehow important information such as this takes a while to reach Broadway, Virginia."

"The women's suffrage movement in Virginia started way back in 1870 before either of us was born and just last year in Virginia, the most vocal supporters organized around the Equal Suffrage League of Virginia," she said excitedly. "This group is working with other women's groups around the country trying to change state and local laws and pass an amendment to the Constitution and I'm right in the middle of it all."

Once again I was reminded how much I enjoyed conversing with Pearl and vowed to be intentional about keeping up our friendship. She had skillfully guided me away from the past and into the future and I so appreciated that in her.

"You know, Charles and I set up a debate society at Shenandoah and one of the debates was about the women's vote," she continued, her eyes sparkling with the pleasure of the memory. "Charles was appointed to argue against the idea and did a great job, even though he actually believes the other side. Shows what a talker he is and how he can argue you down about most anything," she laughed, looking toward the living room where Charles was still going on and on about something with Papa in rapt attention.

"Did everyone in your family go to college?" I asked, wondering about Charles' education and quickly wondering why I cared.

"Some of us—Charles went for a little but didn't go back when Pap died and he had to take over the farm," she said, as if picking up on my interest. But he sure believes it's important. Back when our brother David, who was as smart as a whip, really wanted to go to college, he was discouraged by our father. David had a severe case of dyspepsia, something even worse than Charles' ulcerated stomach and finally asked Father, 'If I get better will you let me go to college?' Father's answer was, 'Oh what do you want in college?' and that was end of that. Charles is convinced that he lost the will to live when he thought there was no hope of continuing his education. He died when he was only nineteen year's old—just gave up and died. Both of our other brothers, Sam and John had serious health problems too. John, who had a congenital weakness of his muscle, actually fell out of a tree while hunting squirrels and broke his neck—he was thirty-nine and that was the same year David and our father died. Now that was a really bad year."

"How very sad," I sighed, thinking perhaps my life and the losses I had suffered were not unusual. Life certainly was difficult for everyone and perhaps it was high time I stopped feeling sorry for myself. "Guess we can put supper on, now."

Pearl helped me carry the steaming dishes of food to the table where Charles and Papa now sat, looking expectantly hungry.

As I set the platter of chicken on the table I took notice of what Charles was wearing. He had dressed in what I assumed were his Sunday clothes, but they weren't the usual Brethren high collared shirt and coat. He wore a tailored suit with a vest, white shirt and a tie. Something John Flory would have worn. I pushed the thought aside as I always did when the memory of him bubbled up from the past.

"This sure does look good enough to eat," said Charles, "Pearl and I appreciate your hospitality and all the time it must have taken to get all this together."

"Would you like to return grace?" Papa asked Charles.

"No, sir, I don't much like to pray outside my own home," he said firmly. "You go ahead."

I thought this was an odd response and wondered what he meant. Every Brethren I ever knew, including Papa, loved to pray out loud anywhere they got a chance, using the prayer as a platform to expound on religion or whatever happened to be on their mind at the moment.

We bowed our heads as Papa began, "Father in heaven, we thank you for this fine fellowship with the Wamplers, who are good people. Bless this food to the nourishment of our bodies and our lives to Thy service–Amen." I was relieved that he kept it short and without any personal reference involved.

During supper Papa continued his interrogation of Charles—and that's exactly what it was, no doubt in my mind.

"So are you going to continue in the horse business?" he asked, as he began passing around the steaming dishes of food. Charles took very little on his plate and I thought there must be a reason. Then I remembered Pearl's passing comment about his ulcerated stomach.

"I'm not so sure about that. Last year I went to a short course at VPI with about forty other agriculture people and I learned a lot. The only preparation I had before I took over our farm was doing what my father told me to do and reading a few farm magazines. At that short course we talked about politics, religion, finance and farming. I think we settled all the world's problems, or at least we tried," he chuckled, looking over at me.

I had to admit that I enjoyed listening to him talk but tried to remain neutral and not show it too much. He looked directly at me when he said with a touch of mystery, "I've been turning over some things in my mind about how we might bring something new to the farm to make it pay."

"And what might that be?" asked Papa, pulling Charles gaze away from me.

"Not quite ready to let it out of the bag," he said quickly, then looked back at me again.

"And how about you, Miss Sadie Zigler, what else are you interested in besides taking care of this household?"

Once again, I was a little taken aback by his forthright approach, so much so that I blurted out, "I want to go back to college and be a school teacher."

Papa gave me such a look and said bluntly, "Sarah, I believe it is a little late for that."

"Nonsense," Pearl piped up, always ready for a good debate, "never too late to get an education."

Papa seemed stunned that he was being contradicted by this young woman who was a guest in his house. I could almost hear him thinking, "Oh heavens, not another one like Sarah," but he held his tongue.

"Certainly not," said Charles, continuing the train of thought, "We need teachers of any gender. I had a wonderful woman teacher once – Miss Pauline Head was her name. Unfortunately, she couldn't control us rowdy boys so she didn't last long," he laughed, seemingly not noticing that his host had gone silent. "Now Pearl here, taught at that one room school for three years and she…"

"You know good and well, Charles Wampler," she laughed, "That I must have run that school right into the ground – closed it right down, they did. After that, they built a big four room school in Dayton and didn't ask me back.

Papa was becoming more and more uncomfortable with the direction of the conversation so, in good Zigler tradition, he changed it.

"So Charles, what do you think about the stand the Brethren Church is taking on peace and war?"

Subject changed, we continued on into the evening after supper talking about various subjects from politics to religion to farming. Pearl and I excused ourselves, cleared the table and went to the kitchen to clean up.

After we finished we came back into the living room and suddenly, Pearl spotted the organ.

"Is that a harmonium?" she asked walking over to the instrument and touching the wood gently.

"It is," I said, "do you have one, too?"

"No, but I have some friends who do – do you play?" she asked.

"A little, I…"

"A little," said Papa, happy to be able to brag on something I did of which he approved, "Why she took lessons from George Holsinger."

"From Bridgewater College, George Holsinger?" asked Pearl, obviously impressed.

"One and the same," said Papa. "Sarah, why don't you play us something?"

Embarrassed by all the attention, I said, "How about we pull out the Hymnal and I'll play and we can have an old folks sing right here in the living room?"

About that time, Robert came in from wherever he had been with his friends. He was now nineteen years old and had graduated from high school, still waiting for Papa to allow him to register for college.

"Pearl, Charles, this is my younger brother, Robert," I said, "Robert, Pearl and Charles Wampler."

"Very pleased to meet you, Mr. Wampler, Miss Wampler," he said cordially, reaching out his hand. Robert had grown much taller but was still frailly–built. He had become very handsome with a head of wavy sand–colored hair. There was a quiet confidence about him and everyone was drawn in by his charm. "The Wampler name is a very familiar one in the Valley and amongst the Brethren here. I understand from my good friend Dr. John S. Flory that you are first cousins."

I was stunned. The Wamplers and Flory's were related? I wanted to ask about the connection but Robert continued, "Hey, Sister Sadie, are we about to have a sing?" I decided to let the matter rest until later – I would ask Pearl.

Until about 10:30 that evening, we sang hymn after hymn from the Brethren Hymnal that Dr. Holsinger had edited. Charles had a good bass voice and was obviously used to singing in part harmony and with gusto.

Our voices finally tired out, we decided it was time for turning in.

We climbed the stairs and I showed Charles to the "Tramp Room."

"Here's where we put all the tramps and hoboes that come through and stay for the night," I said with a laugh.

"Sounds like the perfect place for me," he said, grinning and suddenly taking my hand. "Thank you, Sadie—I certainly did enjoy the evening."

"As did I," I said, quickly pulling back my hand but realizing that I really meant what I had said.

Pearl and I went to Mama's room downstairs where we talked into the night like young girls. How nice it would have been if Lizzie and I had had this much in common.

Early the next morning after a full breakfast of scrambled eggs, country ham, biscuits, pan haus, smear case and strawberry preserves, the Wamplers hitched up and left for Dayton.

As the wagon with Guerier in the lead drove down the dusty lane, I reflected on the previous evening with a warm feeling. Certainly being with Pearl again and renewing our friendship with her was part of it, but I knew that there was something else that had transpired. I had been with a man who was obviously interested in me as a woman. I had enjoyed his company and for once, entertained the idea of wanting to be with him again. I put the thought aside and suddenly I recalled, "Shoot, I forgot to ask Pearl about them being cousins to John Flory."

And then, the thought occurred to me as to why exactly I wished to know this. Charles Weldon Wampler had more than a little of that trait that I had applied to my former mentor and dear friend: Passion.

CHAPTER FOUR

April 1, 1910

Dear Sadie,

Pearl and I enjoyed so much your family's hospitality last week when we came up to Broadway. The meal, conversation and especially the hymn sing were enjoyed and appreciated.

I thought of stopping right here in this letter because after saying thank you, which is the proper thing to do—any more might be taken by you as my being a pest.

I sat on the front porch in the rocking chair on that bright spring day reading the letter that had come in the mail just days after the Wampler's visit. Papa hadn't stopped talking about Charles and how impressed he was with him. Not that I hadn't been, but found myself trying not to dwell too much on the things he had said that I liked, in particular the support for my educational goals and becoming a teacher. I did like his sense of humor and during the evening had become more and more comfortable being around him. I continued reading, wondering whether I might be moving into a situation that would be troublesome for me and then wondering why I thought it would be troublesome. Would he, indeed, become a "pest?"

After we met last January at the Blossers, though I enjoyed it, I, at first didn't' think much about it. Since we had been set up by our nosey sisters, my first notion was to just leave it be. I'll admit I don't' much like to be told what to do or with who (or is that whom — I'll ask Pearl) but as time went on, I found myself wanting to know more about this Sadie Zigler, who, more than just a lovely woman seemed to have a mind of her own. So my request is that I would like to continue to correspond with you to become better acquainted with that mind and share with you some of my thoughts. I want you to know that my intentions are entirely honorable, though I must be honest, I have little idea what those intentions might be. I am an unmarried, twenty–five–year–old man living with his mother and two sisters. Like most of the men in my family, my health is not that good. Apparently I have the worst looking stomach my doctor has ever seen. (you might have noticed I didn't eat that much the other night). In fact, the doctor has also told me that I shouldn't ever get married and certainly not have children because I probably wouldn't live to see them grown. So you see, prospects for my future are a little shaky at best.

What I ask is this: could we write to each other and have no particular purpose except to enjoy the workings of two GREAT MINDS!?

I paused in my reading, laid the letter down on the side table and went into the kitchen to brew a cup of tea. From Charles' letter I was learning a bit more than I really wanted to know about him, and yet, here was a man who seemed to want to be just a friend and was interested in my mind and getting to know me on that level. If he was like his sister Pearl, perhaps we could be just that, and enjoy a correspondence without any personal entanglement, even though he was a man. I boiled the water, fixed my tea, and carried my cup out to porch where I returned to reading his letter.

How about you get started by telling me more about you wanting to be a teacher. If you don't write back, I'll take that as a "NO" and will leave you alone.

Sincerely,

Charles W. Wampler

P.S. As you can tell, I got some help for Pearl on my spelling on this one.

As I finished his letter, I sat looking out toward the barn where Robert and Sam were chopping wood, a job that they had done since they were young boys. Robert was still biding his time, waiting for Papa to come around to agreeing to let him go to college. There was talk of selling the farm if Robert decided to go to Bridgewater, which put him under great pressure that I felt was unfair. But that was the way of our family and our loyalties.

I looked back at Charles' last sentence which gave me a perfectly good way out. I could end it right here, right now.

Yet, perhaps it would be enjoyable to begin a correspondence with this man who didn't seem to be putting any pressure on me for anything but a friendship. At such a distance, I could certainly control the situation and not let anything go beyond my own comfort. And why was I uncomfortable, really? The only real thoughts of romance in my life had centered on a man who was out of my reach. If I were honest with myself, I had to admit that I had been affected by John Flory and the way he came and went out of my life – I knew full well that there was a spark that went both ways when we became adults and his choice to move on to someone else without so much as a look back had hurt me deeply. Maybe I just didn't want to chance being hurt again. I'm not exactly sure what it was that made me decide that it was worth taking the chance.

And thus began a correspondence by letter that would span over a year in which Charles and I shared our interests, our dreams and his "grand idea." This idea would ultimately change the lives of thousands of people in Rockingham County, Virginia, forever. As it turned out, he had other "grand ideas" that would change my own life.

S. J. W.

CHAPTER FIVE
August, 1910

"Papa, listen to this," I said as I opened yet another of Charles' letters to me. We had corresponded several times a month since we began and I was happy about my decision to do it. I felt no pressure whatsoever and sometimes even found myself going to the mailbox and being disappointed at there being no letter. Charles was very busy traveling with a job he had taken to bring in more money after giving up on the horse business. He worked for the county, visiting schools and farmers, and organizing "Boys Corn Clubs," which promoted agriculture among young people. He seemed to enjoy the work and since he was so good with people, he was feeling some success about it. But his mind was still on other things which he shared with me in this latest letter. I began reading aloud to Papa.

> *...which brings me to my new idea. I will share it with you because I would like to know whether you think I am crazy or not. All the people I've talked to so far think I am.*

> *Turkeys! My brilliant idea – yes, Turkeys that 100% American bird.*

First, let me give you a little turkey history so you know where I started my way of thinking. From the beginning of this country the domestic turkey has been an important part of the development of Rockingham County – during the time of the first settlers, it fed farm families. No improvements in these domestic turkeys have been made all that time and the mortality and morbidity rate was very high. My first turkey experience started on our farm when I was about nine years old and was paid seven cents for each turkey nest I could find. Some of the hens were really good at hiding them and since the women of the family depended on the eggs and hens for food and meeting expenses it was important to track them down. My mother was one of the biggest turkey operators, buying and selling the birds as well as using them for meals. I turned out to be a whiz at finding the nests out on the farm so that was my first business venture.

So here's what I've been thinking..."

I stopped reading aloud to take a breath as Papa, who had held on to every word, got up from his chair and exclaimed excitedly, "Your man can sure talk a blue streak, can't he? And I bet I know where he's going with this. Go on Sadie, keep reading.."

"He's not 'my man,' Papa, he's just a friend like his sister Pearl and we're having a good time writing, that's all," I stated firmly, aware that I was not being completely honest with myself or him.

"Well, alright, just keep reading," he said sitting down beside me at the table, his eyes expectant and shining with the interest of a man who loved new ideas.

> *In 1885, Sam Blosser started putting thermometers under the chicken hens, sitting around watching them all day, even sleeping under the house to hear how often the hens turned her eggs. Everybody thought he was crazy. His craziness resulted in today's chicken industry. So I got the thinking, why couldn't we do the same thing with turkeys and their eggs?*

> *As I said before, the farmers at the VPI short course didn't think much of the idea, but I figure if I can be as crazy as a fox like Sam Blosser, I might really have something here. So what do you think?*

"Well, I think it's brilliant, don't you, Sarah?" he said, getting up and pacing around the room. It was good to see him excited about something. The weight of decision about the farm was wearing him down lately. "You better grab this man soon, he's really going places!"

"I really do think it's a wonderful idea," I said truthfully, ignoring, as always, his constant reminders of my chosen spinsterhood. I was becoming increasingly impressed with Charles' forward thinking – much like the spirit of my own father in his youth. "But do you think he can do it without some support from the Poultry departments of the state Universities? He can't just do it by himself."

"And just why not? Nobody thought I could bring back the Harmonia Sacra and I did. Sarah, there are no limits to what one person can do in this world and don't you forget it," he said marching out the door, whistling an old hymn tune."

I was reminded once again that Papa's "limitless possibilities" still applied only to men. I went back to reading the letter, suddenly aware that the man who was writing to me did not have that particular bias.

Now, for your next letter, I wonder if you can tell me a little about your religious beliefs. You signed your letter, "In Christ." Just what does that mean to you? Will look forward to hearing what you have to say about my grand idea.

Until then I am Your Crazy–in–the–head friend,

Charles

As we continued our conversation by mail, Charles and I shared more personal things about ourselves with each other. He had asked about my religious beliefs which I found difficult to express in words. Instead, I told him about growing up in a family where, though we were very Brethren, religious dogma was less important then way in which we lived and treated others, particularly our Negro farm hands and home workers. I told him about the tramps, gypsies and Nadya and how we had taken her in. He particularly liked the story of sneaking her into the Love Feast and I could almost hear him laughing out loud. He did share his own story of a Negro man called "Pete" who had worked on their farm and started stealing from them and some of the other neighbors. There was something about the way he told the tale that alerted me to a touch of prejudice toward Negroes in general. This bothered me. When I mentioned this, he was a bit defensive and we decided we would address the issue when we saw each other in person. "I suppose we can't agree on everything," he said.

I began re–reading his latest letter dating August 10, 1910, after finishing preparations for his overnight visit today. I was becoming a little nervous about the turn of the recent communication on his part. There had been indications that his intentions, though indeed honorable, were beginning to lean in the direction of a formal courtship. I was surprised that I was more open to this than I expected. Our relationship by letter had very gradually grown more intimate in what we shared with each other and so far I still felt comfortable.

> *I feel that have come to know you well in our corresponding even though we have not met since spring. We spoke early on about my intentions or lack thereof. Lately I have come to realize that my intentions are becoming quite plain to me in regards to you and I would like to come to your house to speak to you and your father about them. Please let me know when it would be convenient for me to come up on the train and stay the night. I hope that you are not too surprised at this,*

as I feel that we have become more than friends. I don't know how you feel about this sickly farmer with some crazy ideas, but I am hoping there is some affection there beyond friendship.

I will look forward to seeing you.

With Affection and Hope,

Charles

The plan was that Charles would come up on the night train on a Saturday after he finished his county agent rounds, spend the night here and attend church with us the next morning.

Papa and I picked him up at the station at ten o'clock and by the time we got home it was so late, we decided to wait until morning to begin visiting. I was quite happy to see him again after so long and also somewhat relieved that we could start fresh in the morning after a good night's sleep to reacquaint ourselves.

"Is the tramp room available tonight?" he said as we climbed the stairs, "I feel like one after my week wandering all over Rockingham County."

"Reserved just for you," I answered, feeling like – I wasn't sure what I was feeling. I wasn't uncomfortable, even though it had been months since I last saw Charles. He seemed to have a way of seamlessly connecting our communication through letters to this visit.

"Until tomorrow, then," he said, gently taking my hand in his and looking deeply into my eyes. "We have a lot to talk about. Sleep well, Sadie."

"Tomorrow," I said, my voice catching with what I can only describe as lovely anxiety.

Getting to church on Sunday morning is always rushed at our house and by the time chores were done, breakfast eaten and our dressing for the service, there had been no time for any discussion about our relationship.

I had not slept well at all, turning over in my head what Charles might have on his mind. Well, I pretty well knew what he had on his mind, but just how far was he planning to take it, I had no idea. And I had no idea how I would react to what he might say. Finally exhausted, with a prayer of turning the whole matter over to God's keeping, I fell asleep.

After breakfast Papa pulled Noir and the wagon around to the porch and I got in. Robert and Charles joined us, continuing a conversation they had begun at the breakfast table.

"I agree that there is nothing good about war," Charles was saying, "but sometimes we need to defend our national principles or something we believe in strongly."

"I firmly believe that the peace message of the Brethren Church is the only way," stated Robert, trying to be respectful of his elder guest, but his passion would not let him back down. "Now, Dr. John S. Flory believes a little stronger about that than I and thinks that we should not only refrain from joining the armed services but should preach strongly that war is wrong, period."

"I can see you've been influenced by my cousin. John's a good man but is a little too radical for me," he said, pulling himself up on the wagon to sit beside me. "You're a young man, you need to make the decision for yourself – sometimes war is just plain necessary – I do admire your spirit, Robert."

Knowing Charles love of debate on either side of an issue, I wasn't positive whether he actually believed what he said or was just enjoying the argument itself. We continued on to the church, where there were more wagons than usual tied up owing to the fact that we had a guest preacher for today.

The service was no different than always and from across the aisle, I could hear Charles' booming bass voice on all of the hymns. He glanced over at me watching him and winked. The woman beside me saw this and raised her eyebrows in disapproval. I smiled enjoying the fact that Charles, too, seemed to like to rock the boat.

The guest preacher preached a heated sermon on Grace vs. Works and Salvation in general. Charles and I had discussed this subject in our correspondence and he, as on most issues, had very firm ideas concerning it. The two of us had similar views on this issue. This particular preacher was staunchly in the "Saved by Grace only," corner.

Papa had invited the guest preacher to our home for Sunday dinner after the service so he joined us in the wagon back to the house. Charles was uncharacteristically quiet during the trip and we both remained silent as Papa and the preacher exchanged pleasantries.

At home, as we finished the main meal and I was back and forth clearing dishes and preparing dessert, I could see that Charles was gearing up for a debate with the minister. His brow was furrowed as he bent over his food, biding his time until he could find a way to begin. I quickly put the apple pie and ice cream on the plates and served everyone, sitting down immediately so as not to miss what I expected to be quite a discussion. Eavesdropping would not suffice in this case – I wanted to be in the middle of this one.

The two of them sat across from each other at our dining room table; one, with sideburns connected to a long untrimmed grey beard, no moustache, the other completely clean shaven—one wearing a black high-collared coat with no buttons and a white shirt, the other sporting a tailored navy suit and vest, white wing–tipped–collar shirt and a soft blue tie that matched his eyes. The contrast in appearance was striking and that was only the beginning. I leaned forward, drawn to the electricity in the air.

"Now, Brother Early," Charles began, calmly and with respect in his voice, "do I understand that you believe that we are saved, or obtain Salvation, solely by Grace?"

"Indeed I do, without a bit of doubt," said the preacher firmly, pausing his fork over his hot apple pie. "Do you not believe this Truth?"

"Well, sir, I sure believe in God's Grace, but I must tell you that I believe it's how we live, what we do, how we treat other folks, that makes more difference to God," replied Charles, sitting up tall in his chair as if to make himself more imposing. "I heard Brother D.C. Flory say once that he objected to the idea that you were saved through Grace and then, because you are saved, you do good. He said that you are saved because you do good. He called it Practical Religion."

As I sat and listened to the discourse, I was struck by the passion of this man who had come to visit me as well as agreeing with what he was saying. It was not lost on me that this trait was one I had always admired in other people and particularly the one who had introduced me to it long ago.

Brother Early bristled. "Listen, son, you can't save yourself – it isn't what you do that counts. You are saved only by the Grace of God through the atoning blood of Jesus Christ on the Cross."

"Sir, with all due respect, I do not say we can save ourselves, no, I do not," Charles argued, but was pulling back just to appease the pastor. "We are created and sustained by God's Grace, but to know his will and do it seems to be more…"

Brother Early was beginning to get a little hot under his high Brethren collar. He waved his fork in the air as he said, his voice rising to a fever pitch.

"Jesus died for our sins on the cross — but for that, and only that, are we saved from the fires of Hell," he almost shrieked with his eyes as fiery as the Hell of which he spoke.

Papa, Robert and I were listening intently to this escalating discussion: Robert, with youthful curiosity, wanting to add his two cents worth, but a little intimidated by the two strong debaters. Papa was uneasy, and though I knew that theologically he stood with Charles on the subject, he was concerned that this peaceful Sunday Dinner was getting out of hand.

And I, for my part, was unable to hold my tongue for any longer.

"Brother Early, just exactly what does Jesus' death on...?"

Papa looked at me with that stern fatherly expression, "Sarah, I think perhaps we should let the men finish..."

Charles eyes widened and he choked on the water he was drinking. "With all due respect Mr. Zigler," Charles said with a confidence I had never heard him use with my father, "Sadie here is as well read as any of us menfolk. I believe she has a perfect right to speak her mind."

Everyone at the table was stunned, including me. I looked at Papa who nodded cautiously, "Go ahead, Sadie."

I began slowly, "I've read that atonement theology and practice has a long history, starting with human sacrifice to appease a wrathful God. Then, with the Jews, burnt offerings of livestock and birds was seen sufficient to satisfy God's requirement." I paused, realizing every eye at that table was focused on me – I liked the feeling. "Then comes Jesus who showed us by His life how we must live and by his death, showed us that we might be required to make sacrifices in our lives, even to the point of death."

I looked at Charles, who was beaming at me.

Papa waited, holding his breath as the preacher proceeded to counter everything that I had said. I didn't mind––I had had my say and I was supported by someone I was beginning to admire more and more.

The conversation moved to other theological discussions, in which everyone at the table was included, even Robert. When the last of the dinner dishes had been washed and Charles was due to meet his train back to Dayton, we lingered alone on the porch.

"Charles," I said, "I can't believe what you did for me earlier with Brother Early. I just…"

He took both of my hands in his and looked me squarely in the eyes. "Sadie Edna Rebecca Zigler, you and I may not always agree in the coming years. I am a stubborn and opinionated man, but I promise you, I will never try to keep you from saying your piece or expressing your views. I love you for many reasons, and not the least of these is that quick mind of yours. If I ever try to diminish you in any way because you are a woman, you have my permission to kick my behind."

I didn't pull away my hands as we stood there with our eyes locked for several moments. And then, he leaned in and kissed me cautiously on the cheek, a little like the Holy Kiss of the Love Feast. As he walked away toward the wagon, I suddenly realized what he had said and I froze.

CHAPTER SIX

October, 1910

I was conflicted in the days following Charles declaration of love and his chaste, but certainly meaningful kiss. By all accounts, I would be considered an "Old Maid." I was twenty–eight years old, three years older than Charles. The truth was, I realized, I had become comfortable in the thought that I would never marry – that whether I would live out my life on this farm in Broadway or, by some wild chance, be able to go back to Bridgewater College as Pearl had suggested, I would remain single. If I married… and ah, there was the rub, Charles intentions had moved us headlong into a courtship that might well result in marriage, a home and children. I was sure that he had talked with Papa about his intentions and Papa was almost giddy. He would come in from the mailbox handing me another of Charles' letters with a knowing smile. Was I just being stubborn to prove Mama and Lizzie wrong, or had my feelings for Charles somehow overridden my struggle for independence?

Almost a month had passed after Charles' visit and I had not written him a single letter even though he wrote every couple of days. He had noted in one letter, "I scared you off, didn't I?" I knew that this was unfair to him – if I was having second thoughts about continuing our relationship I certainly should have the courtesy to tell him face to face.

I knew Charles had been encouraged by my positive response to his intervention with Brother Early and my father and I couldn't discount that each time I thought of that scene my heart beat a bit faster.

I finished his latest letter and walked out into the yard where fall was beginning to change the October foliage. I needed to think about this carefully. What was I giving up and what did I have to gain? Charles' persistence alone was a matter to consider. He had set out from the beginning to win me over—no one had ever done that for me and I knew that this, by itself, drew me to him. I tried to imagine moving on without Charles and suddenly, I knew for a fact that I would miss him.

I returned to the house and began a letter to him.

November 1, 1910

Dear Charles,

It is true that I have had to pause and think about whether to continue our relationship. I am not at an age where I expect to be swept off my feet like a young girl in the novels I read. Certainly my affection for you has grown over the past year, yet there are practical matters we have not yet discussed that are important to me. Perhaps we could meet as soon as the roads clear of snow, and I will tell you of my concerns. Please forgive me for my rudeness in cutting of our correspondence with no explanation on my part. This whole thing has moved a little too fast for one who might be considered by some as an 'old maid.'"

With Sincere apologies, Sadie

Not surprisingly, within a few days I received a letter from Charles, who had been amused at my hinting at the speed of our courtship.

...since it has been almost a year since we have been corresponding and I making visits to see you. That said, I respect your wishes and would welcome a chance to address your concerns. I have spoken with the Blossers and wondered if you might want to come to visit the farm for a day or so. They would welcome you to stay overnight if you do not feel comfortable staying here at the house. As you know, Mary has married, so Pearl, my mother and I are here at the house. Perhaps, seeing first hand, the farm and my home situation might give you a clearer picture of a possible future for the two of us. (Oops, too much pressure? – sorry)

Please let me know when you might come, as I do find myself lately traveling quite a bit with the new job I have as County Agent.

Hopefully,

Charles

P.S. You are certainly not an old maid in my mind!"
I look forward to seeing you again. I will do my level

best not to make you feel any pressure, although you do know my intentions which have not changed a bit since we last met.

Until then, Charles

CHAPTER SEVEN

December 31, 1910

I gathered my things as the train pulled into the station in Harrisonburg that New Year's Eve morning. At first, I had asked Lizzie to accompany me on the visit, but she couldn't get away so I had decided to come alone. I supposed some might not think it proper for a young woman to visit her prospective beau unchaperoned, but since Pearl and Charles' mother were both going to be at the house and Pearl would accompany him to pick me up, I convinced Papa that I would likely not cause a scandal. And, as always, I took a little delight in the slight indiscretion.

"Over here, Sadie," I heard a female voice call as Pearl and Charles walked toward me. "Welcome to the big city — glad you could come."

Charles hung back a bit, not quite knowing how to greet me. We hadn't seen each other since his visit in September. Since I was the one who had caused his uneasiness, I went to him and held out my hands.

"It's very good to see you again, Charles — I really mean that," I said.

And I did mean it. In the month or so after I had made my decision to continue corresponding, we resumed sharing our lives and our ideas. There were no declarations of love or plans made, but the fact that he had given me some space to breathe made me not only more comfortable, but endeared him to me in a way I couldn't explain.

He heaved a great sigh of relief, smiled, and took my hands in his. "Sadie, I have missed you. Thank you for coming," he said, taking my bag.

The buggy and Gueriar, looking fine as always, waited for us at the hitching post.

"Let's head to Sunny Slope Farm," said Pearl.

We followed the Dayton Pike from Harrisonburg and turned off to the right on a lane that wound through the farm. On either side lay pastures fallow for the winter.

"The farm on the left all the way up belongs to the Myers family – they've been here as long as the Wamplers have," Charles began his commentary which I was sure he had given many times before. "To the right is the Ralston Farm. Right there," he said, nodding his head to the right as we started up a steep incline, "is an old Mennonite graveyard that was there when my father first brought my mother here after he bought the land from Mr. Harshbarger. The story goes, she said to my Father, 'Are we not coming to the home?' and he said, 'No, we have another big hill to cross.'"

And it was a Big Hill. Gueriar strained to pull us up and over the ridge. At the top of the hill, I saw a view of the home place that I had missed when I was here that first time. The only way I can describe the scene is that there was a sense of utter peace and calm about it. The house sat squarely at the end of the lane surrounded by huge leafless trees. To the right of the house was a large blue spruce. The rise of the hill behind gave a feeling of protection to the house nestled in the manicured yard before it.

"And that's why we call it Sunny Slope," said Pearl, as we observed the mid–morning sun rising full over the eastern mountains, bathing the hill with a yellow glow. As we drew nearer, I saw that the foundation was built of honed blocks of native limestone and the walkways around the house were also of limestone.

"How lovely," was all I was able to say.

"Why don't you and Pearl go inside," said Charles, "I'll take Gueriar and the wagon up to the stable."

Pearl and I got down from the buggy and climbed the steep steps of the front porch where we were met at the door by a tiny woman with a twinkling smile. She was short like Pearl and couldn't have weighed more than ninety pounds. Charles had told me she was sixty–years–old but she looked far younger than that. Her skin was flawless and her blue eyes had that same piercing look as Charles.

"So this must be the Sadie Zigler I've been hearing so much about," she said in a clear young voice, reaching out her hand. "I'm Kate Miller Wampler, Charles' mother.

It sure is a pleasure to meet you. My, you are a pretty thing, aren't you—no wonder…"

"Mother, don't overdo it. Now that we finally got her here, we don't want to scare her off," Pearl said, not altogether in jest. The comment made me laugh, however, and I realized how easily I related to these women with whom Charles spent his life.

"Come on in, then," said Mrs. Wampler. "How about we have a little glass of fresh milk and some cookies I just baked then we can show you around."

The house was spacious and comfortable, the furnishings more modern than most Brethren homes – rather like ours, in fact. As we walked through the dining room to the small kitchen at the back, I saw a staircase leading to the second floor.

As I stood there, I heard the front door close and then Charles came into the room. He immediately took up his family storytelling which I had already learned was an integral part of who he was.

"When my grandfather built this house he put in that staircase – pretty modern it was for the time, and look at this," said Charles, opening a door to another staircase to the cellar, "this was really unusual to have indoor steps to the basement."

After we had milk, fresh from the large crock on the counter, and oatmeal cookies, Pearl said. "Why don't we take your things upstairs where you'll be tonight. Do you need a little rest? I know that train leaves awful early."

"I would like to freshen up, thanks," I said, indeed feeling a little tired.

We walked to the front hall and climbed a second staircase to the floor above. Upstairs there were four nice–sized bedrooms and yet another set of stairs that went to a full attic. Across from the door to the attic was a door leading to a small porch with a wooden railing. It looked out over the lane leading up the hill.

"Can you go out there?" I asked.

"Sure can," answered Pearl. "That's my little reading and writing hideaway – I go out there all the time – makes me feel like I'm above the fray of daily life – my little cloud."

I walked out on the porch and took in the view back from whence we had come. It was spectacular; the bright green of winter rye in the Myers's field was a stark contrast to the fields on the Sunny Slope side of the road.

I decided that I would lie down for a bit, just to settle my thoughts before what, I knew, were going to be important discussions. As I lay there, I went over my first impressions of this place, and, if Charles had his way, would be my future home. The thought of leaving Broadway, where I had spent my entire life, gave me pause and yet, this home, this family, felt very familiar and comfortable to me. There were still questions I had to ask, but in the meantime, I realized I was beginning to entertain the idea of a change in my plans for my life. After about an hour, I went downstairs where Charles' mother had laid out a meal that could have fed a crew of field hands.

"Heaven's Mrs. Wampler!"

"Please call me Mother Katie," she said, with a wink.

"This looks wonderful," I said, "though I'm still pretty full from those delicious cookies."

"Eat what you want – we can take care of the leftovers for supper tonight," she said as she bustled around, obviously enjoying entertaining a guest. I sighed, thinking of my own mother and all the years she spent doing the same.

Charles, as usual, ate little and when we finished he said, "Sadie, what would you think of a buggy ride down to Dayton? We can go over to Silver Lake and talk a little."

"Silver Lake, I don't think I've ever heard of that one – where is it?"

"It used to be called Mill Dam Lake," said Pearl, "One time Charles and I were down there and I said a pretty lake ought to have a prettier name. So I thought a little and suggested the name, Silver Lake, so we started calling it that – it's beginning to catch on. Better bundle up, it's chilly out there."

"You don't think that it would be improper for us to go alone, do you Pearl?" Charles asked, reaching for my coat and offering it to me.

"I think you are both old enough to behave yourself," she laughed, patting her brother on the back. "Do you feel comfortable with that, Sadie?"

"It's the middle of the day," I answered with a grin, loving this woman's wit and gumption, "I do believe we couldn't cause too much of a scandal."

Neither of us spoke as we traveled down the road to Dayton. I thought I was prepared for this, but realized that I had no idea how to begin. I knew that I had moved from a position of completely dismissing the idea of settling down with Charles to more of a "conditional" possibility. He had said from the beginning that his health might be an issue, particularly in the area of having children, so I had to ask myself, did I really want children in the first place? I wasn't sure. There had been my feelings about Nadya and her baby. But maybe if this was not a possibility there would be a chance that I could go back to school and become a teacher like Pearl.

We passed the Grist Mill and just to the other side of it lay a lovely lake, calm and still with a crust of ice near the shoreline where we pulled up the horse and buggy.

"Silver Lake," Charles announced grandly, "well named, don't you think?"

"Yes, I do," I said, looking out over the small crystal clear water surrounded by homes on the far shore. The afternoon sun shone on the icy surface giving a silver sheen to it.

"Shall we talk here?" he asked.

I nodded, still reluctant to begin the discussion myself. As usual, I didn't have to wait long for him to begin.

"You said you have some concerns about us. Where would you like to start?" he said, still giving me the chance to go first.

I looked out over the lake, and tried to form some kind of question to begin. I came up with nothing.

After an interminable silence, Charles turned to me and said, "Well, then, how about I say something to get us going?"

Relieved, I sat forward expectantly and waited.

"Sadie, you know how I feel about you – think I've made that pretty clear. So here is what I can tell you over and above that fact. What I offer you, besides my love and devotion to you, is this: you know what the doctor has told me about my prospects health–wise. I'm planning to do exactly what he says to do as far as taking care of myself and prove him wrong. I am far too honery to die young."

I laughed, once again put at ease by his humor and self–awareness. He paused a moment, giving me a chance to respond. I looked silently out over this lake that my dear friend Pearl had had the audacity to name. She also had fully expected everyone else to call it that – and they did. The mill at the far end was a large wooden building with a huge water wheel that circulated the cold water, providing power to grind the corn or grain inside. Pieces of ice were being carried and spilled over the top with a slight crunching sound, breaking the silence. A few ducks flew over, quacking in frustration, as they looked for an iceless spot to land. When Charles became uncomfortable with the silence, another trait of his, he began again.

"Children, if we're lucky enough to have them, I want as many as you would be willing to have and take care of. I'm gone a lot, so it would most likely fall on you to do most of that." At least he was being honest, but my thoughts immediately went to my mother and Lizzie, who had each had seven children to rear. Was this something, if it came to pass, that I wanted?

He continued his overture, "Pearl will be getting married soon and moving out and my mother will stay. I know this can be a problem for some wives, but knowing both of you, I don't think it would be. If it is we'll talk about it. In fact, I think she would be a great help with the house and chores and would lighten your load."

Several generations living in one home was something I was used to so this didn't bother me at all. I certainly felt after just meeting Mother Katie that I wouldn't have any problem living with her there.

"I don't have much of an income right now and the farm is barely making it, but I am a man of imagination, big ideas, and pure stubborn determination. I want a full partner who will be by my side to encourage my dreams for success – to be my help–mate."

Suddenly, my red flag of independence waved nervously in response to his last sentence. Was I to be just an addendum to his success? I almost said as much as he continued quickly, probably seeing the alarm on my face.

"As for your dreams about college and the like, on Sunny Slope you are that much closer to Bridgewater College and, if you want to go back again, I would fully support that. We may be poor for a while, I feel sure, but that won't last long, I promise you.

Having little was something I had grown up with in the Zigler household and certainly this would not be a problem for me. We had always managed to sustain ourselves as well as many others along the way.

"I have already asked permission of your father to offer a proposal of marriage and I guess this must be it. So now, do you have anything else bothering you?"

I waited until he caught his breath and I my wits and said quietly, "Not for the moment."

Charles flicked the reins and Gueriere made a circle and began to pull onto the road home. Neither of us spoke and that was comfortable, it seemed, for both of us.

After we returned to Sunny Slope, the remainder of the day was spent in relaxed conversations, walks around the farm and much laughter. I felt good about our Silver Lake conversation, though it had been mostly one – way on his part. What he had said, however, gave me a clearer picture of what this new life with him might look like and I had to admit, enough on which to base a decision on my part.

Pearl and Mother Kate teased Charles and me as if we were teenagers in love, which to my amazement didn't bother me. I appreciated the sharp wit and outright fun of this family, much lighter of mood than my own.

Pearl and I, as we had at my house almost a year ago, stayed up late into the night in one of the upstairs bedrooms, talking girl talk. She told me about the man she was about to marry the coming June.

"His name is Arthur Wendell Showalter and he's tall, dark and handsome," she giggled. "Since I'm short, fair and cute, we make a perfect couple. He's well educated and is already involved in the workings of York County where we'll be moving after we get married. I plan to be the first woman to vote up there."

"Oh, Pearl, I was hoping you'd be close around so we would be able to visit more. What am I going to do without you?" I said, already feeling a real loss at the prospect of her moving so far away.

"We can write, Sadie, just like we always have," she said as she yawned and patted me on the back. I do so enjoy your letters. She paused a moment then said quickly as if she knew she shouldn't ask. "And whatever you decide about Charles, I hope that we will always remain friends. By the way, what...?"

"PEARL!" I said in mocked horror.

"Sorry, I'm just about to bust to know…"

"When I know, you'll be the first – well, maybe second."

"He's a good man Sadie, not perfect for sure, but a real good man, yet."

"I know that," I said, smiling in the dark at her familiar Pennsylvania Dutch "yet." I rolled over and immediately and surprisingly, fell into a deep sleep.

CHAPTER EIGHT

New Year's Day, 1911

We pulled up to the little white frame building that was Garbers Church. Above the door was a sign that indicated it had been built in 1822, sixty years before I was born.

We were early for the 11 o'clock service, a trait that we of Swiss/German descent have in common. Sunday school was still in session so we waited along with all the other early-arriving Swiss/German Brethren in their wagons and buggies. The doors to the Sunday school building opened and out ran the children in their Sunday clothes.

"See that weather-boarding up there?" Charles began yet another one of his family stories of which he seemed to have an unending supply. "There used to be a bumble bees nest under that board there and after Sunday school us boys would stir those bees up just to see the girls scream and run. That practice stopped rather suddenly when some of the parents found out about it and the boys got a little stinging that didn't come from the bees. Father just said to me, 'don't do that anymore' and that was always enough for me to stay out of trouble."

Pearl rolled her eyes at me as if to say, "He never stops does he?" and we all laughed and proceeded into the church.

The small sanctuary was like most Brethren Churches built in that era, very plain, no adornments of any kind. Compared to our church in Broadway, it was tiny. The two rows of pine pews on either side were hinged in the seam between the back and seat so as to convert them to tables for the annual Love Feast.

We were greeted by everyone with smiles and hearty handshakes. Of course, everyone knew everyone else. I knew some of the folks from meetings and sings around the area and several people mentioned the Weaver's Church sing the year before and were very complimentary of my song leading efforts.

After the opening prayers, the song leader got up and we began the service with "There's a Wideness in God's Mercy." The four part harmonies rang through the little church while Charles' booming base counterpointed my high soprano. Here, in this ancient church, the men and women weren't separated by gender, a fact that did not escape me.

The service was a regular Brethren one with scripture, long prayers and an equally long sermon, however, on this New Year's Day Sunday, the sermon was uplifting and enjoyable. We rode home in the wagon afterward lustily singing the final hymn on the tune from Beethoven's Ninth Symphony as if we were celebrating the occasion of this fresh New Year.

Sunday dinner back at the home place was, once again, a full meal. The aroma of the turkey already roasting had greeted us when we woke that morning before church. Mother Katie and Pearl had prepared the traditional Pennsylvania Dutch side dishes of dressing, gravy, mashed potatoes, sauerkraut with pork sausage, green beans with cured side meat, cranberry relish, rolls and butter. There were several fruit pies and a coconut cake with boiled custard for dessert.

"Since you missed our Thanksgiving and Christmas Dinner, I thought I'd do it all over again. You can never have too much turkey," she said, looking at Charles with a grin. Obviously, she was also in on his Grand Idea.

"This coconut cake is wonderful – so moist, and the coconut is sweet and tender," I said cleaning my plate and licking the frosting off my finger.

"You must know that preparing the coconut is not a sport for the faint–hearted," said Pearl, gathering up the plates, "Grating the chunks of coconut on the grater can be rough on the fingers – you didn't find a piece of flesh in yours did you?"

"Pearl," scolded Mother Kate with fake disapproval, "Don't ruin a perfectly good meal with your nauseating... you didn't did you, Sadie?"

And with a final group laugh, we left the table to do the dishes and Charles went out to harness up Guerier for the trip to the train station in Harrisonburg.

My train was to leave at three and it was almost one so I went upstairs to get my things together.

As we drove away from the house, I looked back to where I had spent two of the nicest days in present memory. The slope behind the house was still sunny in mid–day, but with a different hue to it. The house itself, with Mother Katie and Pearl waving from the high front porch, exuded warmth and welcome that I had felt so keenly while there. Other than my own home and family, I had never felt quite so at ease and comfortable. As we breeched the top of the hill and looked toward the Blue Ridge Mountains and Massenutten Peak, I knew what my decision would be and I was at peace.

As Charles helped me up to the train, he looked at me with the unspoken question hanging in the air, to which I said,

"Yes, Charles, the answer is yes."

* * * *

If I look back on my decision to marry Charles, I take great pleasure in knowing it was an uncluttered decision on my part, with no pressure from anyone or any life circumstances that gave me little choice. I knew after that New Year's visit that my life with Charles on Sunny Slope Farm would a good one, whatever that future might bring.

On a crisp, sunny February day, Charles Weldon Wampler and I were married in the living room of the Zigler home in Broadway. It was not a fancy affair, but it was joyous by all accounts. Our guests filled the large room that had once been a church for so many in the past – the setting seemed perfectly appropriate. Everyone in my immediate family attended, including all of my older brothers and sister, their spouses and children and, of course, "My Robert," so grown up and serious–faced. I knew he was thinking about the farm and Papa's dilemma about selling it, as well as his own part in this decision. Papa and Mother Katie were beaming as were Charles' sisters, Mary and Pearl. Of course, Liz Canody, Alice Madden, Sam and their families were there. We even convinced them to come into the house for the occasion.

Before the ceremony I stood with my sister looking into that same old mirror where Mama had declared me beautiful at sixteen years of age. Lizzie had helped me dress in Mama's simple white wedding dress, yellowed with age, as we both sighed, knowing how happy she would have been on this day. I was to be a bride in less than an hour, something I had never thought I would be. The reflection of the woman in the mirror didn't show that she was nervous or that she was pondering this momentous step she was taking. I was not experienced in the ways of love or how one decided that she was "in love" or not. What I felt for Charles, I was positive, was a love of some description. The thought of being his wife and bearing his children felt absolutely right. So, were the nervous feelings I was having typical of any bride on her wedding day, or in the back of my mind, did I wonder if I had somehow settled for a life that would be a fine and good one but one that did not include the dreams I had had for myself for so many years? I was twenty–eight–years old, Robert would be going to college and the home where I had spent a lifetime was being sold at auction.

Only time would tell.

As I walked down the stairs, I saw Charles, standing in front of the fireplace next to the preacher, dressed in a brand new dark navy tailored suit, vest and a bright blue tie. Had I never noticed? This man was handsome and his gaze made me feel truly beautiful.

The service was conducted by D.H. Zigler a cousin of ours. It was short and consisted only of our reciting the traditional wedding vows. We looked into each other's eyes. Charles was very serious as he vowed to "love, honor, and obey," though he did smile a little on the "obey" reference. I wanted to be present in the moment but the moment was so full of emotions and memories that the ceremony was over before I knew it. It ended as we each stated the traditional, 'Til death do us part."

Little did we know when we spoke those words that time would come far too soon.

PART THREE

SUNNY SLOPE FARM TO MORVEN PARK

And the strange thing about it was this, that she
was glad. She could not feel one twinge of regret…It was
significant that she did not ask God to forgive her lie."

The Re-Creation of Brian Kent
Harold Bell Wright
1919

CHAPTER ONE
July, 1911

I have no doubt that most young people of Charles and my generation and religious persuasion entered into the bonds of matrimony in the same profound state of ignorance of the intimacies of that institution. As farm folk we are well aware of the circle of life and how that works, but as to how that translated to humans and their relationships, well, we just didn't talk about it.

I don't know whether Mama had a conversation with Lizzie before her first marriage – I rather doubt it. All Lizzie would say to me was, "It's going to be wonderful, Sadie," which wasn't a bit of help. Charles, for his part, having no living father and only his sisters and mother at home, certainly received no council on the matter.

That said, Charles and I fortunately came into our marriage with a deep and trusting friendship which had been developed over more than a year's time. This bond served to ease the awkwardness of our inexperience. Charles was gentle and patient with me and I with him as we learned together how to translate our affection for each other into a loving physical relationship.

Evidence of our successful union showed itself a mere two months after we were married. In April I knew I was pregnant.

"I thought the doctor said you might not be able to have children because of your health," I had said after I announced the news to a delighted Charles when I was positive it was true.

"He didn't say I 'couldn't,' he suggested I probably 'shouldn't' – big difference. And you know me, I've behaved myself when it comes to my ulcers – I never eat what anybody would consider a decent meal and it's paid off. I don't have any trouble when I eat like I'm supposed to." He was right, of course, as he had been about most everything he proposed in his Silver Lake overture that New Year's Day.

"Still having morning sickness, I see," said Mother Katie on a brisk August morning. She smiled a knowing smile as I threw up in the waste basket in the kitchen. She handed me some saltine crackers. "You should be over this pretty soon – you're almost five months along now."

"I certainly hope so," I said, cautiously eating the only thing I could keep down in the morning hours. "How can one little baby make a grown–up so sick?"

Except for the morning sickness, I was excited about the coming baby. When I had accepted Charles proposal and settled down on Sunny Slope Farm, I soon realized that I was ready to let go of the dreams of going back to school and becoming a teacher. I was a little surprised at myself and relieved that I seemed to have no regrets whatsoever about my new life. I was content.

"How about I go out and check the turkeys for you? You go get a little rest until you feel better." said Mother Katie, handing me a cup of chamomile tea, just as Mama would have done.

Charles had been right as well about his mother and me getting along. She and I shared chores inside the house and out on the farm, but there was never any question that she considered me the woman of the home now. She was so like Pearl in her wit and outlook on life and we got along famously. Life here on Sunny Slope Farm was much like at home in Broadway where, though we had little money, we ate well on the various farm animals, the vegetable garden and the orchards behind the house.

"By the way," I said, suddenly remembering, "My brother Robert is coming by for supper tonight – says he has something important to tell me."

"Wonderful, I like that young man so much. He has a good head on his shoulder and a good heart as well," she said already moving around in the kitchen to plan the meal. "What's his favorite food?"

"He's a twenty–year–old boy, he'll eat anything – I think he's missing my cooking since I moved out. How about we get out some of that pork tenderloin and we'll fry that up with…" I stopped and headed toward the waste basket to vomit again.

Robert walked in that evening with a most solemn expression on his handsome young face.

"What in the world is wrong, Robert?" I said, immediately falling into my mother role with him.

"Can we go for a walk outside – I have a few things to tell you – some of it is good and some, a little sad," he said, taking my hand and leading me through the kitchen and out the door onto the back porch.

The Wampler house had been built directly at the base of the hill/pasture behind and had no back yard whatsoever. A three foot tall wall made of large blocks of hued limestone stood there, and, growing in beds at the top where dirt had been brought in, were a variety of teas and herbs I had brought from Broadway, a living reminder of my mother.

"That looks familiar," said Robert, running his hand gently over the tops of the plants.

"I wish she were here so she could brew me up something for this nausea of mine. She'd fix me up in a minute," I said, knowing what he was thinking.

We were silent for a moment, savoring our memories as we walked around the house then down through the front yard. Across the front was a wire fence and metal gate that stood behind and on top of another limestone wall with a hitching post and steps built into it. Robert opened the gate and we walked up toward the old barn. I waited for Robert to begin.

"I've been accepted at Bridegwater College for the fall term," he announced with less than great enthusiasm.

"Why Robert, that's wonderful. I'm thrilled with the news but…why so sad?"

"Because Papa will have to sell the house and the property," he said, hanging his head. "I feel so guilty, but I know that this is what God means me to do. Do you understand, Sadie?"

"Of course I understand, and I'm so happy you've made, what I know, is a very difficult decision," I said, putting my arm around his slumping shoulders. "How is Papa taking it?"

"Pretty well I think, but I know how disappointed he is. He's planning to hold an auction in the fall and then he'll go live with Lizzie and Charles or Edgar. He's still doing a lot of traveling, you know."

"What finally made you decide?" I asked, feeling a mixture of emotions. On the one hand, there was excitement for this boy I had reared myself, taught to read, and encouraged every step of the way about the importance of education; on the other, sadness at the vison of our home passing to another owner and knowing how Papa must feel.

"John Flory is the main reason," he said, breaking into my thoughts. "You know how he is about education in general and college in particular. He's president now so he'll be there which is wonderful for me," he said, finally allowing himself some excitement. His eyes began to shine as he told me how this had come about. "My final decision was made when he came up one day last spring. I was out in the field with the horse, plowing up the ground for the early corn planting, and up he walks in his fancy suit and says, 'Robert, you are an intelligent and gifted young man, and I believe you have what it takes to get a college education—I guess I must have believed him.'"

And there he was again, John Samuel Flory, making a difference in another Zigler's life. First Lizzie, then me and now, because of his guidance, my cherished brother would be able to follow his dreams as I had always hoped he would.

I had finally learned the family connection between John and the Wamplers. Pearl had told me that her and Charles' father, John Wampler, was a younger brother to John Flory's mother, Susanah Wampler. She had married Daniel Flory and John was one of their children. Pearl said that since he was almost twenty years older than either of them they weren't particularly close as first cousins. Though Charles respected his cousin's accomplishments in educa-tion, they tended to disagree on matters of the church, es-pecially John's adamant opposition to war. Charles and John had butted heads on occasion, both being of the same stub-born and passionate nature, and were not in contact with each other very much.

I was so happy for Robert that I only felt a tiny sting of what might have been envy. The constant reminder that because he was born a man, his choice, though difficult, was a clearer one than mine had been on so many occasions.

I patted my slightly bulging stomach, "If you're a girl, I promise, things are going to be different for you."

CHAPTER TWO
November, 1912

"That is the worst idea I ever heard," said Mother Katie when Charles presented his newest plan to her. "Katherine is barely a year old and who in the world will run this farm while you go gallivanting off to Leesville, wherever in the world that is?"

Charles and I had already talked about his offer of a new job at Morven Park in Northern Virginia and agreed it had great possibilities. At first, I was not too keen on the idea. I had settled into life at Sunny Slope as well as being a wife and mother and I loved it. To adjust to another move so soon was not something I particularly wanted to do.

Katherine Wampler had been born on December 19, 1911 at home on Sunny Slope Farm, as had her father before her. When that little blond–headed, blue–eyed baby was placed in my arms, there were no regrets whatsoever. I had chosen wisely and my life was good.

"Charles, are you sure about this? How is this any better than what you are doing here now?" I had asked, as I carried little Katherine to her crib in our room and laid her down. "I know it pays more money, but that isn't all there is to consider."

"This is real opportunity for me," explained Charles, taking his debate stance, "I will be managing Morven Park up in Louden County for a man named Westmoreland Davis. He's president of the Virginia State Farmer's Institute and supposed to be an outstanding farmer. Been losing money, he says, because he's away a lot and hasn't had a good manager. We'll have a real nice house on the property with electricity, an inside bath and I'll be making a decent salary. It's the opportunity of a lifetime."

After a little more discussion, I realized that he had already made up his mind so I decided to do some research on this place in Leesville and what we might find there. I went to the public library in Harrisonburg and found quite a bit of information about both the Davis' history and the history of the farm itself.

What I learned was that this particular farm was actually a huge estate that dated back to 1780 when it had been a plantation. For over one hundred years the estate had been home to the Swann family and they had enslaved at least sixty Negroes until the Civil War broke out. This really bothered me at first. But, I rationalized, that was a long time ago and surely the situation must have changed considerably since Mr. Davis and his wife Marguerite had purchased it in 1903. The more I thought about it, the more the move began to sound like a wonderful adventure. My one lingering regret in leaving would be Mother Katie and the close bond we had forged.

"What about Sunny Slope?" Mother Katie asked, with an unaccustomed touch of fear in her voice. "I sure can't do it all."

"Wouldn't expect you to," began Charles, stating his case, "We've already got good help in Albert and I've got time before we leave to train another man to do what Sadie and I have been doing with the turkey experiments. Charles had hired Albert Thacker to help him with his new work with the turkeys, as well as assist with other chores on the farm. He and his wife Lessie would move in with Mother Kate at the home place as soon as we left.

"Well, Sadie, what do you think of this bright idea?" said Mother Katie, hoping for a womanly agreement from me.

"I actually think it's a good plan, Mother Katie," I said trying not to sound too excited. "I haven't traveled out of this Valley my whole lifetime and living close to Washington, D.C. would be an adventure and it's a real opportunity for Charles to use his managerial skills. If it doesn't work out, we can pack up and come home."

Mother Katie knew she was out–numbered and re-signed herself to the fact that the remaining members of her family would be moving away from Sunny Slope Farm.

We began our planning for the move to Morven Park for an arrival in January of 1913.

That year would be a momentous one for our little family.

* * * *

Nothing in my background, including the expansive array of reading I had done, prepared me for the scene we beheld on that cold winter day. Even Charles' descriptions of his previous visit to Morven Park fell far short of the magnificence of the place.

A fine horse hitched to a fancy carriage had picked us up at the train station in the town of Leesburg. Katherine, all bundled up against the cold, was sitting on my lap. She had gotten fussy after the long train ride from Harrisonburg but as soon as she saw the horse she brightened up. One of her favorite things at home was riding in the wagon with her Daddy.

After leaving the community of Leesburg itself, we wound around roads surrounded by wide open fields as far as the eye could see.

"This be it," said James, the carriage driver, who had introduced himself as Charles' personal "coachman" for his tenure on Morven Park.

We turned into a lane through black wrought iron gates attached to two large stone pillars on either side. The rolling pastures on each side of the lane seemed to go on forever. To the left was a large iced–over pond which enhanced the beauty of the landscape, and suddenly, we saw it.

"That be Mistah Davis house – can you see it?" said James as he flicked the reins, urging on the magnificent black stallion.

"As if we could miss it!" laughed Charles, who was beginning to show signs of acting like a child at Christmas. His blue eyes sparkled with anticipation and I was happy for him and for what this might mean for our family.

"It looks like a Greek palace," I said, looking at the gigantic white pillared building in front of us. What we were seeing today was a culmination of many years of additions by the various owners.

As we drew closer we saw a stone structure, a bit over-grown, in the field in front of the house and to our right.

"What is that?" I asked, wanting to know everything about this place that would soon be our home.

"That be some kinda fountain thing – it were here when the Mistah and Missus bought this place from the Swans. It don't work no more."

Just before we went through another set of pillared gates, there was a large old building to our left made of stuc-co. It had also been adapted over the years and had several wings.

"Slaves," said James softly and I felt something in my soul weep. Even if I already knew about this place and its history, this physical reminder still there was unsettling.

The carriage followed the lane directly in front of a porch where two larger–than–life–size stone lions stood guard on either side of a set of steps leading up to the main entrance.

"So where exactly are we going now?" asked Charles, his head turning in every direction to take it all in.

"To the manager house right up here a space," answered James, pointing about five hundred feet ahead where there were yet two more stone pillars, this time with a white wooden picket gate matching the picket fence leading up to the entrance.

As we pulled through the gate we saw, straight ahead, two beautiful white wooden buildings with a breezeway in between. Above two large swinging wooden doors was a working clock, mounted in a beautiful casing topped by a roof–like structure. On either side of the clock across the top of the breezeway was an ornate railing.

"Is that our house?" I asked, more and more overcome by the elegance of everything we saw.

James chuckled, "No, Ma'am, that the stables – over there your place."

We looked to where James pointed on our right. The two–storied, shuttered house was built of light brown stucco. Though somewhat smaller than our house on Sunny Slope, it looked spacious for an employee's home on this grand estate. I think I had prepared myself for much less.

I stood up with Katherine and James helped me down from the carriage. I waited as the men picked up some of our belongings and then we walked to the little front porch.

Just inside the door was a large room that spanned the entire length and breadth of the house and was completely furnished. In the very middle of the room was a wood stove for heating and cooking attached to a brick chimney that rose to the ceiling. It was organized very like our home in Broadway and at first glance, I began to feel more relaxed. There was no separate kitchen but the room was furnished at one end as a living area, the other, an eating and food preparation area. As promised, there was a bathroom with indoor plumbing. "I could be at home here for a while," I thought with a smile.

Katherine was wiggling in my arms so I set her down on the shiny wooden floor – she started pulling up on everything in sight, happy to be free at last.

"Let's go upstairs and see the bedrooms," said Charles, pleased at seeing my smile and anxious to show me everything there was to see.

I picked Katherine up again and we went up the narrow staircase to two small bedrooms. In every room there were windows looking out on the beautiful views of pasture land and out of one, I could see the mansion. The winter sun streamed through the windows giving a friendly glow to the rooms. The furnishings were not elaborate but certainly very comfortable, and I began to imagine us living here happily.

As we came back down the stairs, James flipped a switch. The light from a milk glass, globed lamp, hanging from a long chain, shone brightly. Katherine, who had never seen an electric light burning in a home, pointed and said one of her very few words, "STAR!"

CHAPTER THREE
February, 1913

L ife at Morven Park was a fairly leisurely one for me compared to all the years in Broadway with family duties and the constant entertaining of guests. Then, on Sunny Slope, I took up farm chores in addition to managing a household and taking care of Katherine. Here, after I had unpacked our things, I had little to do. Charles had a staff of workers in his service so he didn't need me other than doing a little secretarial work. The Davis' had offered someone to help me clean house and cook but I graciously declined. I wanted to do these things myself if only to keep busy and feel useful.

"Thank you James," said Charles after his morning rounds, as he dismounted from the magnificent black horse out in the courtyard of the stables. The coachman took the reins from Charles and waited for further instruction. I watched from the little front porch of our house with Katherine playing at my feet as Charles came through the swinging gate to the house. Never had I expected to live in such luxurious surroundings. Certainly, Charles had not predicted this in his original "Silver Lake proposal." The beautiful horse provided for him reminded us of Gueriar who had died just recently. James groomed, saddled and brought him to our gate at Charles' beck and call.

"You needs 'im later, sir?" James called from where he still stood outside the gate with the horse. His request was asked formally as he ducked his head. His demeanor reflected his status as a worker on this farm, somehow different from the Maddens and other Negroes on our place in Broadway. Certainly they had kept some distance, but there was something about James' approach to Charles that was wary and almost fearful.

"I have a meeting with Mr. Davis in a few minutes. I'll let you know what he wants me to do after that. Thank you James" answered Charles with a pleasant smile that pleased me. At least he was trying to be respectful.

Just then Mr. Davis appeared at the gate. He was on foot and had walked down from his office in the mansion. "Good morning, Charles, I hope I haven't interrupted your work too much but I needed to talk to you about some things," he said, glancing at James who was walking the horse to the stable.

"No sir," replied Charles, "I'm at a good place to take a little break anyway. Mr. Davis, I'd like you to meet my wife, Sadie Zigler Wampler and my daughter, Katherine."

Mr. Westmoreland Davis was a tall, solidly-built man with dark hair and a neatly trimmed moustache. He was dressed to the nines at this early hour of eight A.M. in a black pin-striped, tailor-made three piece suit, starched white collared shirt and tie. Topping off his morning attire was a black fedora pulled down over his eyes. He walked with the air of an aristocrat who was confident in his lofty position as Lord of the Manor. I thought to myself, "Even his first name, Westmoreland , suggests he is in a class above everyone else."

I extended my hand, and he shook it with a limp grip which didn't impress me at all. Papa had always said, "The first impression you make is with your handshake – it needs to be a firm one." I had no doubt that Charles would have observed this little flaw in his character already.

"Very nice to meet you, Sadie," he said with a marked Southern Drawl, "Welcome to Morven Park. I hope that your accommodations are adequate. Hello there little Katherine," he said patting her on the head like a puppy.

"Oh, yes, thank you sir, more than adequate – a bit more than we're used to on Sunny Slope. I picked up Katherine and walked through the door into the house – Charles and Mr. Davis followed.

"Would you like some tea or coffee, Mr. Davis?" I offered, feeling somehow ill at ease with this man. There was something about him that I didn't particularly like. Perhaps I just wasn't used to a Southern aristocrat.

"No thank you, Sadie," he said, dismissively, and I immediately knew why I felt the way I did. He had called me by my first name and had not corrected my addressing him as Mr. Davis, putting me in my place. For the first time in my life I knew how the Negroes and Gypsies must feel when being diminished in someone else's eyes. I did not like the feeling.

"Excuse us please, I need to take Katherine upstairs and do some housework," I said, walking up the stairs, leaving the two men to talk. I put her in her crib, closed her door and assumed my eavesdropping position on the landing.

"Now Charles," Mr. Davis began, "I've been getting some reports about your managing style that you're just going to have to change. These people who work here are of a class below your own and we need to make sure they know their place. Sounds like you are getting way too friendly with them. To keep them under control you must call them by their last name only and insist that they call you 'Mr. Wampler.' You are to hire them as cheaply as possible because the chances are they are going to be worth even less than that."

So there it was. I was beginning to understand James' attitude with Charles. It came directly from Mr. Davis himself. It was clear that he had carried his prejudices from the Deep South with him, even though he had lived in New York for some time before he bought Morven Park. Both he and his wife came from prestige and very old money made before the Civil War on the backs of the enslaved. Mr. Davis' fortune had come from cotton and Mrs. Davis' from shipping lines and hotels in New York.

I could imagine what was going through Charles' head as all this was being said or at least I hoped it was the same reaction as mine. Even with some slight prejudices, his style of management was based on mutual respect for the people he hired and he believed that kind of treatment encouraged better work rather than worse. Charles didn't argue, of course, and after more instructions, Mr. Davis left.

I came downstairs, "Well, that was interesting," I said, waiting for him to give me some idea of what his reaction had been.

"You heard? What a little eavesdropper you are, my Sadie," he said with a smile and kissed me on the cheek.

"I confess, I've had years and years of practice," I said, relieved that it didn't seem to bother him. "A rather pompous man seems to me."

"Well, I think I'll try it my way and see how it goes," he stated with confidence, "Maybe if the farm starts making money, he'll come over to my way of thinking."

I knew well that men like Westmorland Davis rarely come over to anyone's way of thinking.

CHAPTER FOUR
February, 1913

"Sadie, I really appreciate all your help with my office work, but I think maybe I need a full–time secretary," said Charles, as he sat at his desk brimming over with a large pile of correspondence and bills. "This has turned out to be more paper work than I expected. I've asked sister Pearl to come and Mr. Davis has agreed to hire Arthur as a carpenter on the farm while they are here. That suit you alright?"

"Suit me, of course it suits me!" I said, delighted with the suggestion. "You know how I love Pearl and I've gotten a little lonesome here with no family except for Katherine. When will they come?"

"Next week, I think. They have some things to wind up at home in York County first," sounding relieved that I wasn't put out by him replacing me.

In the time we had been at Morven Park I had come to realize that for the first time in my life, I had free time on my hands. Other than the secretarial work I did for Charles and taking care of Katherine and the house, I was simply not

267

very busy. I had not read much at all since becoming a wife and mother and I sorely missed the mental stimulation. I hadn't however, brought any reading material. I knew exactly what to do.

February 5, 1913

Dear Pearl,

I am so excited I can hardly stand it that you and Arthur will be coming to Morven Park soon. You will not believe how beautiful it is here and I'm feeling like a lady of leisure recently. A nice change in some ways, but I find that I am becoming a bit bored for the first time in my life.

Little Katherine is so good and does not require that much time. Here I am, in the middle of winter, stuck in the house while Charles wanders the acres and acres of this estate doing his managing duties. You should see him sitting that horse they provide him — looks like a proper country gentleman yet.

I have a request; when you come, could you bring me some of your old books? Anything is fine, novels, poetry classics, whatever you think I might not have read or would enjoy.

I can't wait to see you and Arthur. Plan to come to supper as soon as you get settled so we can catch up. You haven't even seen Katherine yet. She is sweet most of the time but has a little temper when she doesn't get her way. I have to watch her now with the stairs as she is crawling all over the place. Oops, there she goes!!

See you soon, Sadie

* * * *

Pearl and Arthur arrived soon after I wrote her the letter and when they came over for supper she pointed to a huge box that Arthur carried and dropped with a bang on the floor.

"There you go — ask and ye shall receive," she said with a broad smile and a twinkle in her eye. My, how I had missed that.

"Pearl, you are an angel, thank you — and Arthur, thank you for being the beast of burden," I said, anxious to tear into the box immediately.

"She wanted to bring the whole library but I refused to have any part of that," he joked. We had been at Pearl and Arthur's wedding in June after our own in February and I had immediately taken a liking to my soul friend and sister's new husband. I hadn't seen either of them since they moved to York County but we had corresponded regularly.

I embraced Pearl and when I pulled back and looked into her eyes I realized I was very teary. Not having family around had affected me more than I thought.

"Oh, my," said Pearl, seeing my emotion, "has it been that bad?"

"It's just that here on this place, because of the way the Davis' look at things, we feel like we are isolated between two classes of people, whether we think that way or not."

"What do you mean?" asked Pearl, looking puzzled as she looked around the room.

"Mr. Davis' family lost all of their fortune after the Civil War but he became a successful lawyer in New York and soon was well off again. Both of them were involved in high society in New York City and have continued that here in Leesburg. So they think, or at least Mr. Davis thinks, that they are above everyone else that works on the farm including us. He also thinks we should think ourselves better than those Charles hires to work here. That leaves us with little social life. We don't have a church here either so it's gotten pretty lonesome for me."

"I guess that definition puts me in the latter category—will you be able to associate with the likes of the Showalters you think?" asked Pearl pulling out that wonderful wit that I so loved in her.

"Your dag–gone right," said Charles, joining in the family banter. "Nobody don't have no more class than you do sister Pearl."

I had fixed a big supper for us to celebrate our reunion with as many Pennsylvania Dutch dishes as I could find ingredients for. The room was cozy with a fire in the stove and I found it familiar and comforting to be entertaining once again. Katherine had been put to bed early which Pearl was not happy about.

"She needs to meet her wonderful Auntie Pearl – can't you go wake her up?" she said, pleading with me.

"You can meet her in the morning—she gets up early and I'll give her right over to you and I'll go back to bed," I teased, almost feeling giddy with happiness.

We put the food on the table and sat down. After Charles returned thanks, Arthur immediately began to question him about the farm.

"How do you like working here so far?" asked Arthur.

"I'm having some reservations but I am going to stick it out," Charles began cautiously—he didn't want to say too much since Arthur was just starting, but he couldn't help himself. "Mr. Davis is quite a character. He and I don't see eye to eye about how to treat workers and another thing, he's a rather spiteful man."

"How so?" asked Pearl, spooning some creamed lima beans onto her plate.

"Well, I was all excited about his involvement with the Percheron horse business. He had gotten a lot of beautiful mares imported from France and you know how I love a good horse. The worst shock I got was when I discovered that he got disgusted with the American Percheron Association because they elected as president a neighbor he didn't like. So he bred all the fine mares to a jack and wrote a letter saying he expected them to register his mules!"

"What a Jackass!" quipped Pearl, laughing at her own joke as we joined her.

After we washed the dishes, Pearl went to the box of books and pried it open. She pulled out a brightly wrapped package, "Happy late birthday, Sister Sadie," she said, as she ceremoniously handed it to me.

I opened what was obviously a book. Inside the package was a large volume entitled *Mother, Home & Heaven*. The beautifully bound book was an olive green with an etching of a small cottage set under a tree. In the tree, etched in gold, was a mother bird feeding her babies. A human mother and child stood in front of a structure of some kind watched over by an angel carrying a sheaf of wheat.

"I have one of these that belonged to my Grandmother Miller and I thought you might enjoy it as a new mother. It's mostly poetry, which I know you love – Enjoy!"

"Oh, Pearl," was all I could manage without breaking down, "Thank you, my sister."

This precious book would be inspiration, guidance, solace and comfort for me in the coming years and would be the beacon to another generation who would want to know my story.

S. J. W.

CHAPTER FIVE
March, 1913

"*T*o: Mrs. Sadie Wampler,*" read the elegant script on the envelope that arrived at my door that Wednesday morning, delivered by a maidservant from the Davis' mansion.

I opened the note with more than a little curiosity. Had I done something wrong or offended the sensibilities of our hosts at Morven Park?

Dear Mrs. Wampler,

My husband has suggested to me after talking with your husband several times, that I might want to meet with you.

I would like you to come to the mansion on Friday about 10 A.M. I understand that you have a young child who would need watching. If you can find no one to do this, I would be happy to send one of my maidservants to you.

Please let me know whether you can meet with me.

Sincerely, Marguerite Inman Davis

I noted immediately that she had addressed me as "Mrs. Wampler." Perhaps she wasn't as pompous as her husband.

"Now what in the world could Mr. Davis have said to her about me that would prompt this?" I said to Pearl who had come over to do some work for Charles.

"Who knows," she laughed, getting up from the desk and strutting around the room like a turkey, "Maybe your reputation precedes you!"

"Heavens, I hope not!" I said, always amazed at how Pearl could lighten a situation. "I suppose it wouldn't be too impressive to someone of her estate that I frequently went running after a turkey tom wielding an ax."

"Well, are you going?" she asked expectantly. "I can keep Katherine, and you can come back and give me all the dirty little details of the lives of the filthy rich."

"Why in the world would I not?" I said, realizing that I had already made up my mind to take Mrs. Davis up on her invitation "I'd love to see inside that house and I've never met an heiress before. The adventure continues."

"Atta girl, I knew you wouldn't let me down," she said, going into the kitchen area and taking down a cup for tea as if she were in her own home.

"Did you know," I said, for some reason lowering my voice, "That her family owns the shipping line that built the "unsinkable" Titanic that sank last year?"

"That's a fact I sure wouldn't bring up if I were you!" she said, "You want a cup?"

"No thanks, I'm too excited," I said pacing around, "What on earth should I wear?"

"I think I'd forget your Brethren prayer covering and bonnet," she laughed, motioning tying a bow under her chin.

"Perhaps I could pull out my tiara from storage," I said, parading around in a mock queenly walk.

"Try to behave yourself," she scolded in a motherly tone. "And remember your manners."

This was going to be very interesting to say the very least.

* * * *

Minus my tiara and prayer covering, I arrived at the mansion on Friday morning. I felt like a little girl meeting her first princess. Mrs. Davis had sent James over with a wagon to pick me up, though I certainly was within walking distance.

We pulled up to the white pillared mansion which dwarfed us and as I walked to the front door I began to wonder if I had made a mistake in accepting the request for my presence – or if I indeed had a choice in the matter.

I knocked at the front door and as it opened I was met, not by a maid or butler, but Mrs. Davis, herself.

"Why you must be Sadie Wampler. I am Marguerite Inman Davis. I'm happy you decided to come. Please come in – it's cold out there."

I had expected to see a stately aristocratic lady who matched up with her husband. I was pleasantly surprised to be met by a petite and slender woman with a kind smile and a friendly demeanor. She was dressed simply in a nice house dress which didn't begin to blend with the grandeur behind her.

"Yes, Mrs. Davis, I am. Thank…"

"Please call me Marguerite – I don't stand on formality—even if Morley does most of the time. Do come in," she said, leading me into the spacious entry room. She was not at all like her husband and I began to relax a little.

Never in my wildest imagination had I ever thought I would be in such a house as this. The cavernous room we entered was hung with tapestries and art—there was no empty space anywhere on the walls, nor on the floor where oriental carpets were laid, some two and three deep. There was furniture of every period and from all over the world where the Davis' had traveled and collected. I glanced to the left where the ornate table and chairs of the dining room sat under a huge crystal chandelier. Every table and mantle anywhere you looked was covered with china, porcelain, silver and other elegant decorations. I had in my vocabulary the word, "eclectic" but I had never actually seen it.

"Please come this way," said my hostess as we walked to the room on the right. In the very middle of the parlor room was a full-size Steinway piano. The room was furnished as elegantly as the entranceway and dining room. I kept trying to keep my mouth from dropping open.

"Please have a seat over here, I thought we'd have some tea," said Mrs. Davis, motioning me to a maroon velvet St. Anne chair beside a small walnut table with a marble top.

After settling into the parlor, a beautiful, exotic–looking girl with olive skin and dark eyes came in carrying a silver service with coffee and a plate of petite fours. She looked to be about fifteen. I immediately thought of Nadya.

"Thank you, Kezia, this is Mrs. Wampler."

"Hello, Kezia, such a lovely name," I said noticing quickly that she was quite far along in her pregnancy.

Kezia nodded and ducked her head.

"That will be all, thank you, Kezia," said Mrs. Davis, dismissing her with a wave of her hand. "Lovely girl and a wonderful help but as you can see, she won't be for long. Has no idea who the father is, I'm afraid."

Though used to a similar situation in Nadya, I was unused to this kind of frank conversation especially with a woman I had just met. I remained quiet, waiting for her to explain the reason for my visit.

"You may wonder why I summoned you," she began as she poured tea into our tiny porcelain teacups and handed one of them to me.

"Is that what I had been…Summoned?" I thought, "Heavens, what was this all about?"

"My husband has learned from talking with yours that you are quite a remarkable woman. Charles absolutely worships you, Morley says," she began, holding her cup with her little finger raised in the air.

I smiled, sipping my tea, waiting to see where this was going.

"He says you are well read and has noticed the many and varied books you have lying around your home. He mentioned that you like poetry and play the piano."

"Well, I play the harmonium, not…"

"As you might imagine," she continued as if she had rehearsed what she had to say and was not about to be interrupted. "I have been exposed to higher education and the arts from the beginnings of my life. I was born with a 'silver spoon' as they say, with all of the advantages that affords. But here at Morven Park, even though Morley and I have a rich social life, I find that I am missing something valuable––a woman friend with whom I can share some common interests and provide me with some companionship."

She stopped to take a breath and waited for a response that I was totally at a loss to give her. Since she was a woman who could have anything at her command, did she really expect me to become her "pet" friend to ease her loneliness?

As if reading my mind, she said, with a lovely and genuine smile, "I'm sorry, Sadie, may I call you Sadie, what must you think of me? 'The rich lonely lady begging for attention.' I assure you that is not my intention. I don't know you at all and you don't know me. What I would wish is that we might get to know each other and see what happens. You may decide I'm just a pathetic snob and don't want to have anything to do with me."

I finally found my voice, "Mrs. Davis, though I am a bit mystified at your proposition, I am also touched by your obvious sincerity. I would be pleased to have you as a friend as I, too, have found myself alone with no one but my sister–in–law with whom I have common interests."

We began sharing our love of poetry and reading novels and the classics.

"I'm forever writing favorite lines of poetry in the margins of the books I read. Do you like Longfellow?" she said, picking up a copy of poetry from a basket beside her chair.

"Oh yes, I do the same thing and Wordsworth is another one of my favorites."

"The Old Oaken Bucket…" we said in unison and both of us laughed and relaxed.

On and on we talked until the grandfather clock in the entranceway chimed noon. I had been there for two hours.

"Oh dear, I can't believe it's that late, I said, setting down my cup and getting up from my chair. "I have to go feed Katherine and Charles dinner."

"Dinner?" she said raising her dark eyebrows in a question, "Isn't that in the evening? It's not that late is it?"

"I'm sorry, I forgot, that's farm–speak for the meal in the middle of the day," I said, trying to explain what I meant. "Dinner for you is supper for us."

"Really, well isn't that quaint?" she said with just a touch of the aristocrat I had expected.

"Thank you, Mrs. Davis," I said, letting the little pithy remark go, "This has been so enjoyable."

"Marguerite, please, Marguerite, and I also enjoyed it," she said, warmly and I felt, sincerely, as we walked back into the front hall. "We must do it again soon. What if we set a regular time each week to visit? Not that we can't meet at other times too and there may be times I'll be away, especially as spring comes around. I'd like to show you the gardens, particularly the work I'm doing with the English boxwoods. Do you like gardening?"

"Oh yes, I was hoping to be able to put in some vegetables this spring if I can get some seeds and plants. There's a little patch of ground outside our house that gets good light almost all day."

"I'll arrange for you to have some seeds and starter plants as soon as it's time," she responded excitedly.

"How generous, Mrs. D...Marguerite—I'm not sure I can call you that quite yet," I said, more and more impressed with this woman who had everything, and wanted to share it with me.

"It'll come – it'll come," she smiled as she opened the door for me.

And it did. As time went on, we spent many hours together discussing everything from religion to politics to women's rights and the arts. She allowed me to borrow books from the extensive library where there were four walls of books from floor to ceiling. Like many wealthy people, books were brought in mainly to impress rather than to read. Mr. Davis had arranged the books in sections by subject. There was an entire wall devoted to poetry.

One day while I waited for Marguerite in the dining room, I caught sight of my reflection in a mirror set in a huge, ornate gold filigree frame. The mirror reflected the opulence around the room, the shiny crystal chandelier, the tapestries and portraits on the wall, the sterling silver candlesticks and coffee service. The mirror was hung so high that only my neck and head could be seen. As I looked at the woman in the mirror I realized that slowly but surely, that part of me I had left behind had begun to surface again. My mind was being challenged and respected and I reveled in it. I was no longer just a housewife and mother, which I loved, but felt like a student of the world again. One of the favorite things we did together was taking turns playing the Steinway in the parlor. It was very different from the harmonium but I soon learned to play. Since I could already read music, Marguerite would bring out her collection of printed compositions. I even learned to play the Bach Invention that Mr. Plougher had unsuccessfully tried to play years ago. I could completely understand his frustration with the harmonium's limitations in this kind of piano piece, which, on the Steinway, flew like lightning over the keys. And the light in the eyes of the woman who looked back at me was VERY, VERY bright.

Each time I went to visit Marguerite, Kezia was there, getting bigger with pregnancy every day, and I made a point of interacting with her. Though Marguerite was never disrespectful of her, she wasn't particularly warm either. Kezia seemed to be an intelligent girl and would listen attentively outside the door, just as I had growing up, if we were reading poetry or playing the piano. Occasionally I invited her to come to my house where I would help her with her reading. Somewhere along the way she had been taught to read and had an active mind and a voracious curiosity about everything. As time went on, we formed a close bond, not unlike Nadya and me.

Marguerite and I were an unlikely twosome and both our husbands were perplexed that we became such good friends. I think Pearl was a little jealous, too, but I assured her that no one would ever take her place as my dearest soul friend.

"Now don't you get to thinking you're better than the rest of us, and get all uppity–like," she said, not really joking.

"You don't have to worry about that, Pearl," I said, putting my arm around her to reassure her, "All I have to do is get 'the look' from Master Westmoreland Davis and that puts me in my place."

CHAPTER SIX

Late Night, March 26, 1913

There was a frantic knock on the door in the middle of the night. Charles was dead asleep after a long day, so I went quickly downstairs to answer the door before it wakened Katherine.

James was there, and said breathlessly, "The Missus want you to come to the big house right now. They's a baby comin'."

I knew immediately that it must be Kezia, but why would she have come to the mansion to have her baby and why would Marguerite have agreed to let her in?

"I'll get dressed and come right out. Can you wait for me, please?" I said, shivering and a little embarrassed that I had come to the door in my nightgown. It was still very cold outside on this March night.

"I gots the wagon waiten' to take you over, Ma'am," James mumbled, looking away from my state of undress.

I turned and ran quickly up the stairs, leaving James on the front porch. I put on a house dress and my coat and wrote a quick note to Charles, letting him know where I was going. I was not at all sure he would approve of my leaving in the middle of the night, especially going over to the mansion alone. It had not been lost on me that he was beginning to be bothered by my frequent visits with Marguerite. When I would come back from our visit he had started making comments like, "You sure are spending a lot of time with that woman," or "exactly what do you two do all the time? Seems like you're ignoring Pearl these days – and what about Katherine?" I tried to assure him that we were just friends who had some common interests and that I spent plenty of time with his sister and Katherine.

The lights were on in the mansion when we pulled up to the front porch. Marguerite came running out the front door to meet me in her bath robe and slippers, an unlikely attire for this lady of the manor. No doubt Kezia's appearance had taken her by surprise.

"Thank you for coming, Sadie. I figured growing up in the country you would have some knowledge of birthing a baby. Kezia and I need some help," she said as she wrung her hands nervously. I had never seen her other than completely composed. I knew where she had gotten the idea that I could deliver a baby – I had mentioned my experience with Nadya.

"Come on into the kitchen, she's in there. She showed up at the back door about fifteen minutes ago and I could see she was in labor. Why she thought I'd ever let her in, I have no idea but well, I did. All she said was, 'I need Ms. Sadie right now,' so I sent James over."

History seemed to be repeating itself. I had seen Kezia becoming more and more attached to me in the past few weeks but was still surprised that she would prefer me to her own family in childbirth.

"Thank goodness Morley's away on business," she said, lowering her voice and looking a bit guilty for sharing such a personal fact with an employee, "He'd be having a fit, but what he doesn't know...well, come along, let's get back in there." We walked through all of the elegance to an area I had never been and she, herself, probably didn't frequent often.

Just then we heard a childlike shriek.

We walked into to the kitchen where Marguerite had fashioned a bed on the floor with blankets. Kezia was lying there obviously in full labor. Her young face was twisted with pain and fear – she was sweating profusely. As Marguerite entered, Kezia quickly looked past her – the moment she saw me, her face changed completely, not only with relief, but as if she had fully expected me there.

Compared to the rest of the house, the kitchen was very plain and utilitarian. The walls were lined with white painted cabinets and the floor was black and white, checked-patterned linoleum. This was servant territory and seeing Marguerite there, even in her night clothes, was a stark contrast.

I automatically began to do what I knew was necessary.

"Marguerite, please get some clean towels – we'll need them later," I said noting the shocked expression on her face as I issued orders to her. She left the room, leaving me alone with Kezia.

I knelt down on the floor beside the girl and raised her dress. She drew back, at first embarrassed then, trusting my presence, relaxed a little. She looked at me with those large brown eyes that said, "Thank you for coming."

"Kezia, you need to put your knees up so I can see how far along you are in your labor. I know you're frightened but I've done this before and I'm going to help you bring your baby safely into the world."

I was amazed at how calm I felt and how confident I was that I could do this. Surely, part of it was my experience on the farm with Mama having Robert and Mary, as well as helping with Nadya, but something else had happened that had changed my attitude about myself in the months since coming to Morven Park. I seemed to have a new confidence that had immerged as a result of my new–found independence here.

I checked Kezia as she allowed me to feel for the baby's head. Each process of childbirth, farm animal or human, was always a miracle to me, though I had been party to many of them, including my own child. However, children having children seemed so unnatural and I already worried for this baby.

"Kezia, you're doing really well. I can see the baby's head, just a few more pushes and this will be all over and you'll have a new baby," I said, trying to calm her as the pain became more intense.

Kezia gasped and screamed as the next contraction came hard.

"Breathe, Kezia, hold my hand and breathe and push – one, two three. Good girl. That was a really good push. When the next one comes, really push hard – I think one more will do it."

It was less than a minute when the next contraction came.

"Now push, breathe, push, and breathe!" I held her hand and simulated breathing deeply in and out. She responded by following my lead and with a final scream she pushed out the wet, bloody, child who immediately began to cry lustily with her first breaths. In my hands I held a healthy baby girl.

"Marguerite," I said, "Get me some of those towels." She stood frozen in the doorway as if she wanted to escape. "Marguerite, NOW!" I think she was more undone than Kezia.

She finally moved and picked up the towels she had gathered and handed them to me. I placed the baby girl on the towels as she continued to howl in protest of leaving her safe, warm haven of the past nine months.

We hadn't had time to sterilize anything to cut the cord so I asked Marguerite to find some kitchen shears and run them under the hottest water she could from the spigot. Unaccustomed to being in this area, she frantically opened drawer after drawer until she finally found a pair. She ran the water until it was steaming and let it run it over the scissors. She handed them to me, beginning to regain her composure.

After I had cut the cord, delivered the afterbirth and made sure Kezia had stopped bleeding, I looked over at the child I had just brought into the world. I had laid her on some clean towels right beside Kezia. She was, like her mother, olive–skinned with a head of black curly ringlets. She had stopped crying and was looking around her with large brown eyes. She seemed so aware. She was absolutely beautiful.

I cleaned her off and wrapped her in the towels and handed her to Kezia.

"Here is your beautiful little girl, Kezia."

"I don't want her," she said flatly.

"Of course you do dear," said Marguerite, surprised at this response. "It's your baby."

"No, I don't and neither does anyone else in my family," she said matter–of–factly.

And then she looked directly at me and said, "Why don't you take her?" and I had the strangest sense that this had been her plan from the beginning when she came here to have the baby.

Marguerite gasped in shock – I did not. This was familiar territory for me after my experience with Nadya. In that instance, the baby had died. Had it lived and needed a home, I have no doubt that my family would have gladly taken it in.

"I don't think it's a good time to make that big of a decision," I responded, trying to get her to take baby in her arms.

"I'm too young to raise a baby and I need to get back to work and earn my keep," she said, looking at Marguerite, then, looking directly at me she said with a smile. "You would be such a good mother to her, Ms. Sadie, I just know you would."

I had been correct in what I suspected, and was at once touched and broken–hearted for her to be put in such a position.

"You'll have to nurse her for a while until she gets stronger," I said, thinking perhaps if she bonded with the baby, she might change her mind.

"Maybe you could live with the Wamplers and help out while you do that. I'm sure Mrs. Wampler would appreciate an extra hand," suggested Marguerite, trying to regain control of a situation from which she had been sorely excluded.

I suddenly realized that all of these decisions were being made without the benefit of one very special person's input.

"I need to talk to Charles about this, but I'm sure he'll agree," I said, not at all sure at that moment he would. I had already made up my mind that if this was Kezia's decision to give up her baby, I knew that I would gladly take her – it was as natural to me as delivering the child in the first place. I could surely convince Charles that this was a wonderful opportunity for our family.

This would not be as easy as I thought.

CHAPTER SEVEN
Early Morning, March 27, 1913

A s soon as I was sure Kezia and the baby were stabilized I made the decision about what to do. It was almost three A.M. and I needed to get back to the house — Charles and Katherine would be waking soon and I wanted to be there. So I said, more as a solution than a question, "Kezia, how would you and the baby like to come over to my house at least tonight and tomorrow and then we can decide what's best to do next? We need to tell your family what's going on."

Kezia looked at Marguerite for approval, which she gave with a smile and a nod of her head.

"I think that's a wonderful idea, Sadie," chirped Marguerite, visibly relieved to be rid of the lot of us. "Don't you think so, Kezia?"

Kezia, completely exhausted, merely smiled and nodded as she gingerly held her new baby in her arms like a child holding a doll. Again, I had the distinct feeling that she had this scenario in her mind all along.

I cleaned up the kitchen, leaving the blood–stained

towels in a pile for the kitchen help to attend, and went out front where James still sat in the wagon fast asleep.

"James," I called loudly from the porch steps, "We have a couple of new passengers to take back to my house. Could you please come in and help us?"

James woke with a start and climbed sleepily down from the wagon seemingly not surprised at all by my request. As we walked through the opulence of the mansion to the kitchen, he looked neither right nor left.

Kezia was now standing weakly, leaning on Marguerite's arm for support, still holding the baby. James, a large and strong man, and without any instructions whatsoever, gently scooped up the two girls and calmly walked out of the kitchen, through the house and into the dark early morning.

Marguerite, who had probably never been up all night save for an elegant social event, could only wave limply and close the door behind us.

"What in heaven's name is going on, Sadie?" said Charles as he came down the stairs, already dressed for the day, "The first thing I heard this morning was a baby's cry and it wasn't Katherine!"

Charles hadn't wakened when I came in early this morning. James and I had been as quiet as possible getting Kezia and the baby settled in Katherine's room upstairs. Thankfully, Katherine hadn't wakened either. I slipped quietly into bed with Charles and slept for about three hours until Katherine woke me at her usual time about seven AM.

"Baby, baby, baby," babbled Katherine, pointing her finger at the upstairs.

"Kezia and her new baby girl are just here temporarily, Charles," I said quickly, observing the look of disapproval on his face, "I delivered the baby last night over at the mansion and…"

"You what? You went up there in the middle of the night by yourself? Sadie, sometimes I wonder about you and when that generous nature of yours is going to get you in trouble," he fussed, combining a sideways compliment while treating me like a disobedient child. I knew he had my best interest at heart, but really, sometimes he could be so overly–protective or was it controlling? I didn't like the feeling of the latter possibility.

"James picked me up in the wagon and took me over to Marguerite's," I began, thinking this fact would calm his worries.

Instead, his eyebrows immediately rose in alarm, "You went out in the middle of the night with James? Why that's even more foolish."

I knew several things were bothering Charles that he would not readily admit. The first was that he was beginning to resent my frequent visits with Marguerite and secondly, was his hidden but growing prejudice of other races. I often worried that Mr. Davis' attitude was influencing him, but we hadn't talked about it.

"Charles, this was an emergency. I'm sorry I didn't wake you – that was probably unfair to you, but you were sleeping so soundly and so was Katherine," I began, calmly trying to settle him down. I had learned since early in our marriage that Charles not only didn't mind my doing this, in truth, he knew he needed and almost expected me to it.

"And as far as James," I concluded, "you know as well as I do he's an honorable man and I was completely safe with him."

"Well, I guess so," he grumbled going to the counter to get a cup of coffee, "But if something like this comes up again, please wake me up and tell me – what if I had wakened, and you weren't there or what about Katherine, I would have no idea what to do with her if she woke up." This, unfortunately, was probably a true statement. Charles enjoyed playing with his little girl but rarely helped with her care. My father had been the same way, and I just accepted that a child's needs were met by the mother in the family.

"You're right, of course," I smiled in contrition, sitting down with him at the table after picking up Katherine and putting her in the high chair where her scrambled eggs were waiting.

"Baby, baby, baby," she continued her chant as we heard the new child upstairs cry to be fed.

I still hadn't told him that likely we would have two houseguests after today. I would save that news for another time.

CHAPTER EIGHT
April 15, 1913

"Sadie, you just can't take in any orphan off the street, especially a dark–skinned one who looks nothing like the rest of us," said Charles as he paced up and down the living room, red–faced. "She wouldn't fit in and what in the world will people back home think?"

Kezia and the baby had stayed with us since that night at the mansion almost three weeks ago. Since she immediately began helping me around the house, especially with Katherine, Charles did not object. Katherine and Kezia formed a sisterly bond that was dear and the new baby became 'my baby' to sixteen–month–old Katherine. Kezia fortunately had enough milk and with my assistance teaching her how to nurse, the baby thrived. She had not, as I had hoped, bonded with the baby and had not named her. I knew what I wanted to do – I just had to convince Charles.

"They'll think that we have a beautiful new daughter who looks a little different," I laid out my case, having talked at length to Kezia as well as her parents. I had been correct in my suspicions that Kezia planned to give up her baby long before she delivered. I had gone with her to her parent's tiny cabin in the worker's quarters and her mother had fully supported Kezia's decision. She, like her daughter was olive–skinned and couldn't have been more than thirty–years–old. "She started talking about you when she met you up at the mansion," she said in an accent I didn't recognize. "I had Kezia when I was a little older than she is and it was so hard for both of us and I, at least, was married," said, glancing at her daughter, who ducked her head and I felt so sorry for her having to, with all she had to deal with, to also feel shame.

"You can give her a life that I can't," Kezia told me one day as we washed the supper dishes. "You can teach her to read and go to good schools and learn about art and music. Now that I know her, I'm sure that's what she'd want – and that's what I want for her – I decided this before she was born and after I spent time with your family."

"Nobody need know I wasn't pregnant when I left Sunny Slope," I continued my argument, knowing that Charles was beginning to weaken. "She was born at Morven Park – that's all anyone will ever need to know."

"But I'll know. What if I can't treat her like she's our own or feel about her the way I do Katherine?" he said, re-signing himself to my way of thinking.

"I promise you, you'll take to her just like you would any other children born to us. Just look at her, Charles – she's beautiful," I said gazing down at the precious little girl in my arms. "Some of my kin have dark hair and eyes. No one need ever suspect anything if you don't want to tell them. She's our daughter, period, now what are we going to name her?"

We discussed her naming for a while, Charles beginning to warm to the idea or at least giving up, knowing that my determination would prevail in the end. Adoption at this time was something people often did, but they tended not to talk about it. Silence about these matters was the custom and we would observe that silence.

Since there were Elizabeth's on both the Wampler and Zigler side, we settled quickly on that as a first name.

"What about her middle name?" asked Charles, "What about Pearl after my sister – the two of you are like sisters?"

"I like that idea but how about 'Morven,' since she was born here?" I suggested, knowing I would get some resistance from him.

"That's not a family name. We always use family names. It'll only make people wonder."

"I don't think so, and it might mean something to her one day," I said in the tone of voice that almost always could bring Charles around.

Tired of arguing with me and knowing once I had made up my mind, he'd ultimately agree, he moved on to his next concern. "What about Pearl and Arthur – they'll know."

"I've already talked to Pearl about it and she will keep our secret. She loves the idea," I said with confidence that if his sister approved, Charles would think it must be a good idea. Pearl's comment had been, "Charles could do with a little expanding of his horizons in the matter of racial relations."

"Alright, you win all around, but from this day on, we will never speak of this again. Elizabeth is a Wampler and that's that. Now let me hold our new daughter."

CHAPTER NINE
May, 1913

The hats were called "Boaters" and were made of stiff spinet straw. Around the flat crown was wound a striped grosgrain ribbon, usually navy and red in color. Robert had been wearing them since he was about ten.

There he stood on our front porch in his Sunday suit, bow tie and his Boater hat. He had just arrived by train from the Valley to take up a summer job at Morven Park.

"Well, Sadie, Milady, how is the mistress of the manor?" he said, bowing at the waist, taking off his hat and waving it in a gesture of greeting across his lanky body.

"Quite well, Sir Robert, but that doesn't appear to be clothing suitable for mowing!" I said amazed at how my little brother had matured in the year since I had seen him. He was quite tall, probably over six feet, and still rather thin, but his handsome face had filled out a bit which balanced out his large and protruding ears. His hair was full and rather long in an attempt to cover up that particular feature.

"Well, come on in, don't just stand there," I said excitedly, wondering if he would be embarrassed if I followed my urge to hug him like a little boy.

He stepped through the front door, grabbed me up in his arms, lifted me off the ground and swung me around and around.

When he put me down he burst out saying, with his most outrageous grin, "Guess what, I'm in love!"

Before I could ask him for more details, Katherine came toddling into the room.

"Mama, Mama," she said with eyes a big a saucers at the sight of her mother in a stranger's arms.

I adjusted my dress and my composure and picked her up. "Katherine Wampler, this is your Uncle Robert, can you say, hello?'

She looked at this exuberant young man with a suspicious glare. She seemed at a loss for words, though by now at two–and–a–half, was talking in complete sentences.

"Hello there, Miss Katherine," he said in a reassuring voice, "very nice to see you again. The last time I saw you, you were just a baby."

Finally finding her voice, Katherine said in a commanding tone, "Lizbeth a baby, not K. K a big girl like Mama." She walked over and pushed her way in between Robert and me, making it clear who belonged to whom.

Robert immediately understood the gesture and moved over to the dining room table and sat down.

"I can see that you are a very big girl and I bet you help your Mama," he said taking just the right tone with his defiant little niece. "And tell me, Katherine, where is Lizbeth?" Then he looked and me and mouthed, "Who is Elizabeth?"

At just that moment, Kezia came downstairs into the living room carrying Elizabeth who had finished nursing.

"Kezia, this is my brother Robert who is going to be working here on Morven Park this summer. He goes to Bridgewater College."

Shyly, Kezia said, "Hello," and ducked her head as she placed Elizabeth in her cradle by the stove. "I think I need to go home now," and she scooted quickly out the door.

"And so this is Elizabeth?" he said, looking down at his new two–month–old niece. Then looking at me with a questioning expression said, "Sister Sadie, I think we have some catching up to do."

* * * *

Robert and I spent the next two hours reviewing what had happened in the past year since we had seen each other on the farm. He was the first to whom I told the lie about Elizabeth. Though Pearl and Arthur were aware of the truth, Charles and I decided the fewer people who actually knew the circumstances of her birth, the better off it would be. I told Robert that I had been pregnant when I left Sunny Slope the first of the year but hadn't shared it with anyone yet, even Mother Kate. He accepted the explanation when I told him that I hadn't had enough milk and since Elizabeth was so puny, like he had been, I had engaged Kezia's help.

"Was I that puny?" he asked picking up one of Elizabeth's spindly hand in his now, large masculine one.

"Oh, indeed you were, though not nearly as pretty!" I teased, and I, in typical Zigler fashion, changed the subject and moved on to other matters.

He filled me in on his activities at Bridgewater, where he had been made president of his freshman class. When I exclaimed what an honor this was he laughed and said, "I drew the lucky straw, is all – it could have been anybody."

He told of being a bit of a rabble rouser and bucking the faculty when they refused to allow the students to play intercollegiate basketball. He had already been inducted into a literary society and acted in several plays, however did not fare so well in the glee club where he was eventually kicked out. Apparently his monotone had not improved with age.

Then there was the love of his life, Amy Arnold, who he had met the fall of his sophomore year. "She's the most wonderful girl I've ever known. She's smart and kind and beautiful – about five feet tall and no more than a hundred pounds – reminds me of Mother Kate. They all call us "Mutt and Jeff," he said with the glow of new love beaming in his face.

He also mentioned how much he was being influenced by John Flory who, in addition to teaching had become president of the college.

"More and more I believe that what I learned early on about the doctrines of the Brethren Church are correct. John and I have had many discussions to that effect. I figure that if anyone as intelligent as he is and with as much education as he's had can still hold to those doctrines, why should I doubt them?" he stated, his eyes flashing with the passion of youth and purpose.

Surprisingly, the mention of John Samuel Flory did not affect me so much as it once had. Perhaps the stimulating environment in which I now lived was meeting the educational needs I had associated with John and my marriage to Charles was meeting the emotional ones – I liked the feeling of being free of those particular needs.

Robert looked around at the home where we now lived and sighed, "This reminds me so much of the house in Broadway the way it's arranged with the stove in the middle." I knew he was thinking about his decision to go to college rather than take over the farm as Papa had hoped. There had been an auction and the farm and house had been sold to D.H. Zigler, so at least it had remained in the family. Papa had gone to live with Lizzie and John.

"There were a lot of tears the couple of days of the sale," said Robert sadly, fiddling with his coffee cup. "I'm glad you weren't there."

"It took a lot of courage on your part, Robert, to stand up to him," I said, patting his hand. "I know it wasn't easy for you but you have so much potential – it would have been such a waste."

He paused a minute, watching me, "Of course, so did you, Sadie," he said softly, looking me in the eye. "So certainly, did you. Any regrets?"

I looked over at Elizabeth lying asleep in her cradle and Katherine playing with her blocks on the hooked rug in front of the sofa, "I'd be lying if I said I didn't wish things had been such that I could have graduated from Bridgewater, but regrets, no, Robert, I'm content. Education is a relative term, you know. I'll have to tell you about my new friend."

Before I had a chance to tell him about Marguerite and the life I was leading here at Morven Park, Charles came into the room from his day of work, out of sorts, as usual. Straddling the fence between what Mr. Davis wanted of him and what he knew was best for the farm was putting a strain on him and he was not handling it well. He was becoming very irritable with everyone, including me, and the minute he saw Robert I could see he was gearing up for a debate.

"Well, there's that college man," he said as he reached out his hand to shake Robert's. Robert rose from the table and took his hand. "What are those Brethren professors putting into that head of yours? I bet that cousin of mine is filling it with all sorts of wild ideas."

"So good to see you again Charles," Robert said, trying to take some of the tension out of the room. "Yes, I'm really being challenged at school. You certainly have a nice home here and I see your family is growing."

Charles anxiously looked at me across the room and I smiled and nodded to reassure him that everything was in order.

After supper that night, I was washing dishes at the other end of the room, while in the living room the debate had begun on an old subject. I had put the two girls to bed by then and it felt like old times as I eavesdropped on the conversation between these two men that I loved.

"I'm coming to the conclusion that the original stance of the Brethren about war is the correct one," Robert stated, returning to a debate the two had begun on Sunny Slope Farm before he went off to college. At that time he was mostly parroting what he had heard from John Flory but now, he showed a passion for his own personal beliefs developed from his own research and experience.

"And exactly what would that be?" asked Charles, as he sat in his easy chair and clasped his hands in front of him, ready for battle. His face was set in a firm, patronizing expression. Though only five years older than Robert, he seemed to feel he was somehow more a father figure.

"That war is wrong and we, as a pacifist church, are bound to not participate in any way, period," Robert stated emphatically as he sat down in the chair opposite Charles and leaned forward, his eyes blazing.

"But what about serving as non–combatants?" Charles offered as a compromise. "My father joined the Confederate Army during the Civil War but claimed he never killed anyone – shot up in the air," he smiled and gestured firing a gun. "POW!" He always seemed to have some family story to back up his stance on any given topic.

Robert was not amused. "That's an option, of course, but I believe we need to take a stand morally against war in any form." He folded his arms across his chest in defiance. He was no longer intimidated by his sister's husband, and looked directly into Charles' unflinching gaze.

"I still think," re–stated Charles, from their previous discussion on the farm, his voice rising, "That we have some duty to support our government, especially in a just war that fights against a great evil." His fist came down on the side table knocking over the stack of my books that were piled there.

"And who exactly decides what constitutes a "just war" or a just cause?" Robert countered, lowering his voice and becoming more "peaceful" himself. "Most wars come down to economics anyway. Looks like a war is about to gear up in Europe and President Wilson will soon have to decide whether the United States will get into it. The war machine makes some people very rich. I respectfully disagree, Charles…"

The debate continued as I finished the dishes. I felt such a sense of pride for this young man who cared so deeply about his beliefs. He would be a force for good in the world as I had always known. Perhaps I had had a part in that.

S. J. W.

CHAPTER TEN
October, 1913

"Well, it's about time," stormed a red-faced Charles as I came in the door, "Where the world have you been – dumb question – of course I know where you've been. It's where you always are!" He obviously had had another one of those stress-filled days and this time, I was the target of his frustration. He was standing in the kitchen with Pearl behind him, hands over her ears and a look of mock horror on her face.

"I think I'll be going now, so long, you two," said Pearl, who had been there watching Katherine and Elizabeth while I was at the mansion. She gave me a sympathetic look then quickly went out the door.

I had been in the Davis' library reading a book about the women's suffrage movement and completely lost track of time.

"I'm sorry, Charles, I really am," I said trying to smooth the waters as I always did when he came home tired and upset. This time it didn't work. He wasn't nearly finished with his prepared speech. I was happy that Katherine and

Elizabeth had been put to bed early after Pearl had given them supper.

"You know, I'm getting a little tired of you spending so much time over there with that woman," he continued, his body straight and rigid, his eyes blazing.

"Those Davis' think they're better than the rest of us and if you don't watch out, you'll start acting uppity yourself."

"Charles, I don't spend that much time and I really enjoy Marguerite's friendship. She's not at all like that and it is so kind of her to let me use her library and play her piano," I said, sitting down at the dining room table and motioning him to do the same. He was not interested and continued his tirade pacing the floor.

"Seems to me you'd rather be doing all that rather than taking care of your own children. I thought when I married you this is what you wanted, not associating with a rich woman and all her fancy trappings," he concluded, slamming his hand down on the table and making the dishes rattle.

"Now, Charles, just one minute please," I began, trying to remain calm but in this rare instance, beginning to lose my temper. "I know you aren't happy right now and I'm sorry about that, but please don't take it out on me. You know very well that I take good care of these girls and when I'm not here somebody in the family, Pearl or Robert, has been here to give them plenty of attention and love."

"Well, that Kezia girl isn't family and she's here half of the time and she doesn't even nurse Elizabeth anymore," he spat her name out with such disrespect that I was having trouble controlling myself.

"Kezia has a special bond with Elizabeth, you know that, and Mrs. Davis has sort of loaned her to me to help around the house," I explained, feeling my face getting flushed.

"You ought to be doing the work around here yourself – that's a woman's job to…"

"Charles Weldon Wampler, you stop right there!" I shouted, finally losing whatever control I had maintained so far. I stood up quickly and took a position right in front of him and looked directly into his eyes. "Do you remember that night in Broadway and what you promised me?"

He stood there, unable to speak for once, trying to remember what I was referring to. His face fell and he looked away from my gaze.

"Well let me refresh your memory. You said, and I quote, 'If I ever try to diminish you in any way because you are a woman, you have my permission to kick my behind.'"

He hung his head and placed his hands over his eyes. Heavens, was he going to cry? Had I gone too far? Slowly he uncovered his eyes and in them were not tears but a familiar twinkle as he said softly, "I was out of my mind in love and would have said anything to impress you."

"Well, you did impress me and you still do," I said, regaining my composure, as once again his humor came to save the moment. "I know how hard it's been lately here on the farm with Mr. Davis on your back all the time. I'm sure you feel that you aren't appreciated for the skills you've brought here to use to make the farm better. Think a minute about how you feel when he does that. That's what I'm feeling right now with what you're saying about my wanting to read and expand my mind."

"That's different, it's my job, my profession," he defended himself, never willing to back off completely.

"No, it's not different, Charles. I have always had a curious mind," I motioned Charles to sit down with me at the dining room table and continued in a calm voice, "Since I was a little girl growing up in that Zigler household, I've been exposed to all kinds of books, poetry, music and all manner of interesting people who had the education of the world in their background. You also told me that night that you loved that I have a mind of my own and would speak out my truth." I took a big breath before I continued.

A look of recognition crossed his face as if he had just remembered the woman he had married. He smiled and waited for me to go on.

"Well, this is my truth – yes, I am and wife and mother and I love that part of my life – it is a very important part of who I am as a person. I am and always will be something else, too. I am Sadie Zigler Wampler, who has an active brain and the soul of a poet and musician. When I go up to that house, I don't go to be impressed by the grandeur of it or the high estate of its mistress. I go because there, I'm treated as an equal by a woman who has had every opportunity in life as far as education and every other way. She knows how important it is for women of our time to be informed about what's going on in the world. Your sister Pearl, by the way, is very involved in the movement to get women the vote – did you know that?"

The mention of his sister and her activism seemed to remind him the kind of women he had always admired and he relaxed into his chair as I continued, lowering my voice.

"I love you Charles – I will always love you, and I expect you to live up to the promises you made."

Charles sat there, a slow sheepish smile creeping across his face "Well, that was some speech. Takes me back to when I fell in love with a woman of spirit. Guess maybe I needed to be reminded of that. Consider my behind kicked. It's just that I'm so darn miserable and maybe seeing you so happy was getting to me," he said with a self–awareness that surprised me.

"So are you going to do something about this job of yours? I also married a man of spirit."

There was a timid knock at the door and when I went to see who it was, there stood Robert in his mowing clothes. How long he had been there on the porch, I had no idea.

CHAPTER ELEVEN
Fall, 1913

C harles' work on the farm not only continued to cause him problems but actually got worse. The workers he managed were unreliable and in that, Mr. Davis had been correct. Charles had tried his style of handling the workers with more respect than Mr. Davis, but the whole system seemed to be tainted with an overall dislike of management. And when workers left, Charles found it difficult to replace them because of Mr. Davis' reputation both locally and statewide. Mr. Davis was convinced that the reason the farm wasn't doing well was because he was away so much, but Charles believed it was just the opposite, that Mr. Davis knew so little about farming that his presence interfered with the very thing he hoped to achieve. The last straw was when Charles lost James when he forged a check on Mr. Davis, and the authorities sent him to prison. By fall, things had come to a head, and Charles was informed that he had been replaced as manager. This was apparently Mr. Davis' pattern. We began to make plans to return to Sunny Slope. Pearl, Arthur and Robert had all left after the summer which made it some easier.

I was conflicted about leaving Morven Park. Here, I had had leisure time to read and expand my mind again. I had made an unlikely friend in Marguerite Davis who had respected my intelligence and treated me as an equal in our quest for our best life as women in a man's world.

I visited her one last time in October before we left.

"I'm surely going to miss you," said Marguerite as we sat having our final cup of tea in the parlor. "What a breath of fresh air you are, Sadie. I am sorry that this hasn't worked out for your husband, but I am afraid Morley is not an easy man to deal with. Of course, as the owner, he must do what he thinks is right," she added, a little embarrassed that she had said something negative about her husband.

"You can't imagine how much your friendship has meant to me this past year," I said, my voice catching with emotion. "Your generosity with your library and your Steinway has enriched my soul in a way that will forever change the way I look at myself. I thank you for that." I looked around at this room, full to the brim with opulence that might have been by all accounts, cold and unfriendly—instead, it had been a haven of warmth and encouragement.

"Sadie," she said, putting down her cup and leaning toward me in a motherly fashion, "Whatever you do when you get back home never stop using that sharp mind of yours. From what you have told me, your life on Sunny Slope Farm will be far different from what you have experienced here. Remember to always take time for yourself, always!"

This was the most personal she had ever been with me and she seemed to catch herself when she said, pulling back a little, "Of course, you'll have to be the judge of that; we really have entirely different situations, you and I."

As I left, she gave me a tentative hug on the porch and we said our good–byes. I felt the tears sting my eyes as I walked back to our home that would no longer be our home. Once again in my life, a choice had been made for me.

I was sure Kezia also had strong feelings about our leaving since she had become entwined in the daily life of our family. She was so good with Katherine and Elizabeth and had the best of both worlds as far as her baby was concerned. Even after she had stopped nursing her, she came by the house often, borrowing books and reading to both of the girls.

On a cold November day, a week before we left, she appeared at the door with a large piece of paper held behind her back.

"I have something for Elizabeth," she said quietly, and I could see she had been crying. "I like to draw so I thought she might want to remember where she was born. I know she won't remember me, but I will always remember her."She handed me the paper. On it, in colored pencil, was a beautifully drawn picture of our house. Every detail was there, and I was once again astounded at her abilities.

"Kezia, this is beautiful. I will keep it for her. You know I won't be telling her about you because, well, that's just the way it has to be, but I will always remember what you did for Elizabeth and for our family," I said tearing up and taking her in my arms. I promise you, she will be loved and cared for always. Who knows, perhaps someday she will be an artist like you."

When we had arrived here some eleven months ago, we hadn't brought much from home, so packing up was not a chore. Most everything we needed, right down to kitchen items and linens for the beds, had been provided. Our clothing and other personal items fit into three or four cardboard boxes. One box was full of books that Pearl had loaned me and a few that Marguerite had been generous enough to give me. The last book that I packed was the volume of prose and poetry that my dear soul sister–in–law had given me the first day they arrived at Morven Park. I had savored its beauty and so much of its content resounded within me. I had started putting slips of paper marking pages that spoke to me and with a pencil noted certain passages I wanted to remember. I gently wrapped "Mother, Home and Heaven" in a piece of tissue paper and laid it at the top of the box. It would be the first book I would unpack when we returned to the farm.

As the wagon with all our belongings pulled away, I looked back at the tan stucco house that had been our home for almost a year; I sighed and said to the girls, "Say bye–bye to Morven Park, Katherine, Elizabeth. We're going home."

Katherine, who didn't even remember Sunny Slope, said with a frown, pointing to our house, "Dat home, Mama, dat home!"

S. J. W.

PART FOUR
MOTHER, HOME, AND HEAVEN

"It is not for you to waste your time in useless speculation as to the unknowable source of your life stream, or in seeking to trace it in the ocean. It is enough for you that it IS, and that, while it runs its brief course, it is yours to make it yield its blessings."

The Calling of Dan Matthews
Harold Bell Wright
1909

CHAPTER ONE
November, 1913

Albert Thacker, the man Charles had hired to help Grandma Katie with the farm while we were gone, picked us up in the wagon at the train station. Both of the girls were tired and fussy from the long ride down the Shenandoah Valley. The November air was cold and we bundled up under wool blankets for the ride to Sunny Slope.

As we turned in at the foot of the lane off the Dayton Pike, I suddenly felt a twinge of anticipation and excitement. Prince, the horse that had replaced Gueriar, pulled the wagon up the steep hill and as we came over the rise and looked down at the home place, Charles and I glanced at each other and smiled. "Remember that first time I brought you over that hill?" said Charles. "I did so want to impress you"

I look at the view of the familiar house and the hill behind it, bathed in the bright November sun. "And so you did, Charles Weldon Wampler, so you did!" I said, truly happy to be home.

Grandma Katie greeted us on the front porch landing of the house with a smile that expressed her unbounded joy at our homecoming to Sunny Slope Farm. She had put on her best house dress of a brightly–flowered print and

321

looked even younger than I remembered. At sixty–five she was still spry as she swooped up a surprised Katherine, who had climbed the stairs ahead of Charles and me, and gave her a bear hug. Her granddaughter, who did not remember this woman at all, wriggled loose screaming, "Down, down!" Grandma Katie released her quickly and watched as I mounted the stairs with eight–month–old Elizabeth in my arms. Charles lagged behind, waiting for his mother's first response to our newest family member.

"Well, what do you think of our Elizabeth?" I asked, out of breath from the steep steps. I held her out for Grandma Katie to see, while trying my best to keep a neutral expression. Charles gave me a worried look – this would be a good test of our shared deception.

"October, November, December," Grandma Katie said, counting on her fingers, "For Pete's sake, you were already almost six months along when you left here. How did I miss that? Good thing I didn't know, I would have put up a bigger fuss about your leaving," she said, clucking like a hen who has once again gathered her brood.

She opened the door and we all moved into the front hall and then the living room. "It wouldn't have made any difference," I responded, as I looked around at the familiar surroundings, "Both of us were determined and excited to go. And it was a wonderful experience, maybe more for me than Charles." I glanced over at Charles who was making his best disgusted–face. "And with Pearl, Arthur and Robert there, we had a great family time together. Leaving at the same time made it easier, I suppose," I said, feeling a tug of longing at the life I would surely miss.

She narrowed her eyes and looked more closely at her new granddaughter. "Sure doesn't look a bit like Katherine, does she – she's awful puny–looking but she's a right pretty little thing?" she said fluffing up Elizabeth's black curly hair.

"Yes, she is, isn't she?" I said, relieved that her response had not been out of the ordinary. "It's good to be home again— everything alright with you? You look as fit as a fiddle as always."

"Not bad for an old lady," she quipped as she danced a jig around the living room. She watched Katherine exploring, climbing all over the furniture. "I'm real glad to have you home. You sure were missed around here. It was far too quiet, even with Lessie and Albert living here. And I'm right ready to put you back to work again."

I laughed, feeling more relaxed that we had passed our first test. "Well, I have two pretty good reasons not to do that much, yet."

"No excuses! No excuses! You know Lessie is about to have her baby in December," she babbled on, like someone who hadn't had a good family conversation for a while. "Maybe a Christmas baby. Nothing like lots of children around for Christmas. I have a great big ole turkey hen that'll do for a big meal. Oh, my, isn't all this just wonderful?"

I took a stroll through the house with Elizabeth in my arms and Katherine toddling behind, taking it all in. It had changed little since we left almost a year ago. I looked fondly at the harmonium we had moved from the house up in Broadway when Papa broke up housekeeping and moved in with Lizzie. I hadn't attended the auction because I was busy with a new baby and my work on the farm. And if I were honest with myself, I just didn't have the heart for it. Dear Robert, who felt so badly about his part in the sale of the farm, had come all the way here with the harmonium in the back of a wagon, as it had arrived at our home via George Holsinger so long ago. I looked forward to playing it again after so much practice on Marguerite's Steinway. And there it was – that twinge of regret and even a little resentment that once again, a choice had been made for my life in which I had no say. Would it always be this way for me? Later on that day, I unpacked my box of books. I took out the tissue– wrapped volume of prose and poetry at the very top and held it in my hands. I carried it upstairs to the glass door leading to the balcony where I read and wrote letters to Pearl. I placed it reverently on the little walnut table beside my chair. At that moment I made a promise to myself – I would always continue to expand my mind by reading – I would make the time no matter what. In this one thing, I would always have a choice.

CHAPTER TWO
January, 1914

January 11, 1914

Dear Pearl and Arthur,

The calm has come and I will try writing a while. Katherine is still storming a little, since all the family company has left. There seems to be an unending supply frequenting this house. Reminds me a little of my home growing up.

Grandma Katie and Chas. went to Dayton to church this morning. Had a time getting Chas. started. I had tho't of going but Elizabeth was too sick this morning for me to get away…

Only two months had passed since we returned home to Sunny Slope Farm. Grandma Katie and I seamlessly resumed our co–responsibilities in the house and chores on the farm. I had always been impressed with how adaptable she was. Once again, she seemed to know just how to adjust to her role as second woman–in–command with no fanfare or resentment. For my part, as I wrote my letter sitting at my favorite writing perch on the upstairs landing looking up the lane, I was missing not only my soul sister Pearl, back in York County, but also my friendship with Marguerite, her piano and her library. I hadn't felt as stimulated intellectually since that college semester before Mama died. The confidence I had gained at Morven Park and my feelings of independence there felt a little threatened here in this setting. I had made a promise to myself to continue reading as much as I could, even though with another child on the way and the work on the farm, it wouldn't be easy. Yes, I was pregnant once again. This one would be due in July. Except for a little morning sickness I was feeling well and looking forward to this one. Maybe Charles would get that boy he was hoping for.

"Sadie, could you come in here a minute, please?" called Lessie Thacker, who had had her baby in December. She and Albert had both stayed on until after the baby settled down a bit and Lessie regained her strength. Little Naomi had terrible colic and cried all the time. Albert kept saying she was just spoiled and wanted to be picked up. Lessie and I would look at each other and silently say, "And exactly what is wrong with that?" She planned to go to her parents' home next Tuesday and I supposed Albert would stay here until his wife was ready to take up housekeeping again. I know I should be used to sharing my home by now, but I think I was spoiled having such lovely privacy at our house on Morven Park.

"Yes, Lessie, what is it now?" I answered, a little irritated at my letter writing being interrupted once again.

"I can't get her to stop crying," she whined from her bedroom down the hall.

"Just pick her up, Lessie – don't mind what Albert says," I suggested and followed up with a little sage womanly advice. "He's a man and doesn't know squat about loving up a baby."

I returned to my letter, proud of myself at not jumping up and running to the rescue.

> *…Chas. says to tell you that Katherine and Elizabeth get forty times cuter every day. He said something to K. one day about her 'old ugly Daddy' and she has been calling him 'Old Dad' or in Katherine language "Oda" ever since. She isn't a bit bow–legged anymore and she is growing some. Elizabeth pulls up in her box and can chin it…*

I finished the letter and walked quietly down the hall and then the stairs, hoping Lessie wouldn't hear me. Charles' office was to the left, right at the base of the staircase. It was a large room with windows on two walls and his massive, oak, roll-top desk on the other. He had a wooden chair on wheels in which he scooted all over the room as he moved from one task to another. In good Swiss–German fashion, he kept his workspaces tidy and organized, which I appreciated. When he heard me he came running out the door.

"Sadie, I just talked to Mr. Wenger," he said excitedly, "he has a big ole turkey gobbler for $7.00. I think I'll buy him."

Immediately after we returned home, Charles dove right into furthering his experiments with the turkeys and his plans for making it a full–fledged business. There was an intensity about his efforts now, as if his failure as a manager had given him something to prove about himself. I was excited for him and wanted to help in any way I could.

"That seems like a mighty expensive bird to me. How much does he weigh?" I asked, knowing our finances were not that good at the moment.

"About twenty–two pounds. He would be a good tom to breed the hens. You've been doing such a good job with raising the ones we have and I want to increase the flock. What do you think?" he said, making the effort to include me in the decision, which I appreciated.

"If you think we have the money right now," I answered, knowing that he had already made up his mind – a trait we seem to share. "Sometimes I feel like Old McDonald with pigs and horses, and chickens and turkeys and sheep ee–I–ee–I–O," I sang quite pleased at my ever–evolving Wampler wit. "Where is it going to end?"

"With us making a big pile of money, I hope!" he grinned sheepishly.

"If turkeys weren't so darn stupid it would sure help. Let it rain hard and they'll look up to see where it's coming from, open up their mouths and drown," I teased, opening my mouth and looking upwards.

"You just wait," he countered wanting the last word as always, "This is going to be big."

I walked over to him and kissed him on his slightly balding head.

"The turkey king!" I said leaving him to his big purchase and his even bigger dreams.

CHAPTER THREE
September, 1914

The drums of war were heard by the farmers of the Shenandoah Valley with mixed emotions. Most of us were from traditional Peace Churches like the Brethren, Mennonite and Quaker and were horrified and saddened at the prospect of young men being sent to foreign lands to kill and be killed. President Wilson had been committed to keep the United States out of this "war to end all wars" but was encouraging all citizens to support the war effort with our goods. Therefore, farmers were asked to grow and sell their products to the United States government who would ship them to the allies in Europe. This meant that those, like us, who had been struggling for the past few years financially, had an opportunity to make quite a lot of money.

The hypocrisy of this bothered me more than I let on to Charles, who was more than pleased with the possibility of bringing in more money for us as well as the farmers he was helping as county agent. He had continued this job for Rockingham County which required him to travel quite a bit. His expertise as well as his way with people suited him perfectly for the job. I could see that this success resulted in his feeling much better about himself after his negative experience at Morven Park. His mood had improved considerably for which I was grateful.

This September found Robert entering his senior year a Bridgewater College. He had continued to excel both in his studies as well as extracurricular activities. The Class of '16 had kept him in his position as president all four years. He was a leader, well–liked and respected. The college encouraged students to participate in community service in local churches as well as the community at large, visiting the sick and infirm – Robert's caring nature was well–suited to this. He had also become very active in the Y.M.C.A. and was looking forward to becoming a minister and ultimately a missionary to China. His upstanding reputation was balanced out by a rather mischievous and rebellious side which manifested when he chose to join the "roughnecks" literary society rather than the one which attracted the preachers and missionaries. I reveled in each tale he told about his life there and was always excited when he visited after church some Sundays as he did on one which turned out to be a little more contentious than I had bargained for.

This particular Sunday Robert brought his fiancée, Amy Arnold, whom I had met once the summer's before. As he had described her to me, she was petite and quite beautiful. At first meeting she seemed merely a sweet, gregarious, young woman. I soon learned that she was much more than this.

"Sadie, Robert tells me that he owes you his success in life, as well as his sometimes dubious character," Amy said with a quirky grin as she finished up her cherry cobbler, made from the cherries Grandma Katie and I had picked from the trees in the back orchard. We sat around the dinner table after services at Garber's Church that morning. I was nursing Sarah Ruth who had been born six weeks before with little fanfare as the third girl in the family. Charles sat at his place at the head of the table between the two windows in the dining room, flanked by two large Boston ferns. This position gave him an air of royal authority and I could see he was ready to commence his usual debate with Robert about the war. Grandma Katie began clearing the dishes and the two girls from the room signaling it was time for the adults to begin their conversation.

Charles expression conveyed that he was none too pleased that his guest had already steered the conversation elsewhere but he waited for me to respond.

"I'll take some of the credit and some of the blame, but not all of the credit or all of the blame," I said, buttoning up the front of my dress and putting Ruth over my shoulder to burp. "He's certainly lived up to what I had hoped for him. I am particularly proud of his courage in choosing to move ahead with his education and making the difficult decision to go against Papa's plan for him to take over the farm in Broadway. I know that wasn't easy."

"From what he has told me about you, Sadie, you sacrificed much for him and your family. I don't know whether I would have been as generous," she said, with an honesty I admired.

"Sadie is every bit as smart as I ever was, probably smarter. I've always wondered what she could have done with her life had she the opportunity I was given," Robert said firmly, looking at Charles, who had had just about enough of a conversation of which he was not a part.

"Sadie is a wonderful wife and mother," he said proudly, fully expecting this declaration to swing the conversation to another topic. And you should just see her work with the turkey experiments I'm doing. If this venture is a success, it will be in great part due to what she has done on the farm with me."

Robert gave me a strange look I didn't quite understand. He had, since we had all returned from Morven Park, seemed to be more at odds with Charles than before and it was more than their disagreements over the war and his peace activism. This seemed personal and it didn't occur to me until later why this might have been.

That night as we were getting ready for bed, Charles returned to discussion he and Robert had had after Amy and I left the table to help in the kitchen.

"Your little brother needs to be realistic and stop hanging on to every word Cousin John Flory utters," he fussed, tugging to loosen his tie. "He got all over me about selling farm goods for the war effort. It's good for our family and it's good for the farmers in the area."

"Charles, you just need to understand that Robert is young and idealistic," I said calmly, as I always did when he was riled up over something or another. "His views on peace at this point in his life may seem extreme to you, but his passion for this cause right now is admirable and most probably will change and modify as the years go by."

As it turned out, they only grew stronger.

* * * *

By December our finances hadn't improved even though the work with the turkeys had doubled for me. I fed them, gathered their eggs, and took care of the young ones when they hatched. Grandma Katie was beginning to slow down but did help with the girls while I did the outside work. Albert was still there and helped with the other livestock. Charles had bought a new Percheron stallion and several mares which he bred and sold the colts to good advantage. Charles was gone more and more with his job as county agent and coordinating the goods for the war effort. He had also helped in organizing the Rockingham Pure–bred Livestock Association. He did work for them without pay though they had several sales in which he made a little money. He said the expression, "happy and poor," applied to us at this point in our lives.

Pearl and Arthur still lived in York County on Poquoson Cove Farm. Both were active in the community and in educational endeavors there. They continued to invite us to visit but, of course, with Charles' work, we never did. She and I communicated by letter at least once a week and she suggested books I might read which I, as I had promised myself when we came home, made time to go to the Harrisonburg Library to get and savor. With all I had to do, this was certainly not easy.

Dec.6, 1914

Dear Pearl,

This is a regular old Dec. day; in fact it has been rainy all week. I think the sun shone one day just a little. Last night it sleeted and snowed but is not so very cold this morning.

Strange to say we did not go to church. I think we can get thru' the day without getting lonesome but I do not know what grandma will do when she gets tired reading. Knit I guess. Her needles hardly get cold these days. I think she is nearly thru' making Xmas gifts. As for myself I don't have time to make any and have no money to buy with so Xmas will not make me so busy. I am going to roast an old turkey hen at Xmas. Wish you and Arthur could be here to help us eat her. And you haven't even seen little Sarah Ruth who is almost six months old now. Grandma says she's the prettiest of the lot but I don't think she's any better looking than the rest of them. I think Charles was a bit disappointed at not having a boy this time but the way things are going, I seem to get pregnant every year — there's always next time. This makes me tired even thinking about it...

I paused from my letter writing as three–year–old Katherine came bounding up the stairs yelling, "Yibby won't stop eating my huckaberries dat I needs to make pies, Muder." She had a towel tied around her as an apron. "You writen' Aunt Pa? Tell her I'm makin' pies to beat the band."

We had started calling Elizabeth, "Libby," to make it easier for K who still had trouble with her words. She had been calling Charles O'da but was now calling him "Fader," and calls herself "Toag" because Grandma Katie kept calling her "sugar" and she couldn't say that.

"I'll tell her," I said looking down at her bare feet wondering when we'd be able to afford some shoes for the girls. Grandma Katie had knit some wool booties for all of them to put on when we went out. "Aunt Pa will be so pleased."

"You tell her Toag yikes the P's but don't yike to shell dem so much—too much twubble."

I smiled listening to her Dutch–speak which certainly didn't keep her from communicating. I think she, as I did, missed her Aunt Pearl.

Dear Pearl was forever sending us something or another—peanuts, sweet potatoes, anything to supplement our shrinking income. Charles was so focused on making the turkey business survive and visiting farmers all over the county that he didn't seem to realize we were not doing well financially. I was starting to feel a little embarrassed about it and sometimes when I had to ask Pearl for something, I got the impression she got a little put out. But being Pearl, she got over it quickly. When the apples were ripe in the orchard on the hill behind the house, I planned to trade her for something. I'll feel better about that.

"Now go on back down and bake your pies so I can write Aunt Pa," I said, kissing her on the forehead where I cut her straight blond hair in bangs.

She smiled and patted my knee, "Toag yuves you, Muder."

"I love you, too, Toag," I said, hearing Charles come in the front door and go into his office. I suddenly remembered that I had forgotten a few things Charles asked me to record in the ledger. He'd been away again all week and lately it seemed even his weekends were taken—I'm tiring of it but I know he is doing it for us.

I walked down the stairs behind Toag and entered Charles' office where he sat at his oak roll–top desk overflowing with papers. His former organization skills had flown the coop as he became busier and he did not like for me to mess with his business papers.

"Well, hello there, Sadie, I wondered where you were," he said, getting up from his desk and coming out in the front hall to kiss me lightly on the cheek. These gestures were once a bit of a surprise to me, having grown up in a very loving, but not openly affectionate family, particularly my parents. We were well aware of their deep love for and devotion to each other, but would have been shocked if Papa were to kiss or embrace Mama in our presence. In the five years since Charles and I married, I had become used to his loving touches which conveyed just how much I was cared for by him. It concerned me a little that as Marguerite had put it, "he practically worships you." He did seem to put me on a pedestal in some ways, yet in some areas I was beginning to feel more as if I were the supporter of his plans and dreams. I suddenly remembered that red flag of threatened independence I had raised when we had our Silver Lake conversation. As for me, my love for him had grown and though I showed it in a more reserved fashion, I was content in my decision and tried to learn from him and Grandma Katie that there was a need for this way of showing love. In Charles' hand was the ledger which he had asked me to maintain, in addition to writing letters for him. I really didn't mind doing this because since he didn't talk much about how things were going, it gave me some insight into how good or bad things were.

"I see you haven't done the December turkey orders yet," he said, as we walked back into his office together.

"I just remembered – sorry, Charles," I said resisting the urge to remind him   I did have other duties around the house that kept me busy.

"Don't worry about it," he said, as if reading my mind, "I just like to see it written down so I know how things stand. What do you think?" He handed me the ledger. "Going alright, I guess," I said, flipping to the month of December where Charles had placed the orders for the month. "We sold ten hens and four toms this month and we still have some dandy ones left, yet. But it's the middle of winter, maybe spring will be better. This cold, wet weather doesn't help any."

"And don't forget, we're getting a new Tom for ourselves from Albemarle County soon," he said settling in his chair and rolling over to his desk. He idly fiddled around with the pile of papers.

I sat down at the table he had set up for my work and begin to record the orders. We were selling the toms for $4.00, hens for $3.00. We got $.50 more when we shipped them out to people in crates by train. We had sent four to Joel Wrights, three to a woman in King William County, one to Maryland, and one to Louisa Co. We would ship again about the middle of the month.

When I finished, which sadly didn't take very long, I said, looking up from the books, carefully broaching a subject I had been considering, "Charles, I'm thinking of trying some Toulouse geese this spring. Pearl says she picks them every six weeks and gets about a quarter pound from a goose at each picking. The feathers sell for $.50 per pound. It might bring in a little more income." I was always mindful that Charles liked to be the one to come up with new ideas. "What do you think?" I had learned many ways of bringing him around to my way of thinking – I suppose I had learned this from Mama, though Papa had his own ways of handling Mama as he had with the harmonium. I smiled to myself remembering that evening.

He paused a moment, looking out the window, "But don't geese need a lake or something?" said, always thinking ahead to potential problems and withholding his full approval just to maintain his final authority. I knew that the mention of his sister was one of the ways I could encourage him to agree.

"Actually, she says they don't go to the water much which is good," I answered, having already asked Pearl about that. "If we have a lot of rain that sink hole across from the Blosser house fills up with water and they could use that, which reminds me, I have to finish my letter to your sister."

"Thank you Sadie, I do appreciate all you do to keep things afloat," he said smiling and taking my hand. "Maybe the geese will be smarter than the turkeys. You know what I always say, 'the only thing dumber than a turkey is someone who tries to raise them for a living!'"

I headed upstairs, laughing, always amazed at the famous Wampler humor even when things weren't going well.

...Pearl, how many eggs do your geese lay in a season?"
I think we have a few chickens that are still laying, yet.

Effie Harper is coming to sew for me a few days this week. I have been cutting out dresses, skirts, drawers etc. I get my work done pretty well when I have no girl but I do not get any sewing done.

Well perhaps I have chattered enough for this time. Will write when the things come. Hope you are all well.

Lovingly, Sadie

The afternoon had gotten away from me and I heard Ruth waking from her nap and Libby and Toag asking Charles about supper. He had gone out after his office work and killed a hen for the meal. The vegetables that we canned last summer were running short already. It was not a good season and we ate up most of what we grew. Maybe we'd just have chicken tonight.

Supper was always a festive occasion when Charles was able to be home and we sat around the big dining room table. We had to bring in another high chair for Little Ruth since Libby isn't two yet and still needs hers. Toag, now three, sat on a regular chair atop two pillows. Grandma Katie bustled around making sure each of them had what they needed. Everyone talked at once and as I look around at my family, I felt contentment.

After dinner Charles went immediately back to his office. Toag and Libby went to the back porch to make more pies and Grandma Katie and I cleared the table and began washing dishes. Ruth was still sitting in her chair, playing with her food.

"Grandma Katie," I said as I heard Ruth begin to fuss, "Would you mind finishing up while I put Ruth to bed?"

"I'll be glad to, you go ahead," she said smiling, as always ready to do what needed to be done. I continually appreciated her presence in our home.

"Come on little one," I said, picking up Ruth, who had food smeared from head to toe, "Let's go get washed up and ready for bed."

By the time I came downstairs after getting Ruth tucked in for the night, I found Elizabeth asleep on the hook rug in the sitting room and Charles and Toag piled up together dozing behind the new coal stove. Again, I was touched at how affectionate he was with the children in spite of his tendency to be authoritarian with them at times.

I suddenly realized how bone tired I was. I sat down on the sofa and picked up *Mother, Home and Heaven* which I read each day if I rose early or had a few moments in the evening. I flipped through the pages and stopped on page 117 to a poem called "Home Defined" by Charles Swain. It began:

"Home's not merely four square walls,

Though with picture hung and gilded:

Home is where affection calls,

Filled with shrines the heart hath builded!

Home! go watch the faithful dove,

Sailing 'neath the heaven above us;

Home is where there's one to love!

Home is where there's one to love us!

Before I got to the second verse or was able to mark the page, I fell asleep in the chair.

Grandma Katie, finding everyone in her family lying all over the house, roused us and directed us to our respective beds.

CHAPTER FOUR
May, 1915

"Why don't we take Colonel Carter and the wagon and go up to the Love Feast at Mt. Clinton tonight? They're not having services at Garber's Church tomorrow for the third week in a row so we'll be at home again on a Sunday with the kids," I said hopefully, as I came into the house from feeding the geese and turkeys.

Charles had been gone so much lately, I rarely saw him. He rode Col. Carter, his favorite horse, all over the county checking on the farmers clubs he had started, attending his other duties with the county agent job and the farmers growing food for the war effort. I had decided to just let the matter go even though I still felt it crossed a line spiritually for me. He would have to deal with his own conscience himself.

"I think that's a wonderful idea, Sadie," he said with a boyish grin." We haven't done anything just us for a long time. It'll be like our old courting days in Broadway."

To hear him agree so quickly to my plan was a surprise and I was thrilled and touched that he held such memories. Those days seem so long ago.

"Let me see if the new girl can stay the night with the kids," I say excitedly, feeling like teenager girl.

I had recently hired a very good girl and was really pleased with her. The girls and I all loved her and call her "U.U." She had a more pleasant disposition than some of the help I've had over the years – I have surely needed the help. Once again "morning sickness" has visited me. I'm feeling more and more like my mother and Lizzie and sometimes I catch myself resenting the comparison. Ruth doesn't even walk yet. So much for the doctor's recommendation that Charles not to have children! But now, this little gift—maybe Charles is more sympathetic than I thought in agreeing to our outing.

With U.U. helping in the house, I could get out to tend the geese I bought and I've had great success with them. Three lay fifty–four eggs the first laying. I set a turkey hen and two of the geese on the eggs and got twenty–three geese. One of the larger geese got in the hog pen and all we saw was feathers! I must say they are the dirtiest things I ever saw, even though I think they are a bit smarter than the turkeys, which aren't doing that well right now.

"U.U., could you stay over tonight so Charles and I can go to the Love Feast up at Mr. Clinton?" I asked, going into the kitchen where she was feeding the three girls.

"Would you like that Libby?" she answered, picking up two–year–old Libby from her high chair. Her dark curly hair was getting long and was a stark contrast to her two sister's blond straight hair.

"We make pies, U.U.?" Libby said in her still faltering speech. She and Toag both seem quite content to talk "dutch" and understand each other perfectly. Half the time we didn't know what either of them was talking about.

"Of course we can," said U.U., "And Toag. and Ruth can help us."

"Rufe too yittle – her make messy," she said as the three of them went to the little back porch.

As I got ready for the Love Feast, I stood in front of the mirror, looking at the woman I had become in the past five years. I was now thirty–three–years old and had lost not only my girlish figure, but my girlish sparkle–my tiredness showed. I had gotten a new black suit that didn't wrinkle as much as my grey one. It also was a little roomier as I had put on some weight after Ruth. Now, I'd need even more room! Will I ever get my girlish figure back?

My hair was still dark and curly and parted down the middle but no longer did I have a full head of hair. I think of a photograph of me in the back yard of our home in Broadway. I was probably around eighteen. I was kneeling on the ground in front of the picket fence, teaching my little dog to sit up on his hind legs. I wore a long dress and a white apron and oh, the hair! Piled on the top of my head was a sumptuous bun. The remainder of my hair was wavy and, even the photo, shiny and healthy looking. Now, I saw instead, a short bob that was cut above my ears. It was still very curly and perhaps because it was so short, a bit kinky. I had decided one day that all of my house and farm duties did not afford me the time it took to mess with a head of hair. Charles was none too pleased but the truth was, he hadn't even noticed until a week after it was cut.

"You look just grand!" Charles said as he came into the bedroom, dressed to the nines in a navy suit, vest and blue tie. He put his arm around my shoulders as he looked at both of us in the mirror. "We look almost too good to be just going to church."

The wagon ride up to Mr. Clinton was spectacular on this May Saturday evening. We traveled up to Hinton Grove Church on the Rawley Pike, by way of New Erikson Road.

The Love Feast was a traditional Brethren one with feet washing, the meal, scriptures and bread and wine (well, grape juice.) Afterwards, we departed the church as the Bible instructs, "singing a hymn." And oh, the singing – somewhere along the way I had pushed aside the music in my life. Except for the lullabies and nursery songs I sang with the girls, I hadn't thought of that time when I trained to be a song leader and led the singing at Weaver's Church – the night I met Charles. Was that dream altogether a thing of the past? I would have to think about that.

On the way home, we took the long way, through Dale Enterprise, Hinton, Mr. Clinton and then turned off on Silver Lake Road toward Dayton. I had never been up that way.

It was almost dark when we passed by Silver Lake.

"Remember?" Charles said quietly as he pulled in the reins and we stopped along the road next to the lake.

"Of course, I remember" I said, the memories flooding back. "You were a pretty convincing suitor, I must say."

"The moment I met you at the Blosser's that night, I knew I could not let you get away," he said as he took my hand in his. "Any regrets?"

The stars were coming out and the new moon reflected on the lake Sister Pearl had named. I thought about my younger self, the girl in the photo with the shiny hair atop her head. I thought of the dreams she had then and where I was now, a wife, pregnant with my fourth child. And I looked into Charles expectant blue eyes and said, "Not that I can think of, right now," which was only partially true. I didn't have any regrets, but I couldn't honestly say that buried under the full life I was leading weren't yet lurking some yearnings from those unfulfilled dreams.

CHAPTER FIVE
November 25, 1915

I woke that Thanksgiving morning planning to do what I always did, prepare the holiday feast for our family. I was due in less than a week and was as big as a barn and moving slow.

The traditional menu since Abraham Lincoln declared Thanksgiving a National holiday had always been headed up by a big fat roast turkey.

Benjamin Franklin had even tried to make the wild turkey our national bird but it lost by one vote to the eagle.

Turkeys on Sunny Slope Farm were more than a symbol of Thanksgiving, they were a living hope of becoming this family's livelihood. That "Grand Idea" of Charles was still in its brooding stage as Grandma Katie and I readied for days to prepare, what we all called now, "A Wampler Turkey" for our meal.

"I put it in the oven at five this morning," said Grandma Katie as she bustled around the kitchen. "Doesn't it just smell dandy?"

"That smell actually woke me up, or maybe it was this baby rolling round in my belly," I said walking into the kitchen where she was not only fixing the side dishes for the meal, but breakfast for us as well.

"Must be a boy, this one," she smiled and patted my belly, "the way he's moving and kicking all the time. Now wouldn't that just tickle Charles?"

"It would," I said, secretly knowing I hoped for a boy myself this time. "I know he loves his girls, but a man always wants a son to carry on the name – I mean Owen, of course."

We both laughed, sharing the old family joke. Once again, I was thankful to be a part of this witty family and I seemed to be picking up the trait myself.

One by one the girls appeared in their flannel nightgowns. Toag was almost four, Libby, three and little Ruth was sixteen months and walking now. She still slept in a crib by the stove in the sitting room and crawled out on her own when she heard the others. What a brood!

"Muder," said Libby, coming over to me and looking at the floor beneath my dress, "you make piddle on floor like Rufie?"

I looked and suddenly realized that my water had broken.

"Oh my, girls," said Grandma Katie excitedly, throwing her dish towel over her shoulder, "Looks like we're about to birth another baby."

* * * *

"Mr. Wampler, you have a son, congratulations," announced Dr. Dyerle ceremoniously and smiling as he placed the newest Wampler in my arms. As with our other children, this child was born in the very room where his own father, as well as his brothers and sisters had been born.

"Thank you doctor," Charles said beaming, as I lay in our bed exhausted from another long, all-day labor. "We appreciate your coming out in the middle of the night."

"Not at all," replied Dr. Dyerle, packing up his things, "It's always a pleasure to bring another Wampler into the world."

Charles walked him to the door as I looked down at our new son. He was plump and healthy with brown hair and blue eyes like his father.

"Thank you Sadie," Charles said as he came back into the room, "Thank you." He kissed me on the cheek – as if I had anything to do with finally having a boy.

"Charles Weldon, not Owen, Wampler, Jr... Yes, Sadie?" he asked, knowing my answer.

"Of course, Charles, of course."

There was no big Thanksgiving meal that day around the dining room table. Grandma Katie made plates for the girls and they ate at the "children's table" on the back porch. U.U. came over and helped her keep them busy and out of the bedroom. From that day on, I would always associate Charles Weldon Wampler Jr. with the odor of a turkey roasting in the oven and Thanksgiving would be a double celebration.

CHAPTER SIX

June, 1916

In the months after Charles Jr. was born that Thanksgiving day, we were up and down. The turkey business was at a stand–still so Charles got involved in the Duroc hog business. As with everything he did, he went, pardon the pun, hog wild. He was part of the State Duroc Association and went to all manner of meetings throughout Virginia.

The turkeys were left almost entirely to me. Grandma Katie's health was failing and she was hardly able to do anything outside anymore. I set out the eggs in the incubator and hoped and prayed they'd hatch. I had gathered them from the hen's nests and put out seventy–five just today.

In addition to the Duroc Association, Charles was on the road working his county agent job and still working with the farmers to grow and sell goods for the war effort. He had bought a used Ford that I do believe he loved as much as any horse he had ever owned. It provided him with quicker transportation for all of his travels and I had hoped that this would result in his having more free time to be at home. Unfortunately that didn't turn out to be the case – instead, he used it as an opportunity to be gone even more. I began to resent his absence and planned to talk with him about it. I knew it was important to choose the right time to broach the subject—Charles' moods fluctuated from his immediately being open to what I said, or closing down completely when there was a conflict. He rarely raised his voice or argued with me about anything because he knew I could often bring him around to my way of thinking. Our communication with each other was not what I had hoped it would be and I felt it was important to address the issue before it got worse. As it turned out, I should have found the time before someone else beat me to it.

In June of 1916, Robert graduated from Bridgewater College. I went to the ceremony on that Saturday afternoon with Papa. As I watched my brother receive his degree, I felt such a sense of pride in "My Robert." In the class history portion of the program were written these words, "Our president is a born leader. He was elected to that office four years ago by receiving the lucky straw and has held that position successfully ever since that time. He also takes great interest in all kinds of religious work. He has been President of the Y.M.C.A. for the past three years, and is now looking forward to the time when he will be elected to the ministry. Bob is known and loved by all." I pointed this out to Papa, who patted my hand and said with a knowing smile, "We all make sacrifices don't we Sadie?"

President John Samuel Flory challenged the Class of 1916 with these words: "Use your powers in the service of God and humanity. Live for others, and, in so doing, make your own lives the truest, the noblest, the most useful. In the altruistic spirit of the twentieth century you will wish to have a large share. And in your unselfish service you will reflect credit upon yourselves and your Alma Mater."

My eyes stung with tears of both joy on this festive occasion as well as the irony that though I had tried my best to live the kind of life of which he spoke, I would never have those words spoken at my graduation. I noted as he sat down that my feelings about John Flory seemed to have settled into a comfortable place. He was someone who had been an inspiration to me and especially to Robert along the way. I was grateful to him and cherished the years when we had been in contact. I told myself that I no longer needed from him whatever it was that so captivated me years ago. That's what I told myself.

Charles hadn't wanted to go and stayed home to work in his office. My new help, Beulah Miller, was there with the four children. She attended school but was good help when she could be here. My sewing was piling up and I didn't even try keeping the house clean, but Charles didn't seem to mind. A tidy house was not high on his list of priorities.

I had invited Papa, Robert and Amy over for supper after the graduation. I had considered asking John Flory to come as well but decided against it. The dining room table would already be crowded and I certainly couldn't have accommodated his whole family. I still received regular periodicals from Bridgewater and kept up with his comings and goings through them. He and his wife Vinnie now had five children, very close in age to our four. Their youngest was about the same age as Charles Jr. John, like Charles, traveled quite a lot, promoting his books and preaching here and there so with his work at the college and our busy schedule, we hadn't seen them at all since we had been married. I thought of his wife, Vinnie, who was in the same situation as I, yet was a college educated woman. I wondered how she felt about that – I wondered how he felt about it. If Charles agreed it was a good idea, perhaps we could have the two of them for supper one night when Pearl and Arthur followed through on their promise to visit us – that might prove to be an interesting family get–together.

Beulah had been there all the day before so everything was ready when we arrived home. There was a great ruckus as the children greeted their Grandpapa and their Uncle Bob. Papa rarely visited us but the girls always remembered him because he sang with them around the harmonium. He alternated living with Lizzie and Edgar and much of the time was on the road in his horse and wagon, traveling far and wide and continuing to promote The Harmonia Sacra. At seventy–three he was still active and healthy.

I knocked on the closed door to Charles' office. I was certain he had not ventured out since I had been gone. He came to the door, sleepy–eyed, "Guess I must have dozed off—sounds like a war zone out there," he said grumpily. I gave him my "look" and he adjusted his clothing and his attitude as he went to greet our guests.

I had asked Charles before I left to please refrain from bringing up the subject of the war. "Well I won't if he doesn't," he said with a certain edge to his voice. I sometimes wondered if he were a little jealous of my close relationship with my brother.

Yesterday I had baked a ham we brought in from the smokehouse. We had butchered one of the Duroc hogs the fall before. I had also put together the scalloped potatoes so all Beulah would have to do was run them in the oven. Fresh spinach from the early garden provided our green vegetable and there was a large bowl of applesauce we had canned last year. I had bought rolls at the store since I had no time to make them. I so missed the outside oven in the yard in Broadway where we baked bread each Saturday.

The talk over the meal was congenial and, true to his word, Charles didn't bring up anything about the war. He asked Robert about the graduation and what he would be doing next.

"I applied in February of this year for a scholarship at Vanderbilt," Robert answered, buttering his roll. "They have a graduate program there to train students for ministry and mission work and have accepted me for the summer session. I'll be leaving in a few weeks." I noticed the reserve in his voice. He was very respectful but there was something about the way he approached Charles that was odd.

"I suppose," said Charles, continuing to keep the conversation light "that means you two will be getting married before you go."

"Oh, heavens no," piped up Amy in her cherry voice. "I'm not going with him to Nashville. I graduated a year ago and have continued with my teaching job at Milo School in Morgan County. We'll keep corresponding by letter like we've done while he was still at Bridgewater."

"That sounds like Sadie and me the year we were courting," he said, smiling warmly at me from the other end of the table. "I couldn't wait for the mail to come to see if I had a letter from her. With my spelling it's a wonder she ever agreed to marry this old farmer."

"Sister Pearl saved you on that score," I said, laughing, relieved that the conversation was keeping to a friendly family banter. Now this was the Charles I married, cordial and a perfect host. I relaxed feeling that today's visit would go just fine after all.

"Take a little advice from me, Bob," Charles said with a wink and a smile, "you better corral that pretty filly while you have a chance." He nodded Amy's way. "She might decide that she'd rather be a school teacher than settle down with a missionary."

I had watched Robert throughout this entire conversation and could feel he was coming to a boiling point. He had ducked his head and on his face was a look of disapproval, but he had held his tongue. This last statement was just too much for him and he said in a quiet voice with an undercurrent of anger, "Amy is more than someone who settles for something or someone in life. She is her own woman and has her own dreams for herself. Our plans for a life together include both of our dreams and goals, not just mine. Every man owes that to his partner." He glared at Charles.

Charles looked like he had been slapped across the face. The table grew silent and nobody moved. Even the children knew something was going on and stopped eating. Papa cleared his throat, nervously as he had done years ago at the table when Charles had taken up for me with the visiting pastor. Robert had been there that day. And he had been there another day, another place, regarding this particular subject. A sudden awareness came over me about Robert's attitude toward Charles since Morven Park. He had certainly heard Charles and my discussion as he stood outside on the porch of our house. He had been observing what was happening with my life since then and he was not happy with what he saw. The implications of his words were clear, "You are not respecting my sister and I have noticed."

Charles had developed two modes of discussion when the subject was sensitive or contentious. He had been well-schooled in the art of debate in which he took a stance, stuck to it and was not expected to compromise or change his view. The other was something fairly new – he would withdraw into silence, thus abruptly ending the discussion. For this particular situation, he chose the latter for which I was grateful.

"Well, now, how about some dessert?" chimed in Grandma Katie, jumping up from the table – and thus the silence was broken and at least some civility restored.

I suppose in some way I can thank Robert for his youthful outburst at the table on graduation day. As much as I loved my brother and respected his opinions, I felt he was out of order in what he had said to Charles and I told him so. But on some level what he said had penetrated Charles' consciousness and we finally had that conversation about what was going on between us. I was able to tell him the toll it was taking on me and the children that he was gone so much and he promised to try to curtail some of his travels. Whatever I could say about Charles Wampler, I knew he loved me, I knew he loved his children and if pressed to a certain point, he could admit he was in error and would try to rectify the situation. His intentions were noble and sincere and for a while things were indeed better. Then in the fall of 1916 he was asked to be emergency County Agent for Page County. He drove his two–seater Ford over the Luray Mountain every Monday, worked through Saturday, came home exhausted late that evening and left again on Monday morning. The children called his overalls his "Sunday Clothes."

CHAPTER SEVEN
1917–1918

Pearl had been only half–kidding when she said to me on the phone soon after Charles Jr. was born, "Well, seems to me that brother of mine drops by Sunny Slope just long enough to get you with child." When I didn't get pregnant for almost two years after that while Charles gallivanted the state in his Ford motor car, I decided she had been just about right.

The break gave my tired body a chance to strengthen and gave me an opportunity to do a few things for myself, even with the four children. Grandma Katie's health continued to deteriorate, but I still had good help with Beulah. I found more time to read and began practicing the harmonium again. Our new telephone gave me opportunity to talk to Pearl at least once a week, and even though we continued to correspond by mail, hearing her cherry voice was balm to what could have been a lonesome time.

The United States finally entered World War I in April of 1917 after President Wilson came under great pressure from a strong Anglo–American lobby. Unrestricted submarine warfare and German's diplomatic maneuvers with

Mexico prompted him to change his mind and break his campaign promise.

Robert was not exempted from the draft as he was a theological student rather than a ministerial student. He continued his efforts in promoting peace and non–combatant service to the military. His college work with the Y.M.C.A led him to a position as national Y.M.C.A Secretary and after a training period he was assigned to a huge Marine base at Paris Island, South Carolina. There he worked to boost the morale of the men who were being trained to kill and die in the war. The irony of this would strengthen his resolve to fight for peace. Amy remained in Virginia teaching school until August of 1918 when they were married. She went with Robert for a short time to Paris Island but the limited housing for dependents led her to the decision to return to Frederick, Maryland where they had been married in her home Church of the Brethren. She resumed her teaching career and the first year or so of their marriage they would remain apart. This seemed very strange to me but a new generation had their own ideas that seemed to work for them. It gave me pause to reflect on my own situation. I decided that perhaps I could be a little more understanding of Charles' absence—after all, in his own way he was also serving his country.

* * * *

God has a way of using a particular situation to teach his creatures what they have perhaps been too blind or in my case, too busy to see. Thus did God give me back my purpose.

I had become weary of feeling sorry for myself concerning my choices in life, particularly those associated with my education or lack thereof. With more time to read and reflect on life as it was, I recalled what John Flory had told me after my mother's death when I dropped out of college. "Your education needn't stop just because you are not in school," or something to that effect.

I was now thirty–five years old and the mother of four wonderful children under the age of seven for whom I was their world and their guide. Toag, now seven, had begun school in Dayton a year ago and was smart as a whip. Libby was five and could already read. Ruth was four and Charles Jr., who we now called "Buster," was three. I read to them constantly and taught them hymns and children's nursery songs. They were all quite musical and could memorize verse after verse easily. I began to revel in my role as teacher, because that, I suddenly realized, was what I was – and much more.

I returned to reading the book of prose and poetry, "Mother, Home and Heaven," that Pearl had given me. I poured over the section called "Mother." Passage after passage was dedicated to the vital importance of a role I had somehow thought of as secondary, as if it had happened to me, rather than something I had chosen.

One evening after everyone had gone to bed, I sat in the upstairs hall outside the children's rooms at my favorite reading and writing post. In the bedroom to my right slept Toag and Libby in single brass beds covered with colorful quilts made by Mama and Lizzie years ago on the farm. To the left and down the hall, in a small pine bed, surrounded by her rag dollies Grandma Katie had made for her, dozed Ruth. In the back bedroom at the top of the kitchen staircase slept Buster nestled in a feather mattress on the floor. I had checked each one of them to make sure all was well and just to watch them sleep.

For some reason I turned to the Introduction by the complier of the volume, Rev. Theodore L. Cuyler. He wrote: "If I were asked to name any one principle that seems to have an almost universal application, it would be this one – show me the mother and I will show you the man! Next to the sovereign grace of God, the influence of a mother's teachings and example is the most effective in molding character and shaping destiny. Intellectual power even descends most commonly on the maternal side. Nearly all the most remarkable men have had mothers of more than ordinary mental caliber. Great men often have weak children; great women seldom have."

CHAPTER EIGHT
Fall, 1919

My break from having children ended in May of 1918 when Edna Frances was born. I had had an uneventful pregnancy and because I was much stronger physically and bounced back after she was born. With my new sense of purpose I was enjoying my life.

Sadly, in June of this year, Grandma Katie died at the age of seventy–one. I had known her death was coming, but I wasn't prepared for the emotional loss I felt when she was actually gone. For almost ten years, we had shared the duties of Sunny Slope Farm. She had been present at the births of our children and loved each of them unconditionally. She sewed and cooked for them and made toys we couldn't afford to buy. In the past two years, she had been my companion while her son traveled, leaving us all at home. She never complained and was always quick with the Wampler wit to lighten any situation. Her absence would leave a tremendous void for all of us.

Pearl and Arthur's promise to visit hadn't happened last year as we hoped. Every time they planned to come, Charles was away and then Pearl became pregnant with their first child. Pearl Catherine was born in May which prevented them from even coming to Grandma Katie's funeral.

* * * *

In the fall of 1919 Charles called me into his office. I could tell by the tone of his voice that he was upset about something.

"Just a minute, Charles, let me make sure Edna is occupied and not into anything," I answered, looking around for our youngest child, now eighteen months old and into absolutely everything.

"I think that child has reached a critical time in her life when she needs to learn to obey," barked Charles, in his most authoritarian voice. With his being away so much, when he was home, I think he felt obligated to state his views on child rearing which I mostly ignored. Though his mother was pretty relaxed in her approach to the children, Charles' father, John, had modeled a sterner attitude.

"She's just a curious child and that's a good thing," I replied as I pried a piece of coal she had just taken from the coal bucket out of her dirty little hand. "Here Edna, let Mother wash your hands and you go on the back porch with Ruth."

I guided her to the narrow enclosed back porch where Ruth and Buster were arguing about who was going to stir the pot of blueberries.

"Buster grabbed the spoon right out of my hand. I'm the cook, I'm the stirrer," said an irate Ruth.

"You always think you're boss," countered Buster. "I quit – Charles Weldon Buster Jack Wampler Jr. is going to be a farmer like my daddy. Who needs sissy old cooking anyways?" Unlike his sisters before him, he had learned to talk early, plainly and in complete sentences. He knew his mind and could articulate exactly what he wanted. I could already see him as a public speaker or a politician.

I watched his chubby frame as he stomped manfully out the back door. He was getting so pudgy that when Charles took him to town he had to get a ten–year–old size overall to go around him.

"Sadie, will you get in here right now – this is important," Charles yelled impatiently.

"I'm coming," I said, feeling a tug of resentment at being pulled in every direction.

I walked into the office and sat down. Charles was frowning and pouring over the farm ledger.

"We're going to have to make a decision about Sunny Slope," he looked up and began, matter–of–factly.

"What about it?" I said, knowing already that the farm had been divided up between Charles and his brothers and sisters when Grandma Katie died. His brothers, Fred and Joe had taken the back part with buildings towards Silver

Lake and Charles and his sisters, Mary and Pearl had gotten the front part with the big bank barn and other out buildings.

"Mary and Pearl want me to buy them out but I don't have the money, and I don't want to borrow what that would take to do," he stated, and I could tell he was making a case for something I was not going to like.

"But you do want to keep the farm, don't you?" I said, getting a little nervous about the way this was going.

"I'm not even real sure I do. Maybe I'll just quit farming for a few years and land will be cheaper," he continued, not meeting my eye. "The Ella Wenger place sold for $10,500 to Mr. Sam Heltzel from near Sangerville. He has nine children, and I hear he has his eye on this farm. He offered $30,000 for his farm," he said, talking faster and faster as if to get it all out as quickly as he could. When he stopped, he finally looked at me hopefully, knowing what a shock this must be.

"But what would you do, where would we go?" I said, the weight of what he was proposing sinking into my whole being.

"You know me, Sadie, I'm always finding new work somewhere," he said trying to be positive and seeing I was beginning to panic. "We could take the money from selling the farm and get a smaller place and…"

"Smaller place, SMALLER, Charles," I said shrilly, losing all of my composure. I rung my hands and looked out the office door at the living room. "We hardly have room for the family we have now!"

Charles' face relaxed into a slight smile trying to calm me down, reversing our usual roles. "There's always a way, Sadie, you know I'll take care and provide for you and the kids—haven't I always? Now don't you worry, things are going to work out just fine," he stated with confidence and somehow, he managed to make me believe him.

"I know Charles, thank you for letting me in on what's going on," I said, taking a deep breath and calming myself, "Now I need to go check on the children."

When I went into the kitchen, Edna had just finished stuffing Pearl's last letter into the molasses jar!

CHAPTER NINE
November, 1920

T he war in Europe had ended and on June 28, 1919 the Treaty of Versailles was signed. However, the battles I would face in the next few years were only beginning.

First was the matter of the farm. Charles had made the difficult decision to put Sunny Slope up for sale. I knew that for him this was as much an emotional decision as it had been for Papa when he sold our place in Broadway. Both of our families' history had been tied up with the land and homes which then sadly became merely business transactions. I wondered what Grandma Katie would have said about it. I tried to be positive and supportive and keep both our spirits up but I wasn't succeeding very well. Writing and talking every once in a while with Pearl was some consolation. I had had to cut down on my calls to her since York was long distance and expensive. I went to the front room and sat down in the stuffed chair beside the fireplace.

November 24, 1920

Dear Pearl,

They say the circus people are asked most, 'where do you go from here?' and that sure has been put at us. We do not know. It all depends on what Charles does. The Bridgewater College teaching job alone does not pay enough, or not as much at least as the demonstration job. I don't think Chas. likes it quite as well altho' I think things are going along well. He hears occasionally that they are pleased with his work. I think when he could count off his car expenses he would have about as much at the end of the year but I don't think he likes the idea of being home so much.

I paused suddenly realizing what I had just confided in Pearl. The implications and the irony of my ramblings did not escape me. Bridgewater College had hired Charles to teach agriculture there, even though he not only had no graduate degree, but no college degree. I was fairly sure no woman would have ever been allowed to do such a thing.

Then there was the disturbing realization that Charles would rather be traveling than being at home with me and our now, six children. Margaret had been born in October of 1920 and though Cora had come back to fill in when Beulah couldn't be here, I felt overwhelmed. I hadn't realized how much I depended on Grandma Katie for both her help but her emotional support and wit. The chaos that ensued after Margaret was born drove Charles, when he was home, into his office more and more. My own father had not been that much involved with the day to day care of my siblings and me, but his very presence and emotional support around our home gave me a firm sense of security. Now, my security and the security of family was being threatened and Charles seemed to be withdrawing from us on a daily basis.

And there was another issue that I didn't want to acknowledge to myself or anyone else: after Margaret's birth a month ago, I had noticed pains in my abdomen that I hadn't experienced with any of my other pregnancies. I didn't want to bother Dr. Dyerle, not to mention that we certainly couldn't afford any more medical bills. I knew part of it was my workload and the pressure of the farm situation but my intuition told me it was more than this. And then my mind reluctantly drifted to Mama and the problems that had led to her death. She had had six pregnancies before the age of forty and was forty–four when Mary Ruth was born.

Just then I heard Margaret cry from our bedroom where she slept in the cradle all of us had used in the Broadway house. Before I could sink too deeply into the implications of Mama's and my similar history, I decided to just put it aside for the present. I had too much to do to think about it.

"I'm coming, honey, I'm coming," I said getting up from my chair wearily. "There, there, Margaret, you're going to get fed," I said, sitting down in the rocker and loosened the top of my dress to nurse her.

When I looked around, I saw the shadow of a little girl standing in the doorway with a pouting expression on her face.

"Why do we still have Cora's baby?" demanded Edna, who associated Cora's return with the arrival of what she considered to be her replacement. "We needs to give her back real soon—I wants to be the baby."

"Edna, I need you to be the big sister and help mother take care of little Margaret," I said trying to soothe her insecurity.

She stomped out of the room yelling, "I not big – I yittle – too many babies!"

Well, I did have to agree with her on that one

I finished nursing Margaret and laid her back in the cradle. I walked into the kitchen, looking at the gold watch round my neck that Mama and Papa had given me for graduation from high school. Charles would be home sometime today since Bridgewater was closed for the Thanksgiving holiday weekend.

I had Albert kill an old tom turkey, and it was stuffed and ready to go in the oven bright and early tomorrow morning. It would probably be tough as leather but that wouldn't keep it from smelling good as it baked. The garden and the orchard had done well last season so I had put up plenty of vegetables and fruit to bring up from the basement shelves. I had made certain the boards were strong and solid, remembering the disaster in Broadway that day. We would have a feast in spite of everything.

"Mother," I heard Buster cry as he came bounding through the back door onto the porch, "Libby says that I'm not getting anything for my birthday because we're poor – are we poor, Mother?"

"No my darling boy, we're rich, we're very rich. Libby is just teasing you. You are going to have a wonderful birthday. Only special boys are born on Thanksgiving Day."

CHAPTER TEN

June, 1921

B y the first of the next year, we still hadn't sold the farm. We had hoped when we put on the big livestock sale last September that it would show well, but the lane was so muddy from the constant rain we had to keep two wagons hauling men up from the Dayton Pike. All the cars that tried to get in got stuck so the crowd wasn't so much. Most everything went very cheaply although the cows brought more than expected. The two three–year–old colts brought $420 and we sold some old turkey hens for $2.00 each. The whole sale had earned only a little over $2000.

"Sadie, I just got off the phone with Pearl. She called and said she and Arthur wanted to come for a visit," said Charles coming into the living room from his office. He had finished up his year teaching at Bridgewater College last month and resumed his job as Rockingham County Agent. This was a rare day at home.

"That sounds wonderful, Charles," I said as I wiped the sweat from my face with my apron. I had been canning green beans all day and was hot and tired. Toag and Libby were old enough to actually help a little – Ruth and Edna were not, but wanted to be, so were just a plain nuisance. I had stopped nursing Margaret when my milk dried up and was giving her cow's milk which upset her stomach. She cried all night with colic so I was getting little rest. This news was a balm for my soul.

"What in the world prompted this?" I asked, not really caring why they had decided to come. "We haven't gotten together for years."

"Not really sure about that, but she hinted it may have something to do with the farm," he said hopefully, and I knew what he was thinking.

"When do they plan to come?" I said excitedly, already planning meals and activities. The tiredness just seemed to melt away with the prospect of my dear Pearl being close enough to touch. I had so much to discuss with her.

"Well, she'll be done teaching in a few weeks, so they can come pretty much any time it suits us. I figure the sooner the better, how about you?" he answered with an enthusiasm I hadn't heard from him in a long time.

I suddenly remembered what I had wanted to do the last time they had planned to come around the time of Robert's graduation.

"Charles, what would you think of asking John Flory and his wife over for supper while Pearl and Arthur are here?" I began cautiously. "John retired from Bridgewater and is doing a lot of research and writing. He is your and Pearl's first cousin and Pearl has told me she keeps up with the books he's published about the history of the Brethren.

I've never even met his wife and they have five children now and…" I stopped myself, realizing that I was talking faster and faster to make my case. Charles was looking at me with an expression I couldn't quite interpret.

"Well, I guess that would be alright," he said slowly, running his hand through his thinning hair. "You know he and I haven't been particularly close and we don't see eye to eye on a lot of religious issues, but I know he meant a lot to you and Robert growing up—why not?" he declared, pleased with himself for being so magnanimous.

"Thank you so much Charles," I said feeling lighter than I had for months. "Why don't you give a call to Pearl and set up a time. Anything is good for me."

* * * *

Pearl and Arthur had arrived on Friday about noon the second weekend in June. Charles had made arrangements to be home for their entire visit. It did not escape me that when Charles really wanted to be home, he could somehow work it out. I let the thought pass. This was too joyous an occasion to spoil with petty grievances.

"You look so much like your mother," I said to Pearl as she bounded spryly through the front door. She was still pretty and a little plump, carrying some of the weight she gained with their first child. Two–year–old Pearl Catherine was in her father's arms, an adorable mini–version of her mother.

Toag, Libby, Ruth and Buster rushed into the room to meet their new first cousin. Edna, who was still put out about Margaret usurping her position as baby, hung back, suspicious of yet another little girl in the house. The older girls took over Pearl Catherine and went to the back porch where, no doubt, the pie–making would commence.

"Why don't we go somewhere where we can sit down and talk," said Arthur with a slight smile. He still towered over Pearl and had remained handsome but his dark hair was beginning to grey some.

"How about the dining room table," Charles said with anticipation in his voice. "Sadie maybe you and Pearl could boil up a cup of your famous tea."

Glad to have Pearl to myself, we walked into the kitchen. As soon as we stepped into the room, Pearl pulled me into a big hug, which I gratefully returned.

"Oh, Pearl, how I have missed you," I said, holding back my tears. "It's been way too long."

She held me for a moment and then pulled back looking at me strangely. "Sadie, is something wrong, you don't look well? Your color isn't good and you've lost some weight."

"Just running after six kids will do that to a body," I said lightly, vowing not to share my concerns. I would not spoil this visit talking about something that was probably nothing anyway. "I'm fine, just tired, that's all."

I could see she knew I was not telling her everything—she knew me too well, but she also let it go.

We joined the men at the table with steaming cups of chamomile tea made from the plants out back. As we sat down Arthur cleared his throat and began, "Do you want to tell them, Pearl?"

"I think I'd like to if you don't mind," she said, with a mischievous grin.

"I'll get right to the point," she said in her right-to-the-point voice, "Arthur and I would like to take a note for my share of Sunny Slope. That way you could probably get together enough money to buy out Mary's share and the farm would be yours." She paused and gave Charles the dearest look. "As it should be."

Charles jaw dropped with surprise and then his face lit up like a Christmas tree.

"And don't worry about paying us back," added Arthur, indicating that he was a full partner in this particular deal.

After Charles recovered from his initial shock, he sputtered, "Are you two sure? And of course we'll pay you back in full – oh Pearl, Arthur, this is just so generous of you – Sadie, can you believe it?" He suddenly realized that he was rambling and stopped a moment, breathed and said, "Thank you, Pearl, Arthur. You have no idea what this means to Sadie and me."

I smiled at him from my end of the table feeling relief all the way down to my very tired bones.

* * * *

Pearl and I spent the day catching up and herding children while Charles gave Arthur a tour of the turkey "business." She was full of stories about her work with the women's suffrage movement.

"And you know what, Sadie, last November I was the first woman to vote in York County, Virginia," she said with excitement.

"That's just wonderful, Pearl. I'm so proud of you," I said thinking, *I didn't even know there was an election last November.*

"By the way," I said, "I've asked your cousin John Flory over for supper with us this evening," I said, suddenly realizing I hadn't told her yet. "We haven't seen him for years and you know how Charles is about him – thought you'd make a good buffer!"

"My dear brother, God love him, can be such a poop sometimes," she said with sisterly affection. "That's wonderful Sadie, I haven't seen him either and I'd love hearing what he's doing since he retired from Bridgewater. He's got a big family now doesn't he?"

"Yes, he and Vinnie have five children about our kid's age. She can't come tonight because a couple of them have chicken pox," I said, knowing I was not disappointed at that particular fact. "I really would have loved it if Robert could have been here but he and Amy are at Brethren Headquarters in Elgin, Illinois now – you know he was asked to be Secretary of Home Missions there."

"I think that young man is destined for great things. I know how proud you must be of him, Sadie," she said getting up from her chair a starting toward the kitchen. "Don't we need to be putting together some supper?"

The day had gotten away from me – it was almost four o'clock. "We do indeed," I said grimacing as I stood up. Pearl saw me and frowned but didn't say anything. "I've got Cora coming over to feed the kids early and keep them occupied while we eat and visit. You remember her don't you?"

"She's the one that got kicked by the horse and was out for a while, right?" she said remembering a letter I had written about the incident.

"That's the one. The children said she's been a lot crankier since she got kicked in the head." I laughed as we went into the kitchen to get together a light supper of fried chicken I had already prepared and a variety of summer vegetables.

* * * *

"Good evening, John, it's certainly good to see you after such a long time," I heard Charles greet our guest in the front hall.

"Good evening, Cousin Charles, I appreciate your invitation and am looking forward to catching up with you and your family," his still sonorous voice drifted into the kitchen where Pearl and I were finishing up. I had mentally prepared for this moment ever since I had come up with the idea in the first place but I was nervous and wasn't quite sure why. I needn't have worried as John came strolling into the kitchen just as he had done so many years ago in Broadway, picked up a chicken wing off the plate, took a bite and said, "Well, Sadie, I see you haven't lost that Zigler touch!"

And so it came to pass that Charles Weldon and Sadie Zigler Wampler, Pearl and Arthur Showalter and John Samuel Flory gathered around the dining room table on a warm June evening for a family supper and fellowship.

The conversation was spirited, varied, and congenial, moving from family to religion to politics and back around again. Everyone participated and no one dominated the interchange.

Pearl gave us a detailed account of the day she was the first woman to vote in York County. After a long fight that began to gain strength in the 1840's, women in Virginia had finally gained the right to cast a ballot in August of 1920 when the Nineteenth Amendment was added to the Constitution.

"I marched right past all those men and went into the voting booth and marked my ballot. I felt like Susan B. Anthony!" she proclaimed, standing up from her chair and raising her fist in the air.

We all cheered her success, although Charles seemed a little embarrassed at his sister's overt boasting.

When I asked John about his contact with Robert, he said, "Robert really wanted to be a missionary to China. He thought that it was his calling but many of us who knew him and his particular gifts were not so sure." He smiled, a little guiltily, and added, "And I may have had something to do with him not being approved right away. I felt that his skills in public speaking and preaching were weak."

I was surprised at this admission as John had always been such a staunch supporter of Robert in all his efforts. Yet, if there was anything I knew about John Flory it was he could be brutally honest.

"As it turned out, he did finally get a position and was all ready to go to China," he continued almost as a justification of his actions, "when Amy got the measles. I truly believe he's right where he is needed."

Charles caught everyone up on the turkey experiments. "Did you notice the little frame houses being built on the right side of the lane coming in?" he said excitedly.

Everyone affirmed that they had.

"In these houses we will put the newly hatched turkey chicks under lights. They've done that for a long time with chickens and it keeps them safe from predators and bad weather," he explained, getting more and more animated. "And daughter Ruth is beginning to get really interested in helping with the project," he said proudly. He looked at me and grinned, "And if Sadie calls me the Turkey King, I suppose that would mean Ruth might be a turkey princess some day!"

Everyone chimed in their approval and congratulated Charles on his success and wished him well in his further efforts.

Arthur filled us in on his work with the York County education system and his fight for women teachers in the schools. "The bureaucrats still have a firm grip on the system and the bureaucrats are all men," he explained as he looked at Pearl who was making a face. "They are scared to death of all that's going on with women's rights – threatens the heck out of them."

Throughout the banter, I responded, I questioned and only had a little twinge of envy that I seemed to have nothing exciting to add. My life was good and I was content with it, but in comparison to the people around that table…

Cora came in to announce that her time was up and she needed to go home. "I really don't know how you do it alone, Sadie," she said, shaking her head.

"Thank you, Cora," I replied brushing off her observation, "I so appreciate your making it possible for us to have this adult time. When will I see you again?"

"I'll have to recover from today first," she said whining and rubbing her forehead. "I have a terrible headache." She walked to the front door as Buster, Ruth and Toag with Pearl Catherine in tow, came bounding into the dining room.

With chaos again replacing our adult time, everyone began getting up from the table.

"Well, it's about time I get back to my family," said John and I realized that he hadn't told us much about them during the evening's conversation. "Jane and Margaret both have chicken pox and Vinnie is a little overwhelmed," he said, glancing my way.

Pearl and Arthur said their goodbyes and started clearing the table. Charles and I walked John to the front door.

"Enjoyed seeing you again and catching up, John," said Charles, shaking his hand. With that, he ducked quickly into his office leaving me on the porch alone with John.

There was a long pause and John turned to me and took my hand gently.

"Whatever it is, Sadie," he said looking deeply into my eyes, "please find someone to talk to about it."

He dropped my hand and his gaze and as he started down the front porch steps he said, "And this time, this time I'm sorry, but it can't be me."

And there it was again. This man, who had always known me better than I knew myself, had seen into my soul. What was I to do with the realization that the love I had for this man defied explanation? The love I had for Charles was just as real but different. I was learning that love is a very complicated thing.

CHAPTER ELEVEN
Sunday, August 7, 1921

I t was Sunday evening and I was hiding in the bedroom while Beulah was here to take care of the kids. I put down the novel I'd been reading since yesterday and decided to write a letter to Pearl. I was still reveling in the joy of their visit last June.

August 7, 1921

Dear Pearl,

I guess I won't wait quite so long as you did to write. I thought I was going to write this morning but Beulah sent me "The Re-Creation of Brian Kent" and I didn't do anything but read today. Chas. has been at Blacksburg since last Wed. and this has been a long old Sunday. Joe's and Fred's were here about an hour yesterday evening. Fred's had not been out here since New Year's.

The children walked to S.S. this morning and they were pretty good and tired when they got home. Toag spent last week at Joe's and Mary's. Libby is going this week. This gives me some relief although the older girls help out a lot with the little ones and do I miss that.

Margaret is cutting two teeth and has not been quite so gay for a few days. She has eight now.

I lifted my pen from the paper and debated whether to tell Pearl more about how I'd been feeling lately. I decided not to do it – not yet. I considered what John Flory said about talking with someone but I was just not ready. I have an appointment with Dr. Dyerle in November and until I know a little more I won't tell anyone, even Pearl.

I went back to my book, finishing up the last chapter. Immediately following, was a biographical sketch of Harold Bell Wright by Elsberry W. Reynolds. He began, "The biography of a man is of importance and interest to other men just to the degree that his life and work touches and influences the life of his time and the lives of individuals. Only in a feeble way, at best, can the life story of any man be told on the printed page. The story is better as it is written on the hearts of men and women and the man himself does the writing. He lives longest who lives best. He who carves deepest against corroding time is he who touches with surest hand the greatest number of human hearts."

I sat, pondering these words about writing, about life, about legacy. What would be my legacy? If the coming days and months didn't go well, perhaps I should begin writing a little about my life. I reached for the poetry book, *Mother, Home, and Heaven.* A piece of paper dropped out. On it, in my handwriting, were the words, "From lonely silence, from rich quiet, Words rise from our hearts to be shared..."

* * * *

"Mrs. Wampler, I'm not really sure what's wrong with you other than the fact that, from what you've told me, you are probably suffering from complete exhaustion rearing six children practically alone and doing farm chores in addition to that," said Dr. Dyerle, scribbling notes on a piece of paper. He had been my physician and had delivered several of the children, but I couldn't remember ever actually being in his office – if I felt badly, I took care of it myself.

He sat in a swivel chair behind a large walnut desk piled high with papers that he was fiddling with—the walls were lined with shelves and shelves of medical books—had he ever read all of them, I wondered?

"Well, there is that," I said, wearily, checking to make sure I was properly put together after his thorough exam.

"Any chance you could slow down a little? Do you have any help at home now?" he asked, already knowing the answer.

"A little now and then, but in recent years it's been pretty sparse," I replied, realizing how little help I had had lately. Both Cora and Beulah were unavailable most of the time with other jobs and, to be honest, our finances were still such that I couldn't offer much for someone to come and take care of six children.

"Well, I can give you something for the pain and the constipation, but you're going to have to take better care of yourself for a while. What about Mr. Wampler – can he help you out a little more?" he asked hopefully.

I felt myself stiffen at the mention of Charles. After the worry of losing the farm was ended, he went right back to being gone all of the time. The doctor fidgeted as he waited for my answer.

"Not really," I said finally, "I'll just try to slow down as much as I can. I sure wish my mother was still around – she had a cabinet full of herbal medicines that could cure most anything."

"Speaking of your mother, how did she die? "he asked, looking again at my chart.

"She had tumors of some kind that were removed surgically. They kept coming back and she finally died at home," I said, and something about saying this out loud made my stomach churn uncomfortably.

"Hmm," he said with more concern than before. "We'll need to watch this closely. Come back to see me after Christmas and we'll see how you're doing. Maybe I'll do a few tests. In the meantime, try to get some rest. Call me if anything changes, all right?"

"Of course, thank you for seeing me – I'll try my best," knowing there would be little change for me.

As I was leaving the doctor's office, I caught sight of myself in the waiting room mirror. The woman I saw there was hardly recognizable to me. This woman's face was not full and rosy with health and vigor, but had cheeks that were pale and sunken in. The blue cotton dress she wore hung loosely over a frail body. No longer full–breasted and hippy, this woman of forty appeared much older. And most of all, I observed that this woman who looked back at me from the mirror looked terrified.

S.J.W.

CHAPTER TWELVE
December 15, 1921

I sat on the landing in the upstairs hallway with my pen and paper ready to write Pearl. It was early morning – Charles was away, and the children were still asleep. I watched as the sun rose over Massenutten Peak. The view was better this time of year with the leaves gone from the trees out front. The sun had moved to its winter post down the mountain range to the south. The clouds in the bright blue sky magnified the gold rays of the sun, changing colors each second as it made its way into the morning sky.

There it comes! Over the ridge, steady and bright, promising a new day ahead.

The floor was cold on the wide pine boards under my stocking feet – the thermometer outside the window said twenty–one degrees but it felt colder with the wind whipping around the house.

As I began to write, I wondered how many sunrises I'd yet to see on Sunny Slope Farm. I said a little prayer before I began writing, "Dear God, help me through whatever this is."

I looked again out the window at the comforting view. I remembered the first time I toured this house with Grandma Katie, Charles and Pearl standing in this very spot. It seems so long ago, yet it could have been yesterday.

I needed badly to see my soul sister, Pearl. She and Arthur had surprised us when they let us know they were planning to make a return visit over this Christmas. I had not told her of my visit to the doctor and I wondered if somehow she had picked up on my situation and wanted to check on me in person. It would be just like Pearl. I had decided she needed to know and I needed her to know. I hadn't told Charles or the children anything and Charles hadn't even noticed the changes in my body. He was gone so often and things were going very well for him. I tried not to resent his absorption and pleasure in his work. With the weight of the farm sale off his mind, he seemed to be even more absorbed in his work, both at home and on the road. He had struggled for so long to provide for us and all of his work was beginning to pay off. Even the turkey business was picking up and more and more people became interested in what he was proposing.

I knew I was worse, but tried to ignore my symptoms. I had been able to hire some help so was trying to rest more but I knew I didn't look well at all.

* * * *

I heard the knock on the door that I had been anticipating all day.

"Whoo-Hoo," came the familiar voice from the hall-way, "Merry Christmas!"

I went through the dining room and sitting room where I saw Pearl and Arthur on the porch, laden down with gifts and little Pearl Catherine in tow.

She looked at me and as she hugged my frail frame she whispered in my ear, "Sadie, what on earth?"

"We'll talk later," I whispered back, feeling such relief that she was here.

The four older children clambered to the door, not knowing which to explore first, the presents or their first cousin.

"Come on, little Pearl," said Ruth, "Let's go out on the back porch and make some pies for Christmas Day."

Buster, the only boy in the crowd, was obviously not interested in making pies and went straight for the presents. "Which one is for me? Can I open it right now?"

"Later, Buster, after we eat," I said, "Why don't you and Uncle Arthur put the presents under the tree in the sit-ting room."

With everyone occupied, I turned to Pearl, "I need to tell you something before Charles gets home. Let's go up-stairs to Buster's bedroom."

We climbed the back stairs from the dining room to Buster's room at the top of the landing. His room, as usual, was a disaster.

"Have a seat over there," I said, pointing to a stuffed chair in the corner full of dirty clothes. She picked up the clothes and threw them ceremoniously on the floor.

I sat down on Buster's unmade bed.

Pearl waited while I caught my breath from climbing the stairs. In days past I could run up and down those stairs without missing a beat. Now I was completely winded.

"What is it, Sadie?" she asked, knowing she didn't want to hear what I was about to say.

"I think I'm really sick, Pearl – I think I may even…" I stopped, unable to utter the words.

"Oh, Sadie, no, no, please, you… Have you been to the doctor? What does he say? Why didn't you tell me?" she said her face turning white with panic and her voice cracking with emotion. She got up from her chair and came to where I was sitting. "Does Charles know anything? How could he not? Look at you; you're wasted away to nothing. Oh, dear God, I can't believe you didn't tell me. I…"

"Settle down Pearl, please," I said as calmly as I could manage, but feeling as panicked as she looked. "I need you to be calm and help me through this. You've been my rock since the day I met you at the Harmonia Sacra training sessions in Dayton." She sat down beside me on the bed as I continued, laying out what I would need from her. "You've got to help me and you have to help your brother. He will not do well with this. He's always felt that he was in control of his life and this is way beyond what he can control. I should have told him sooner, but I guess I hoped he would notice on his own and when he didn't, I felt hurt and angry."

"As well, you should be," she said with a frown. "Damn that brother of mine—as much as he adores you, he's too caught up in his own business to even take notice of what's right under his nose!"

Always ready to defend him, I said, "Now, don't be too hard on him, he's going to have enough to deal with when he finds out without both of us spreading a cloak of guilt over him. He is what he is and he's a good man. He'll need us both to get through what lies ahead."

"Well, alright, if you can be magnanimous, I guess I can too," she agreed, "Does the doctor...?

"You know as much as I know." I said, truthfully, already feeling better that someone else knew.

"When are you planning to tell Charles?" she asked, finally settling down.

"I thought we'd get through Christmas Day first. Let's not spoil the festivities. I'll tell him the next day while you and Arthur are still here for support – I'm so glad you're here, Pearl."

"As am I," she said as she walked over to the bed, took me in her arms, and we both wept.

* * * *

Christmas Day was a wild and wonderful one with seven children ripping open packages and screaming with delight.

Pearl and I put on our best festive faces and pretended there was nothing at all different from any other Christmas.

We began the morning with a huge country breakfast of scrambled eggs, Canadian bacon, and sausage patties made from the pigs on our farm. There were baking powder biscuits that were rolled out and cut by Toag with a round tin cutter. Libby and Ruth layered the scalloped oysters with butter, milk and saltine cracker crumbs. I had made smearcase, a Pennsylvania Dutch version of cottage cheese, a couple of days before. It would be served with strawberry preserves we put up during the summer.

Ruth had set the dining room table with the good china and made a centerpiece of holly and greens from the blue spruce in the side yard.

Charles had come home late the night before but got into the spirit of things by putting a special gift for each child under the tree, something we hadn't been able to afford in Christmases past.

"Come on in, we're ready," I called from the dining room. The children were occupied with their gifts and had to be called several times.

Finally, we were all settled around the table, Charles at one end, I at the other. Pearl, Arthur, Toag, Libby, Ruth and Buster were also at the big table while the three little ones, Edna, Margaret and Pearl Catherine sat in wooden high chairs, handmade gifts from Arthur.

"Let us pray," said Charles in his best preacher voice.

"Father in heaven, we thank you for this wonderful family and for this Christmas Day when we celebrate the birth of your son, Jesus. May we all be thankful for all our blessings and for this food and the hands that prepared it. Amen."

He looked at me from the other end of the table and for the first time in a long while, he saw me. His expression changed from the joy of blessing to an awareness of something very wrong.

"Sadie," he whispered with what I can only describe as grief.

* * * *

We got through the rest of Christmas day somehow – Charles hovered over me like a turkey hen with her chicks. Through the full turkey dinner with all the trimmings on into the evening, the atmosphere had been, at least with the adults, pretty solemn .

When we finally fell in to bed, exhausted, I had said to him, "Tomorrow we need to talk."

"Alright," he murmured, "if we must."

Right after breakfast I asked Arthur to take the older kids for a walk out on the farm. It was an unusually warm day for December and the sun shone brightly on the brown winter fields. Pearl took the three little ones onto the back porch to play.

Charles had avoided me all morning, hiding out in his office, pretending to work. As soon as the kids and the Showalters were out of the way, I went into his office. I wondered if this was the best place to have this discussion, but decided Charles was more comfortable in this space than almost anywhere in the house.

"Charles, I need to tell you something I should have told you a month ago," I began, doing my best to be calm.

"Then why didn't you?" he snapped. His first reaction to anything emotional was always to get defensive or defiant. Quickly, he recovered and said softly, "Sadie, I'm sorry, what's wrong?" The dread in his voice was palpable.

I pulled a chair up next to his roll – topped desk where he spent hours upon hours dreaming up new projects and plans and conquering new obstacles. I knew that this would not be an obstacle he could conquer.

"Does this have something to do with that you're so thin these days? You look like you've lost a whole lot of weight. I noticed it yesterday at the breakfast table," he said, his expression contrite, trying to cover his obvious negligence.

"Well, that's part of it. Now I don't want you to be alarmed, but I saw Dr. Dyerle last month because I've been having some health problems I couldn't explain.

"What did he say – I bet he says it's because you're overworked, and I'm never at home to help. Well, I have to…"

"Charles, settle down," I said in the calm voice I always used to bring him down from his high horse. I could see how his mind was working – he was feeling guilty and needed to justify his lack of observation of what was going on.

"That's not the problem, even though he did say I needed to slow down some"

"Exactly what did he say the problem was," he asked, nervously messing with the papers on his desk.

"He doesn't know yet. I'm supposed to go see him in January, and he might do some tests."

"Tests, tests for what, what is he looking for?" he said, frowning and his voice rising.

I paused, wondering whether to go to the next level, whether to mention my mother's illness. I chose not to do it. Something held me back from the dreaded "cancer" discussion. I'd wait until I saw the doctor in January and I had a definitive answer. We could deal with it then if it was really bad. As it turned out, I probably should have paved the way a bit, though nothing really would have made it any easier.

S. J. W.

CHAPTER THIRTEEN
January 18, 1922 4 A.M.

I was sitting by the fireplace in the living room with my Bible and "Mother, Home and Heaven." I flipped through the pages of this precious book where I had, over the years, marked pages and passages that fed my soul. I allowed myself to turn to a section I had been avoiding, "Heaven," on page 379. On the left is an illustration of an angel embracing a young child. Underneath is written, "The Angel of Peace," by Kaulbach. The first poem in this section was by Fanny J. Crosby and began:

> *"Oh! Where shall human grief be stilled*
>
> *And joy for pain be given,*
>
> *Where swells the sunshine of a love*
>
> *In which the soul may always rove?*
>
> *A sweet voice answered–Heaven."*

I looked out the front window. The big oak tree in the yard was bare of leaves so I could see up the lane where I first arrived as a bride, a mere twelve years ago.

"I'm not ready for Heaven, God!" I said aloud to the dark, empty room.

I'd been praying a lot lately – not that I ever stopped. Since I was a little Brethren girl in Broadway, I had had a rich spiritual and prayer life. Recently, however, I was at loss as to what to pray for. I supposed a true Christian should be praying for God's will to be done as in the Lord's Prayer. And of course, there was always that little book that had guided my adult life since Robert gave it to me Christmas of 1906, "Kept for the Master's Use." In it I was encouraged to place my life in God's Keeping. I'd asked myself so many times these past few months, "How could it possibly be God's will that I would be taken from a loving husband and six young children? What kind of God would want that?"

Silence was my only answer.

I had a doctor's appointment scheduled for today. Cora would keep the little ones after the older chaps had gone off to school. Charles came home early from Page County to take me in to Harrisonburg. He had been very attentive since Christmas and even helped some with the kids when he was home. He was trying not to "get the blues" as he called it and I'd done my best to keep things on an even keel. The children knew nothing still and both Charles and I had agreed to keep it that way.

"Mother, what are you doing in here?' said Libby as she came down the stairs into the room. She was wearing her favorite red flannel nightgown. "Isn't it time for breakfast?" She rubbed her sleepy eyes.

"Come over here," I said, motioning her to come sit on my lap – at eight she was still small for her age and liked to cuddle. Her black, curly hair was tussled from sleep and I looked into her dark brown eyes and marveled at this precious gift we were given. She looked nothing like our other blond–haired blue–eyed children and had a will and personality that was stronger in many ways. After that day at Morven Park, Charles and I had never spoken of the circumstance of her birth. Even Pearl and I had never mentioned it. No one need ever know. She had never been other than our daughter since that day in the Davis' kitchen. Perhaps someone would figure it out someday but until then there would be only my silence.

"Let's go into the kitchen and start breakfast," I said, placing the books on the side table and getting up, slowly and carefully—the pain was much worse today. "It'll be time for school before long. You can help me before everyone gets up."

One by one the older children came down the stairs – Toag and Ruth down the front steps and Buster down the back stairs from his room. Cora, who came last night and stayed over, came down with Edna and little Margaret. Charles had come down while I was in the living room and gone immediately into his office without a word. When he heard all of the children, he came into the dining room.

"Good morning everyone," he said with a forced smile on his face.

There were "Hello Daddy's" all around – the children adored their father, but kept their distance emotionally.

He was not the hugger Grandma Katie and I were and they tended to see him as the disciplinarian in the family.

After breakfast, the children got ready for school. They were thrilled when Charles offered to take them down to Dayton in the Ford. Usually they walked to the end of the lane and caught a hack provided by the county.

With everyone settled where they need to be, I went in to the bedroom to get dressed. I looked again in the mirror at my emaciated body. My ribs were sticking out, even though my stomach was distended and bloated. I had always been full–figured and with each child, until Margaret, I had gained a pound or two, which I carried on afterward.

What, I wondered would today bring? Deep in my soul, I knew it would not be good. I had continued to feel worse and worse. Only Libby had really noticed the changes in me when one day she said, "Mother, you look different and you seem so sad. Why?" I answered that I was just tired and realized that this was not fair to her or any of the children that I had not prepared them in any way for what I felt sure was about to happen. I promised myself that when I got home from the doctor, I would tell them.

I quickly grabbed my dress as I heard Charles come in the front door.

"What time is your appointment?" he asked, looking away from me as I put on my dress.

"Nine o'clock," I said as cheerily as I could manage.

"It's going to be alright, I'm sure of it, just wait until tomorrow, we'll all feel better," he said with a confidence I know he didn't have.

* * * *

After the preliminaries of checking in at the office and a short exam, Dr. Dyerle asked us both to come into the office.

"Mr. and Mr. Wampler, please have a seat," he said as he walked slowly behind his large walnut desk, as always, overflowing with papers. He cleared his throat several times as if he didn't know exactly where to start. When he finally spoke, he said with a serious face, "This is not what you're hoping to hear, I'm afraid. You don't seem to be any better than when I saw you last month – if anything you are quite a bit worse. You've lost more weight, and my physical exam shows that you are even more tender in the area of your abdomen than you were previously. Your bowels are seriously backed up. I think that we need to get you into the hospital immediately and take a look surgically at what might be going on. Can you be ready to be admitted tomorrow?"

"TOMORROW!" Charles and I said simultaneously, completely taken off guard.

"I have six children to take care of. I just don't see how…"

"Mrs. Wampler, you'll have to make some arrangements," he interrupted and said bluntly, "This needs to be done and done now. I'm sorry that's just the way it has to be."

With nothing else to say, Charles and I left the office in shock. We barely spoke on the way on the way back to the farm and when we got there Charles immediately went to his office and closed the door.

In a fog myself, I called for Cora, "Cora, could you please come here for a moment, I need to ask you something."

CHAPTER FOURTEEN

January 20, 1922 10 A.M.

Some part of me is floating and I can see myself, my body–self, down there on the operating table. I observe doctors and nurses dressed in hospital white surrounding my body. I hear beeps and blips from a variety of machines hooked to me and muffled orders being directed by Dr. Dyerle wearing a mask. All is very orderly and calm as a gloved Dr. Dyerle takes a scalpel from a gloved hand of the nurse. I seem to be suspended in time.

There is an oxygen mask over my face and the rest of me is covered with a sheet, save the area over my abdomen, lined with stretch marks from five pregnancies.

The doctor moves the scalpel toward my belly and cuts an incision from my navel to my pelvic area. Was that a gasp I heard from those who surround me or did I imagine it, and why am I up here looking at myself in the first place? Why can't I feel anything?

The doctor looks carefully into my organs, poking around, shaking his head as the beeping accelerates dramatically.

I am aware suddenly of a bright light in the distance. The light is brilliant, more so than a summer sun, and I am aware that the light is a Presence of some kind. The Presence beckons me. I so want to go meet this light, but something is holding me back, and there is a choice in it. I can go to the light right this moment or not. I have an awareness of my children, though I cannot actually see them, and immediately I am back in my body on the operating table where the doctor is stitching up my stomach. I had felt no pain floating, but now the pain is excruciating. I not only have the pain I have felt for months, I now feel the cut the doctor has made down my body. I am still under anesthesia, but I hear the doctor say, gravely, "I'm afraid there's nothing to be done."

* * * *

For the next seven days, I am in and out of consciousness. The sensation is different from the floating in the operating room, and there is no bright light, only a dulled pain, the result of powerful medication of some kind.

I am aware that Charles comes in and out of the room during the day and sometimes in the evening. He talks to me softly with pain in his voice and tells me about the children and what they are doing.

"Libby brought home chicken pox from school and now they all have it. Cora is doing a wonderful job with them. It's almost easier than getting them all off to school every morning. She has them all down in the sitting room during the day so she doesn't have to climb stairs all the time."

I want to reply but nothing comes out but a few mumbles.

Charles holds my hand and just keeps rambling on.

There are times when he begs me not to die – the doctor has told him the worst. "I can't do this by myself – please, Sadie, you have to come back to us. We need you – I need you. Without you I'm just a crabby, no–account shell of a man. Who else is going to pull me out of the blues? Who else can keep me from being too hard on the kids when I come home tired and cranky? Please, Sadie."

I want to reassure him, to comfort him the way I have always done, but I can't stay conscious long enough to do it.

I suddenly am overcome with a grief that is unbearable. I haven't prepared anyone for this – not Charles, not the children. When I left them on the day of my surgery, they didn't even know I was sick and now I'm going to just disappear out of their lives without even saying goodbye. What kind of a mother does that?

"Dear God, please forgive me for being such a miserable coward and not telling them. How will they ever know how much I love them? I must find a way to let them know. I have to wake up long enough to at least send a message through Charles. Please God, give me a chance to do that, at least that. I'm not afraid of death; I know that the light I saw will receive me into your arms. You have been with me since I was born. You have guided me and blessed me so richly. If we're being honest with each other right now, I am a little angry that my life is to end so soon and that I won't see my children grown – I won't see my grandchildren or great–grandchildren that will come from the union that almost wasn't except for You. All that I sacrificed, will it have been worth it? I have to believe that it was. I have to believe that bringing those six children into the world will make a difference, that they will make a difference in the world someday. And how will they remember me?"

I drift off again, with my questions unanswered.

* * * *

January 27, 1922

There is someone in the room, and I am aware that it is not Charles or a nurse. I try to open my eyes but I cannot. I hear a man's quiet, comforting voice drift into my consciousness.

"Robert called me from Elgin yesterday and told me. I would have come sooner but I've been away on a speaking tour promoting my new book on the Wampler family and, Oh Sadie, I'm so sorry…" his voice breaks as I realize immediately who it is.

John continues, as I try once again to open my eyes, to see this man who has meant so much to me and my family. I want to look into those eyes that so captivated me once.

"The nurses say I shouldn't stay too long but, there are some things I want you to know before…" his voice breaks again and he gently takes my hand in his.

410

"Sadie, I have watched you all these years, sacrificing your dreams out of duty to your family. You may even be wondering whether those sacrifices were worth it. Nobody can answer that question but you, and I don't presume to answer it for you. Yet, I need to tell you this for the record."

He pauses as if waiting for me to, in any way, respond, which I cannot. My hand lies limply in his as he continues.

"There are countless people who have benefited from your sacrifices: Your parents, your siblings, your husband, Charles and those six wonderful children, not to mention those along the way I don't even know about after we lost touch with each other.

The one person who has benefited most, I truly believe, is your brother, Robert. I have watched that young man struggle to work for peace in this world. I see his passion, his drive, his unrealized dreams. Sadie, it is because of what you gave to him from the moment he was born to this day, that he, without doubt, will change this sad world for the better. Do you hear me, Sadie?"

I have heard every word, as once again, the man who has always known me better than I know myself, gives me some peace about my fate, lying in this hospital bed about to die. We stay there in the quiet for some time, him holding my hand and my shallow breathing making the only sound. I have no idea how long we were there before he said, "Sadie, may I say a prayer for you?" I was able to squeeze his hand in response.

"Dear God, I ask that you bless Sadie Zigler Wampler this day. Please be near to her and sustain her through this difficult time. Please let her know that her faithfulness and sacrifice has not gone unnoticed and has not been in vain. And I pray that she will be remembered for her selfless service to You by the generations to come. In Jesus Name, Amen."

"Amen," I hear myself say as I open my eyes, surprising both of us.

I look upon my dear friend, John, and he looks at me with those piercing dark eyes, which all of a sudden take on a look of pure affection.

"One more thing, Sadie – you must be very grateful that I did not follow through on the beatings of my heart that day in Broadway when we had our little "revival." Men like me, who follow their passion, tend to get wrapped up in their own lives and forget those at home who need them. Vinnie fusses at me all the time about it. She deserves better and so did you.

My mother, Susanah Wampler, used to make up words combining German with English. One of my favorites of hers is "sonderful," a combination of the German word, 'sonder,' meaning special, and the English, 'wonderful.' Sadie Edna Rebecca Zigler Wampler, you are certainly that."

"I…" I begin and then everything fades away as I go deeper into the abyss that will soon swallow me up.

* * *

Januaray 28, 1922

Charles comes in this morning early. He gives his usual report on the children. I want so much to say something, but I can't. Just before he leaves, he takes my hand, lifts it to his lips and kisses it saying, "I love you Sadie Edna Rebecca Zigler – and I always will. Please forgive me." He breaks into a sob.

I want to say "I love you Charles, I have loved you since that day when you stood up for me at my Father's dinner table." I want to make up for all the times I hadn't said it, the times I resented his being away, but I can only squeeze his hand and remain silent. I simply pray my last prayer that, someday, somehow, my Silence will be broken.

EPILOGUE

That morning at 10 A.M., Sadie Edna Rebecca Zigler Wampler went silently into the light she had experienced on the operating table a week before.

At home on Sunny Slope Farm, six children were wondering where their mother was. Libby had brought home chicken pox from school, and everyone had caught it except four–year–old Edna and baby Margaret. Cora had stayed on after Sadie went to the hospital to take care of everyone. When someone asked about their mother which they did frequently, Cora would merely say, "She's away for a while – she'll be back soon." The chicken pox left the older four bewildered children itchy and irritable, and Cora, just plain irritable, her nature even in normal circumstances.

In the week or so after Sadie's death, their father just disappeared into his office and was completely at a loss as to what to tell them.

* * * *

There was only one person still living who could explain what happened that January morning and this is what my Aunt Libby at 104, related to me, Sadie and Charles' granddaughter, in 2017. She recalled it vividly and with little emotion:

"Cora had us down in the living room to take care of us, because we all had chicken pox. I remember the phone rang. Daddy answered it, and he started crying. He put down the phone and told us Mother had died – we didn't even know she was sick."

After Sadie died, Granddaddy tried to keep the family together on Sunny Slope, but the complications of traveling and County Agent work, as well as trying to get help at home, soon forced him to farm the children out to family and friends. In a letter to Pearl in February 1923, he stated, "I don't know if I could stand to live this way or not if it were not for the fact that I know that it won't be long until we can all be together again." Within that year he had found someone who would make that possible. He married Zola Huffman, a school teacher from Luray, Virginia, and the children all were brought home. Sadie would have loved his intention in this marriage, which was to gather in his brood. What she would not have been so pleased about is that Charles made it perfectly clear to this new wife that she could never live up to his "Sainted Sadie," and looked on her as more of a replacement for the job of managing the children and the household than a love match. Knowing this must have been difficult for her and, as a result, became difficult for Sadie's children growing up.

I have no doubt that Sadie would love knowing what she had inspired in those six young children, who had many children, who had many children, who had many children. She would be pleased to know that all of her daughters went to college. Katherine (Toag) became a teacher, Elizabeth (Libby) was an accomplished painter and helped run the Wampler Foods turkey dressing plant in Hinton. (Libby also didn't think it beneath her to work on the "line" gutting turkeys with the rest of the girls.)She would have appreciated that her namesake, Sarah Ruth, continued into her adulthood promoting the turkey industry that Sadie herself had been so instrumental in starting. Sarah Ruth actually fulfilled Charles' prediction that she would be the "Turkey Princess" one day. She was the Turkey Queen in the first Rockingham Turkey Festival. She also became active in leading 4-H work (the outgrowing of the corn clubs her father had organized) in the county and state.Margaret worked for years in Brethren Relief Service and the Heifer Project with her "Uncle Bob," Sadie's own "Robert," who was by then famous worldwide for his peace activism and Hunger Relief Work. Edna was the only sibling who earned her college degree. She worked with relief efforts like Margaret and spent her life serving others. There was my father, Charles Weldon "Buster Jack" Wampler, Jr. – his list goes on and on, but then he was a man. He continued and expanded the turkey business that Sadie and Charles had begun by co-founding Wampler Foods, Inc. with his half-brother, William Wampler. He served on many boards including James Madison University, Virginia Tech, Virginia Board of Agriculture and Rockingham Memorial Hospital. He served in the Virginia House of Delegates from 1954-1966. With his sister Libby, he co-founded the Rockingham County Fair and served as its President and General Manager for twenty-five years. With my mother, Dorothy Liskey Wampler, he founded the United Way in Harrisonburg/Rockingham County. He volunteered in the hospital cafeteria until his death at 101. He was most proud of the fact that he had over his lifetime given 171 pints of blood. "I've done a lot of things anyone else could have done, but no one could have given my blood but me," he stated near the end of his life.

In the generations after, there are many teachers, nurses, professors, missionaries, professionals of all kinds. I think she would have been pleased that her grandchildren still get together every year for what we call the "Cuzdo." And she may have even liked the fact that her Granddaughter Elizabeth became a writer and tried to tell her story. I only hope I have come even close to revealing the wonderful woman she must have been.

There are many things I still wonder about my Grandmother Sadie. But what I know is that she was a remarkable woman who could have done everything any of the men in her life were privileged to do. I know that I, as a woman of the 21st Century, have been able to live into the potential I was granted at birth to choose my way and live out my dreams.

With Sadie as my inspiration, I will take the opportunities afforded me by the times in which I live. I will not take for granted the things I have that she did not, and I will live out my life with purpose and thanksgiving, that out of Sadie's Silence came a whole new way of looking at my world and how I could make a difference in it.

S. J. W.

AUTHOR'S NOTES

T hanksgiving of 2016, which would turn out to be my father's 101st and last birthday, my husband Harry and I drove up to an Old Order Mennonite farm on Mossy Creek to see a litter of Golden Retriever puppies.

Throughout our 58 year marriage, Harry and I always had one kind of dog or another. We'd had German Shepherds, Collies, Sheep Dogs, a variety of mutts and two years ago we lost two "designer dogs" called PBGV's, a cross between a Petite Griffon and a Bassett Hound. Traveling with animals had always been a joy, but we had come to like the freedom of being dog–less after Molly and Roo died and we made the joint decision not to get any more, at least for a while.

Then, a Facebook friend posted a photo of a litter of Golden Retriever puppies that were available. I showed the photo to Harry and asked, "Are we interested?" Harry hesitated, "Maybe," he said, "find out where they are. I'm not sure I'm ready to put up with raising a puppy at this time in my life, are you?""I'm not sure either," I said. For some reason, I felt compelled to look further into the matter.

As fate would have it, the dogs "just happened" to be located three miles from Sunny Slope Farm where we were planning to be for Thanksgiving the next week. We called and made an appointment to see the puppies and learned of the one female puppy that was still available, but there were "issues." Round and around we went – did we really want the responsibility of a puppy, not to mention the possibility of a puppy that might have lifelong health issues? That would mean vet bills, and who knew what else. The time it would take to house train a puppy as well as other training requirements would be a major shift for us. Harry had more reservations than I by the time we finally decided to go see the puppies. After all, we were just looking, right?

The farm was a typical one for the Shenandoah Valley of Virginia – a large, plain, white frame house, a bank barn and several out buildings of various sizes and utility. The fenced–in yard and the fields surrounding were pristine, not one thing out of place. Like my own Brethren heritage, originating in Switzerland and Germany, Mennonites must have everything in order.

As we pulled into the driveway, a pretty young woman in her twenties, and a young boy and girl appeared from the back porch of the house. Patricia, with whom we had been communicating, wore a long print dress in the plain fashion of the Mennonites. Her hair was braided, pinned up on her head and covered with a net "prayer veil" required of women in her church. The children wore regular clothes.

We heard barking and walked with the three of them down to a kennel where a Golden Retriever mother and nine puppies rushed to the gate of the kennel, clamoring to greet us. Patricia opened the gate, and the whole tribe of them barreled out.

"That's the one I've been telling you about. She's the only female not promised for sure. I've already told you about her inverted vulva problem which may or may not be a big deal. There are two people still ahead of you, but if they don't take her, she's available and I'll take some off the price for her defect."

I picked up the one she had pointed out. Lighter colored, she had been running around playing and frisking with her siblings. The moment she was in my arms, she literally grabbed me around the neck with her paws and rested her head on my shoulder. If there were ever any reservations about whether or not we wanted a dog, they disappeared as I held this golden ball of fluff with soulful brown eyes and a Zen–like calm.

When I put the puppy down, she again romped and rolled around, as frisky as the others. We watched her as the children interacted with the puppies and noted how gentle she was with them. The little girl picked up the one we were considering and said to Harry, "Do you want to hold her?" Harry hesitated, knowing his resolve was crumbling. He took the puppy and, once again, she grabbed onto him around the neck and settled quietly in his arms. Resolve crumbled!!

"Well, I guess if the other people don't want her, it must be a sign she was meant for us," he said with a sheepish grin.

"She can't leave for a couple of weeks yet. I'll check with the others and let you know."

As we left the farm, I suddenly said, completely out of the blue, "SADIE!"

"What?" said Harry, looking at me as he drove across the narrow Mossy Creek Bridge.

"Sadie," I said again with confidence, knowing somehow she would be ours, "That's her name—after my Grandmother Sadie Zigler. She's spunky the way they say Sadie was and also has that wonderful calm, peaceful nature. Sadie is her name."

And thus, Sadie came back into my consciousness. At the time, I thought nothing of it.

A year later, in August of 2017, a KKK, Neo-Nazi, and White Supremacist rally was held only an hour away in Charlottesville, Virginia. It resulted in several people being killed and many others injured. Horrified at the specter of this kind of racism being flaunted in today's political climate, I was determined to find a way to combat this old and pervasive threat.

I had been in touch with an organization called On Earth Peace which my Uncle Bob (M.R.) Zigler had founded in the 50's. I went to the website where there was a short biography about him. Wanting to know more, I went to the top shelf of my bookcase and took down an extensive biography, *Pragmatic Prophet* by Donald F. Durmbaugh. Flipping through the pages I saw this sentence on page 22 "...the last two names mentioned significant by Zigler were his sister Sadie, who cared for him after the death of Mary Zigler..."

There she was again, trying to get my attention.

In the fall of 2017, I planned a retreat with my dear spiritual friend, Sue. We were to meet for several days at a Jesuit retreat center, Loyola on the Potomac.

Just before I left, I was sorting out some papers left over from the cleanout of Mom and Dad's house after my Dad's death in January. Out of the folder dropped a piece of paper. I recognized it as something I had taken out of a book of poetry and prose called "Mother, Home & Heaven" that had belonged to Sadie. Mother had given it to me many years before.

On the yellowed piece of paper were two typewritten poems, untitled and with no author cited.

With Sadie on my mind, I read the second poem over and over, feeling there was a message of some kind in it for me. I looked up the poem on the internet, finding no hint of authorship. I began to wonder if Sadie had written it herself.

When I showed it to Sue, an English teacher, at our retreat, she also could not place the poem or its author and said she felt like it might have been written by "a regular person."

As I sat on the bank of the Potomac River that afternoon, reading the poem over and over, I fell into what I can only describe as a meditative state. There, I felt Sadie's presence so strongly that tears began streaming down my cheeks. My awareness was that I not only carried Sadie's physical DNA but also her spiritual DNA.

I read over the poem and each line of it spoke to me. And out of Sadie's Silence came her voice, "WRITE MY STORY!"

Nearly a year later, after extensive research, family connections and interviews, I realized there were few primary sources concerning Sadie's life story. Only one of her six children, Aunt Libby, was still living. Such was the plight of women of that generation who were defined by the men in their lives—fathers, brothers, husbands.

Thus, my choice to write this as a fictional biography.

I continued to feel her presence as I wrote. I was intentional about listening and getting out of the way. I could hardly wait to sit down each day, letting her voice speak through me to the page. I would be amazed as I read back what I had written, that the story I was writing felt true.

So I offer, with some fear and trepidation, my interpretation of what came out of Sadie's Silence. Until now, her story has remained a mystery. I hope that I have somehow remained faithful to her and the words of the poem she revealed to me.

Sadie's Silence is a work of fiction based on a significant amount of fact. Aunt Libby died August 11, 2019 at the age of 106. I spoke with her several times in the years before her death and though she was quite sharp and articulate, did have huge gaps of memory. The memories she had of her mother, however, were vivid and emotional. Aunt Libby had never been known for being emotional. But when I interviewed her about Sadie, her wrinkled face radiated a warmth and love I had never seen there. It was she who said, "She was the most kind and loving person I ever knew. I never heard her raise her voice." She also recalled an incident that illustrated this. "I had done something really bad – I don't remember what. She took me into the kitchen and said in a calm voice, 'you know what you did was really bad, don't you?' I said, 'Yes.' And she said, 'Don't do it again.' And that was it. It was the way she always handled me."

My own father was seven when Sadie died, and he didn't remember her much at all. I think what he did recall was from what others said about her. So I was left to find other ways to illuminate her personality and character.

I formed my initial ideas of what might have illustrated who she was from her own books that had been passed down to me. From her childhood books there emerged a certainty that she was exposed, from an early age, to fine literature and poetry. One of her childhood books was *Beside the Bonnie Brier Bush* by Ian Maclaren published in 1895. Another, *Plants and Their Children* by Mrs. William Starr Dana was published in 1896. Neither of these was an easy reader children's book. On Christmas of her twelfth year, her parents gave her a beautifully illustrated volume of John Bunyan's *Pilgrims' Progress*. As an adult she read spiritual books such as *Kept for the Master's Use* by Maria V.G. Havergal and *Throne of Grace* by John Newton. Both of these suggest a faith journey that was deep and mature. Every one of these were inscribed, in her own hand, her name or initials, a sign to me that each was treasured by her. This signature has been used throughout the book at the end of chapters and sections.

She also enjoyed reading the novels of well–known authors of her day such as William Allen White, Mrs. Elizabeth Prentice and Harold Bell Wright.

Finally, the book *Mother, Home & Heaven*, was most likely given to her after she was married since the inscription of her initials is SZW. It was published the year she was born in 1882. In it I found passages underlined, small slips of paper with scripture references, favorite quotes and the poems I have cited.

There was also a book about the training of Sunday School Teachers.

There is no doubt that she was an intelligent, well–read woman.

Sadie's early life is well–documented, though not actually written about her, but in books about the brother she reared from boyhood to adulthood, M.R. Zigler. I used two books as my sources; one was an extensive biography, *Pragmatic Prophet* by Donald F. Durbaugh. The other was a transcription of a series of speeches Uncle Bob gave at *Tunker House*, the name given to the house in which he and Sadie grew up. This was on the occasion marking the designation of the home by the Virginia Historic Landmark Commission and National Registration of Historic Places by the National Park Service of the U.S. Department of Interior. During the week of July 16-23, 1972, when Uncle Bob was eighty–one, he gave a speech twice a day, every day, about growing up in Tunker House. The detail is impressive and his memory remarkable. I soon realized that these details were not only about Uncle Bob's life, but Sadie's as well. She had been exposed to everything he had and could have, but for the times, her sex, and circumstances, have done everything her brother had done in his remarkable life.

The sources I used for the remainder of Sadie's life were copies of the actual letters she wrote to Granddaddy's sister, Pearl. Much of the detail in Part IV and the letters I included are taken directly from these letters. In particular her last letter she mentioned reading *The Re–Creation of Brian Kent*. I immediately got a copy of the book and read it, which gave me a whole new side of what Sadie had thought about certain issues and also revealed that romantic streak I used. There were some letters also to Granddaddy's mother, Katie. In addition I used Granddaddy's autobiography, *My Grandfather, My Grandchildren and Me*.

In the first draft of my fictional biography of Sadie, I tried to stick mostly to the facts I knew or could glean from my sources. When I sent the manuscript to my dear editor, Kate Hopper, she was very clear that I must, in the next draft, "Go with the fiction and enjoy it – don't hold back." So I didn't hold back, and I did enjoy the fiction, that, to be honest, feels incredibly possible from what I do know about Sadie's personality and her life.

I think this best illustrates my view of the relative importance of facts in a novel. In May of 2019 I was invited to play the role of Heidi Schiller in Stephen Sondheim's show "Follies." Heidi is an Austrian, eighty-something, aging soprano showgirl whose memory is a bit sketchy. A waltz, "One Last Kiss" had been written for her many years ago and she relates the story in detail:

> *Franz Lehrer wrote it for me in Vienna. I was having coffee in my drawing room. In ran Franz, straight to the piano. 'Liebchen, it's for you! Or was it Oskar Strauss? (Big sigh) Facts don't interest me—what matters is the song"*

And so I offer Sadie's song, some fact, some fiction but ultimately, what matters is that out of Sadie's Silence I might have composed a melody as beautiful as she was.

I do feel that I need to make clear several of my choices in fictionalizing Sadie's story because of the living relatives who may take issue with my flights of fancy.

First of all, the circumstances of Aunt Libby's birth and Sadie taking her in is pure fiction. She was in fact born at Morven Park, March 27, 1913 while Granddaddy worked there for that year. The entire Wampler family, including Aunt Libby, her children and grandchildren, has joked about how different in looks, personality and behavior she has always been. I even asked her once if I decided to make up a story about it in one of my books, would she mind. Her exact words, "Write whatever you want." So I did.

As to her UN-romance with John Flory, that too is pure fiction. The facts are that he did date Sadie's sister Lizzie in high school, spent a great deal of time at the family home in Broadway, brought books for her and Robert to read and was involved in Robert's development his entire life. Considering Sadie was twenty–eight when she married, I couldn't imagine that she hadn't had any romance in her life before that. Everything I read about him (and there is much written about him) and having looked at his picture, I certainly fell in love with him so he made a perfect choice for Sadie.

The reader might be surprised that the facts I did use in the book are sometimes as fascinating as the fiction I invented. Practically everything that I wrote about the stream of humanity that flowed through the Zigler house in Broadway while Sadie and Robert were growing up was absolutely true. The Nadya character is fiction but certainly something that might have taken place and the story of Sadie's mother and the Negro women at the Love Feast is documented by Uncle Bob in his speeches at Tunker House.

Sadie's letters revealed much about her and Granddaddy's relationship and life together and some of it was not as rosy as the Wampler clan might have hoped. I knew my Grandfather from my birth in 1940 until his death in 1976. He lived within walking distance of our house, and I spent much time there with him and at family functions. He was a complicated man who accomplished much in his full life. I knew him as a generous and kindly grandfather with a wonderful wit, who could be very opinionated and stubborn at times. One characteristic I remember well is that when I had a conversation with him about something, I observed that instead of listening to what I was saying at the time, he was preparing what he was going to say next. I often wonder how different he would have been had Sadie lived longer. Would he have been a softer person? I know from my father that he was a very strict disciplinarian and could be difficult, but he loved his children and thought they could do no wrong.

So to the reader, I invite you to believe in the whole story, which whether it be fact or fiction, paints a picture of this wonderful woman I have grown to know and love.

ACKNOWLEDGEMENTS

With a grateful heart, I thank dear Kate Hopper, my editor, who provided me with the best creative writing course I could have imagined. From the very first "shitty draft" (Anne Lamott), she understood what I was trying to do and say with *Sadie's Silence*. She began, and continued throughout the editing, with a perfect balance of encouragement and tough love critique which enabled me to trust her and move ever forward.

At this writing, I am still in the process of getting to know Wayne Dementi of Dementi Milestone Publishing. We have had to adjust our working together to develop *Sadie's Silence* into book form. The year 2020 gave us a Pandemic of the virus COVID-19 and "working from home" was the only way we were allowed to collaborate. Through phone calls and emails, I continue to learn to respect and thoroughly enjoy this delightful man. By the time we reach our goal, I'm positive I will have much more to say but then it will be too late. Thank you, Wayne. You are a gift to me and to Sadie.

ADDITIONAL THANKS TO:

Writers of the following books about women who lived in the shadow of famous men:

Most especially, *My Dear Hamilton*, by Stephanie Dray & Laura Kamoie, which gave me an early model for the form I used for my book and how to go about researching someone who lived in a time when little was written about them .

> Others were: *The Other Einstein*–Marie Benedict
> *Mrs. Poe* –Lyn Cullen
> *The Aviator's Wife* –Melanie Benjamin
> *Call Me Zelda* –Erika Robuck
> *The Paris Wife* –Paula McLain
> Members of the Wampler/Zigler family:
> Elizabeth Morven Wampler Custer

Some of my Wampler Cousins: Larry David Bowers, Linda Logan, Susan Logan, Dorothy Strate Harper, and Anne Strate Egge, who supplied me with books Sadie owned and pictures of Sadie I had never seen. Judy Custer Huslander who allowed me to interview her mother and ask her anything I wanted even though she may think I have gone too far.

My eternal thanks to Elizabeth Morven Wampler Custer (Aunt Libby) who has, from my birth and naming, been my hero. As a little girl, with a mother who wished her first born to be perfectly dressed and behaved, I needed a model of someone who was just who she was. Until her death at 106, she remained a unique and wonderful example of just that. Though she gave me her permission to "write what I wanted" about her origins, may she come back to haunt me if I have in any way offended her memory.

Jan Stover Miller, a Zigler cousin, Granddaughter of Edgar, Sadie's brother who took me to the Broadway house (Tunker House) for a tour.She also took me to some of the Zigler graves and showed me her scrapbooks full of information she had gathered. She arranged for a tour of the Linville Creek Church of the Brethren archives room where I saw pictures of the Zigler family I had never seen.

Information on Harmonia Sacra: Sam Showalter and Dale McAllister for vital information on Harmonia Sacre.

The staff at Morven Park: For a wonderful and personal tour of the estate, including the mansion, the grounds and the home in which Sadie and Charles lived for that year. They also answered my many specific questions about the history of and the time in which they were there.

Lastly, to my husband Harry of 58 years, who has always been the kind of man who respected me as a woman, encouraged my independence, rejoiced in my adventures and listened to me talking constantly about what I was learning about my family. He is a very good listener. Thanks as well to family members and many others who took an interest in the project and asked questions these past years as I plodded along. At eighty years of age, I'm sure I repeated myself many times and yet they always seemed to be excited about it.

SOURCES

Tunker House Proceedings – 1972, Edited by Joseph B. Yount III, Privately Published, Waynesboro, Virginia 1973

My Grandfather, My Grandchildren and Me – An Autobiography of Charles W. Wampler, Shenandoah Press, Dayton, Virginia, 1968

Pragmatic Prophet – The Life of Michael Robert Zigler, Donald F. Durnbaugh, Brethren Press, Elgin, Illinois, 1989

Wamplers 1871–1971 – 100ᵗʰ Anniversary of John Wampler Family at Sunny Slope Farm, June 13, 1971, Compiled by Katherine Bowers, Roseline W. Bryan.

S. G. W.

1916 - Sadie and Charles Wampler with their children: left to right - Elizabeth (Libby), Catherine, (Toag), Ruth and Charles Weldon "Buster Jack" Wampler, Jr.

AND THEN THERE WAS SADIE

Much has been written of M.R. Zigler, "Man of Peace,"

Who worked his entire life to promote justice

and peace.

Was involved the beginnings of The Heifer Project,

Brethren Volunteer Service,

Conscientious Objectors to war and in the 1970's,

founded "On Earth Peace," And on, and on, and on....

M.R. Zigler was my Great Uncle Bob.

M.R. Zigler was Sadie's brother.

Much has been written about Charles Weldon

Wampler, Sr.

Who founded the modern turkey industry,

Was county agent of Rockingham County,

President of the First National Bank of Harrisonburg,

President of Wampler Feeds Inc.

Involved in the poultry industry his entire life in

Virginia and around the world

And on, and on, and on...

Charles Weldon Wampler Sr. was my grandfather.

Charles Weldon Wampler Sr. was Sadie's husband.

Much has been written about Charles Weldon

Wampler, Jr.

Who continued his father's work in the

poultry industry,

Served on every Board in Virginia,

Was Chancellor of James Madison University,

Founded the United Way in Harrisonburg,

Helped found and organize the

Rockingham County Fair,

Served in the Virginia legislature,

And on, and on, and on...

Charles Weldon Wampler, Jr. was my father.

Charles Weldon Wampler, Jr. was Sadie's son.

AND THEN THERE WAS SADIE!

Written by Libby Layne right before she decided to

write a book about Sadie

S.J.W.